Lifeworlds of Islam

Lifeworlds of Islam

The Pragmatics of a Religion

MOHAMMED A. BAMYEH

OXFORD
UNIVERSITY PRESS

OXFORD
UNIVERSITY PRESS

Oxford University Press is a department of the University of Oxford. It furthers
the University's objective of excellence in research, scholarship, and education
by publishing worldwide. Oxford is a registered trade mark of Oxford University
Press in the UK and certain other countries.

Published in the United States of America by Oxford University Press
198 Madison Avenue, New York, NY 10016, United States of America.

Library of Congress Cataloging-in-Publication Data
Names: Bamyeh, Mohammed A., author.
Title: Lifeworlds of Islam : the pragmatics of a religion /
Mohammed A. Bamyeh.
Description: New York, NY : Oxford University Press, 2019.
Identifiers: LCCN 2018045603 (print) | LCCN 2018049495 (ebook) |
ISBN 9780190280574 (updf) | ISBN 9780190942243 (epub) |
ISBN 9780190280567 (hardcover) | ISBN 9780197584323 (paperback)
Subjects: LCSH: Islamic sociology.
Classification: LCC BP173.25 (ebook) | LCC BP173.25 .B297 2019 (print) |
DDC 306.6/97—dc23
LC record available at https://lccn.loc.gov/2018045603

1 3 5 7 9 8 6 4 2

Paperback printed by Marquis, Canada

Contents

Illustrations

Tables

Figures

Acknowledgments

This book came to life gradually, over many years of public and academic engagement with the sociology of Islam, and while I was pursuing parallel research projects. In the process, parts of it appeared in less polished forms, or were delivered as research notes in public lectures. In its current shape, the book distills what I have learned over the years from countless engagements with colleagues and publics across many countries. Earlier versions of chapter 2 appeared previously in *The Macalester International* (vol. 14, 2005) as "Between Activism and Hermeneutics: One Hundred Years of Intellectual Islam in the Public Sphere," and in *Third World Quarterly* (vol. 29, no. 3 (Spring 2008)) as "Hermeneutics Against Instrumental Reason: National and Post-national Islam in the Twentieth Century." That version was republished in Radhika Desai, ed., *Developmental and Cultural Nationalism* (Routledge, 2009). A condensed summary of chapter 3 originally appeared as "Global Order and the Historical Structures of *Dar al-Islam*," in Manfred Steger, ed., *Rethinking Globalism* (Rowan & Littlefield, 2004). With minor modifications, that summary was reprinted as "What Would a Global Civic Order Look Like? A Perspective From Islamic History," in Scott Nelson and Nevzat Soguk, eds., *The Ashgate Research Companion to Modern Theory, Modern Power, World Politics* (Ashgate, 2016). These pieces, along with previously unpublished materials, have been expanded, revamped, updated, and integrated in this book into a cohesive narrative.

The list of friends and colleagues who helped develop my thought on the sociology of Islam is just too long to list here. What proved most crucial, however, was the sheer diversity of the publics I encountered over the years, ranging from elite university gatherings to working-class community colleges, and stretching in geography among North America, the Middle East, Europe, and East Asia. Those audiences showed patience with some of my ideas in their less polished form. Through their engage-ment, they helped those ideas grow into fuller maturity, and taught me how to communicate across different agendas and explore connections that otherwise would not have been apparent. Particularly helpful were participants at the Chicago Humanities Festival (Chicago, 2017); UNESCO World Humanities Conference (Liége, Belgium, 2017); Oxford University (2014); George Mason University (2013); the American University of Beirut (2013); University of North Carolina, Charlotte (2012); Cornell University (2012); Franciscan University of Steubenville, Ohio (2012); University of California, Santa Barbara (2012); the Egyptian Philosophical Society (Cairo, 2011); the American Research Center in Egypt (Cairo, 2011); Seton Hill University (2009); Duquesne University (2008); University of Pittsburgh (2008); Takween Institute (Amman, Jordan, 2008); Minnesota International Relations Colloquium (2007); Century College (Minnesota, 2006); Saint Thomas University (2006); Georgetown University (2005); University of Victoria (2004 & 2003); University of Minnesota (2004); Macalester College (2004); European University Institute (Florence, Italy, 2003); University of Hawaiʻi-Manoa (Honolulu, 2002); State University of New York-Buffalo (2002); Institute of Ethnology of Academia Sinica (Taiwan, 2001); and the Swedish Collegium for Advanced Study in the Social Sciences (Uppsala, Sweden, 2001).

Everyone cited in this book played some role in giving direction to its arguments. But for special inspiration I would like to thank such friends and colleagues as Asef Bayat, Armando Salvatore, Ahmad Dallal, Charles Kurzman, Sami Zubaida, Said Arjomand, Göran Therborn, Richard Bulliet, Jeanette Jouili, as well as the late Janet Abu-Lughod and Saba Mahmood, and my teacher Fazlur Rahman. I would also like to express my gratitude to the staff at Oxford University Press, and especially James Cook. And as usual, I owe much to the perceptive eye and care of Randall Halle. His role, as so happens to be conveyed by the cover image graciously supplied by my friend Hisham Bizri, gave more meaning to what I had wanted to explore in this volume: less the finished structures of things than the dy-namism of life, and the worlds that make it possible.

Lifeworlds of Islam

Introduction

ISLAM AS LIFEWORLDS

WHY DOES ISLAM appear to persist as a powerful reference point for so many believers? This is the question of this book. Like any other question, an answer makes sense only to the extent that we clearly understand what is being asked. I wish to explore how an Islamic perspective on common affairs, among other perspectives, takes shape and becomes established in public life. In charting out this process, I will focus only on the sociological aspects of Islam, being aware that this focus leaves out vast areas of religious life—including the nature of belief, theological reason, and juridical debates. I will, however, address these areas whenever they have some bearing on the sociology of the faith.

The processes described in this book are probably not unique to Islam. Still, the focus on Islam allows us to explore contexts that, while specific enough, are also part of contemporary structures of global life. Recent history gives us ample reasons for this focus, but the question concerns how to discuss it and what might be the most appropriate questions to ask. For example, 1979, 2001, and 2011 provide three cataclysms that punctuate our approach to Islam in the contemporary period: the Iranian Revolution, the September 11 attacks, and the upheavals of the Arab Spring. Each of these events has provided sufficient reasons for a sharp reorientation of focus in its aftermath, but all have played an undoubted role, until now, in enhancing our attention to the role that Islam as a discourse, and Muslims as peoples, play in shaping political, cultural, and economic realities around the world.

Each of these events caught most observers by enough surprise to suggest that the available knowledge up to that point about the sociology of

Islam was lacking in some profound way. The Iranian Revolution, for example, reawakened interest in Islam as a potent revolutionary force. That revolution was all the more remarkable given that at that time, Islam was widely ignored as a factor in any mass politics, when it was assumed that the main influence and the most movement was likely to be in the domain of already mobilized secular forces. Political life in most Muslim countries was then still overshadowed by Cold War perspectives. The apparently viable and already mobilized political forces then were largely secular: Before 1979, various strands of nationalist, anti-colonial, liberal, socialist, and communist movements and ideas appeared to describe the range of existing political realities or perceived political futures in the vast majority of the Muslim world. The Iranian Revolution completely altered that perception.

The two decades of intense interest in Islam that followed 1979 gave rise to some of the best studies of Islamic sociology, before another inexplicable event led the world, and much scholarship, to an undeserved low point after 2001. Unlike the Iranian Revolution that took nearly two years of constant mass mobilization, September 11, 2001, was a single-day event. Also unlike the Iranian Revolution, which mobilized millions in Iran and inspired many more millions around the world, the 2001 attacks were carried out by 19 individuals, and the network surrounding them was a small, easily isolated group hiding away at the margins of the world, not a mass movement in a central Muslim country. But it triggered the two lengthiest wars that the United States fought, generated far more world turmoil than the Iranian Revolution (even if we factor in the eight-year Iran–Iraq war), cost several trillion dollars in military expenses and postwar "reconstruction," and an increase in the security prerogatives of the state in both the United States and much of the Muslim world. The catastrophic failure of such a response, guided as it was by a fatal combination of feeble intellects and boundless arrogance, became very clear a little more than a decade later, when the erstwhile small band of scattered fanatics mushroomed into tens of thousands of Da'esh (aka ISIS) fighters operating as an effective force in multiple countries.

That sequence showed how poorly informed politics or publics may deliver far more expensive disasters than any act of terror and any revolution. For there was in fact no coherent strategic reason, nor enough social transformations among Muslims, for the September 11 attacks to galvanize the response they did. Under more enlightened conditions, we would not have treated them very differently from Breivik's terror assaults in Norway that killed 77 people on July 22, 2011. Appropriately, the violence meted out by Breivik and right wing groups in the West was typically explained as the outcome of personal pathology or small group recluse paranoia. In such cases, no world wars against terror were declared, nor a broad demand to sacrifice civil liberties in the process.

That event proves the point above about the high cost of ignorance: Acts of personal pathology may become national crises *only* when we do not know the community out of which the actor has emerged. Norwegian society, for example, recognized Breivik as one of its own, which meant that it could easily see him as not representing its own norms. A lone white European or U.S. terrorist may always be regarded as an anomaly by his society, since it is assumed that such a society is different from him. This is not the case with migrants or outsiders whenever they are not integrated enough into a host society and thus remain unknown to it. In such a case, it is much easier for such a community to be stigmatized by the action of even a single individual among them. Informed differentiation between personal pathology and common tendencies, therefore, can only happen when we all know each other, and at the personal rather than theoretical level. Part of the spirit of this book derives from the fact that we are far from that reality.

While in the aftermath of September 11, 2001, questions of terrorism and security became far more present than ever before in the study of Muslims, a decade later we were awakened to another surprise that somewhat alleviated this gloomy perspective, namely a wave of revolutionary events that collectively came to be known as the Arab Spring. These were the first real popular revolutions in the Middle East since the Iranian Revolution some three decades earlier (apart from the Palestinians' uprisings in 1987 and 2000, and the popular uprising in Sudan against Numeiri in 1985, all of which remained local events). This surprise was even deeper than any other, even though all area experts were well aware that grave and widely shared popular grievances had been simmering for many years. After three decades of intense attention to Islam as the only discourse presumed to be capable of mobilizing large numbers of people in Muslim-majority societies, and after Muslims have become identified with their religion rather than with any other loyalty or identity, it was difficult to explain how out of such reality there should emerge a series of spectacular mass movements with *no* religious character. All of the 2011 movements called for a civic state; none wanted an Islamic republic. That

standpoint of the 2011 uprisings was accepted even by the religious movements that have joined them.[1]

This book is motivated by our inability to anticipate these events and,
more specifically, understand the actual role of "Islam" in them. This inability should serve as an invitation to knowledge. In this book, I would like
to pursue the thesis that Islam has served as a guide for a wide range of
ideas and movements not because it has any essential meaning, nor because it determines anyone's behavior in specific ways. Rather, Islam was
useful precisely because it *lacked* such qualities: It could be made to say
whatever anyone who lacked an alternative language of participation had
wanted to say. This conception of Islam is clarified in the following three
chapters, which respectively address the role of Islam in social movements;
how it is elaborated as public philosophy; and the historical structures that
gave it resilience as a common discourse of global citizenship. Collectively,
these spheres of practice (social movement, public philosophy, and global
orientation) may be considered as the *lifeworlds* of any ideology: they are
the everyday methods, the pragmatics if you will, that sustain its life across
vastly different times and spaces.

What is a lifeworld?

When an old idea appears vigorous again today, when just yesterday it appeared to be on the verge of extinction, suggests that something has given
it a license for a new life. For about three decades after World War II, the
secularization thesis predicted that as societies become modern, they also
become secular. Much has since been written about the apparent failure
of that thesis, and its detractors were all too happy to see it so thoroughly
discredited in recent years, almost everywhere in the world (Berger 1999).
Yet the thesis may actually be more true than it appears to be, especially if
what is meant by it is the replacement of one form of religiosity by another,
which is precisely how the defenders of the secularization thesis continue
to argue its relevance (e.g., Bruce 2011). That would be the case, for example, whenever we observe that old-fashioned, traditional, ritualistic,

---

1. As mentioned a little earlier, the fundamental sociological dynamics of the Da'esh
Caliphate, established after the Arab Spring, should really be considered a result of the reaction to September 11, rather than as part of the original 2011 dynamics, in which Da'esh
played no part. This point will be addressed at more length in Chapter 1.

taken-for-granted religion has disappeared and been replaced by a new variety: action-oriented, nervous, instrumental, reified religion.

If this is true, we may first propose two likely sources that feed the ability of religion to overcome prophecies of its doom: first, its capacity to reinvent itself, the means for which are the subject of this book; and second the failure of alternative ideologies to solve problems around which there is sufficient social consensus. The proof of the last point is Western Europe, where the secularization thesis seems true even in its traditional form, likely due to the historical success (up to this point) of social democracy in establishing a new social consensus centered around liberal values that require no religious justification.

Barring that accomplishment, religion reinvents itself in order to tackle *new*, never ancient, problems. It does that in its *lifeworlds*, the true social laboratories of invention. The first two chapters explore the grand contours of two such lifeworlds, one oriented to action and the other to thought: social movements and public philosophy, respectively. The third chapter explores lifeworlds as historical structures that had allowed religion to reinvent itself as needed for many centuries and across the entire world.

Lifeworlds are what anything that is expected to live forever and everywhere must have. That is to say, lifeworlds are ways for doing two fundamental tasks of life: avoiding death, and going around irrelevance. Lifeworlds do their work, this avoidance of death and circumnavigation of irrelevance, at moments and in places where that which is supposed to be omnipresent and eternal, that is to say a universal religion, hits its limits, meaning that it sees both dangers. Without lifeworlds adequate for exploring or navigating the new environment, the old will expire at the gates of the new.

Since its foundations in phenomenology, the concept of "lifeworld" highlighted the world as an *experience* rather than a set of doctrines and structures external to consciousness, and in such a way that individuality itself gained meaning out of its immersion in the world of perceptions and practices, that is to say, the world shared with others. Jürgen Habermas (1987) in particular shows the analytical virtues of "lifeworld" as a concept by opposing it to "systems," which are the economic and political techniques of standardization that seek to arrest the free flow of lifeworlds and deliver them in static formats that reflect bureaucratic and managerial preference for predictability, constancy, and impersonality. This opposition between "system" and "lifeworld" may at first glance appear evident in the history of any religion, where we see two basic approaches to religious life: one governed by systematic doctrine and another by situational experience. Sometimes the two are contrasted as the "rational" versus "mystical" variety of religious life: one oriented to following divine rules, the other to experiencing divine substance. However, it would be inaccurate to say that the former approach provides the system of religion and the latter its lifeworld, since as we will see in subsequent chapters, both can be present in the same mind. The concept of lifeworld, therefore, is not limited to mystical experiences but refers to the entire range of acts and practices through which an old idea continues to generate voluntarily accepted meaning (rather than enforced rules).

I found it important to focus on lifeworlds of Islam since much has been written about the "systems" of Islam: the legal structures, political parties, educational institutions, economic enterprises, and so on. All these will of course be discussed insofar as they have bearing on our understanding of the lifeworlds of Islam. But lifeworlds are more fundamental to our understanding of religiosity, since without lifeworlds to speak to, systems can only be maintained as authoritarian structures, whose authoritarianism reflects the fact that they have no persuasive power. This lack of persuasiveness was evident, for example, when Abu Bakr al-Baghdadi declared his caliphate from the old mosque of Mosul. He made it clear then what Islam meant to him: Islam could only be an authoritarian system. It required an effective authority to enforce it, he stated, since otherwise it will not be followed.

The new "caliph" was hardly original here, since the same principle has already been enunciated by other modern dictators who simply imposed themselves like a dead weight on their societies, from Omar al-Bashir of Sudan to the Saudi royal family. The principle of "necessary enforcement" is likewise perfectly acceptable to many modern Islamic movements that are far less extreme in their practices than the caliphate and far less cynical than the Saudis. Such movements reflect, again, another variety of the same authoritarian conviction that religion is now unpersuasive without sheer force. Among modern religious people, therefore, the real divide is not so much between those who want doctrinal sobriety and the others who prefer the mystical experience. It is rather between those who do not believe that faith has enough of a persuasive power on its own, thus *needing enforcement*, and those for whom faith is a pragmatic compass of *meaning* in ordinary, transactional life. The former perspective always leads to conflict, since it insists on living atop a world in which it knows that it does not fit. Only the latter may be adequate for life. Not because it is "true," nor because it necessarily solves any problem, but because its own life derives from one lifeworld or another.

Lifeworlds are not beautiful utopias, however. I do not think that we can properly understand modern religiosity by separating religions into good and evil varieties, nor by fixating on trying to make religiosity "safe" for liberalism or democracy, for example, when a vast history of political modernity shows how thus far world wars, the worst genocides, and most dictatorships have been thoroughly secular in nature. Danger comes from all sides. It may be true that modern Islamic movements are dangerous—some explicitly so, others only when they have enough power perhaps. But a broader historical perspective shows us that everyone else is dangerous just as well, including secular imperialism, both in its classical colonial form as well as in the newer form experimented with during the first decade of the twenty-first century, and probably again at a later point. Thus it is important not to lose perspective and fixate on one thing: Religion is the problem; no, it is modernity; perhaps colonialism? Maybe, but now it is globalization, and so on. There is no shortage of simplistic answers that pin modern danger on a single idea and thus appear to offer us a clear solution. But in a world in which there are *systems* that have large enough power, such as modern states, danger is equally distributed across *all* ideologies, secular *and* religious. That is because, as I have argued at length elsewhere (Bamyeh 2009), large power structures tend to encourage either a total struggle to take them over, or a tendency to use them to control more of the world. In the final analysis, our fundamental problem is power structures, not religion.

A lifeworld must be differentiated analytically from such power structures, since otherwise it is impossible to understand how any idea acquires a persuasive capacity on its own terms—that is, without coercive power. In an earlier book (Bamyeh 1999) I tried to understand how Islam, as a new idea in the seventh century, had itself acquired a persuasive capacity across multiple societies within a relatively short period. The transition from polytheism into monotheism paralleled a transition from a tribal to transtribal society that had already been underway, in part due to the rise of urban settlements, the increasing economic importance of long-distance trade, the rise of poetic transtribal culture, and the need for new methods of conflict resolution in light of new patterns of tribal warfare. Monotheism in its Islamic version knitted those elements together, and thus acquired a persuasive capacity. Islam acquired its social life not because it produced a harmonious society, but precisely for the opposite reason: It allowed all social conflict to go on, just as before, but under the mantle of a single regulatory discourse. A discourse that acquires persuasive capacity is one that speaks to all social groups and classes, and in a way that allows each social segment to imagine the discourse (a specific faith in this case) to be intimately its own.

Understood this way, we begin to approach religion on its own terms, that is, not by starting out from a problem defined by non-religious people, i.e., how can Islam be made "democratic," compatible with liberal values, or modernized in one way or another. Islam cannot be made to be anything that it is not. And what it is, is a *plenum*. That means that since it covers, or claims to cover, the entire spectrum of sociability, it will always house pathological demagogues, liberation theology, dictatorial tendencies, democratic sentiments, instrumental rationality, contemplative mysticism, feminism, and patriarchy—all at the same time and just like all other religions. Religion may be said to be "pure" in essence and "harmonious" in intent only from a religious perspective. But from any other perspective, religion must be seen to be a mix of tendencies that are not naturally reconcilable—but are able to communicate because they share the same reference points.

That mix is due to the social vastness and historical depth of religion. Anything that is large in space and deep in time must become exposed to "impure" matter: ideas and practices that were not part of its origins—an accurate observation of all puritans, who therefore tend to be a recurrent feature of religious life. Islam, therefore, cannot be made other than what it is, other than what Muslims would allow it to be. And that is true of any other faith. But what is important to note is that we do not speak of Islam the same way we speak of Christianity, or Judaism, even though we know that both teem with demagogues, authoritarian tendencies, anti-democratic sentiments, patriarchy, and calls for violence. And that is because they, too, are distributed across a large space and extend into deep time.

With that in mind, the book is written with the aim of being useful for general educated readers. I have attempted to navigate a path between two pitfalls that always surround this kind of work and invite descent into them: on the one hand the lure of essentializing Islam, that is, presenting it as a system of belief whose meaning appears independent of the human activity that generates questions about meanings; and on the other, the lure of getting lost in Islamic apologia (e.g., "Islam is compatible with human rights," "women's rights," and so on). Throughout, I thought it would be more enlightening to highlight distinct larger meanings that Muslims themselves appeared to imply in some way or another, whenever they identified in Islam a longing for an intimate dimension of their common life, and in ways they may have found wanting in alternative discourses.

These meanings are covered in three chapters, each of which offers a large compass around a key dimension of the sociology of Islam. The last chapter offers the broadest perspective, approaching Islam as the namesake of a globally networked, historical social reality. As such, it offers an opportunity to revisit contemporary globalization debates from an unusual angle, by asking the same question but in reverse: not whether Islam lives well or poorly with global processes, or whether Muslims are suffering or benefiting from globalization. My concern, rather, is whether Islamic global history teaches us something about the basic structures of globalization processes, including those of our times: How do people anywhere cultivate a sense of living in a global society—one that feels close, intimate, and controllable by *relatively* humane, less faceless forces and uncoerced dynamics? Readers familiar enough with Islamic history may want to start with that chapter.

The second chapter explores the ground structure of Islamic public philosophy for the past century—in particular, the era witnessing the most intense exposure of the Muslim world to European colonialism, as well as the decline of traditional Islam in the public sphere in favor of modernizing ethos, both religious and secular. The focus is mainly on the most influential intellectual systems that defined modern roles for Islam in the public sphere of several central Muslim countries. The two general varieties of contemporary Islamic public philosophy, namely "instrumental" and "hermeneutic" Islam, define the work of globally known Muslim intellectuals, some of whom are identified with Islamic social movements. That chapter explores the globality of Islamic thought in how various public intellectuals, working independently of each other and in different contexts, converged on two strands of thought in *each* region, even as they used different methods.

This public philosophy often takes organizational forms that are evident in modern Islamic social movements, whose common features are explored in the first chapter. Islamic social movements must generally be regarded as unfinished experiments rather than as prepackaged ideological bodies. They must be so since they express not so much standard religiosity, but a myriad of ways by which participatory claims are laid down by erstwhile apolitical social segments. The desire of such social segments for some form of participation is in one sense a response to crisis, and in another, a response with minimal means. A "response with minimal means" is what one does when one pulls a familiar discourse out of its hibernation, so as to ask through it new questions: "How do I become a citizen of this environment that is changing everyday around me?"; "what is my real community today?"; "is it enough to help my neighbor as needed, or do I need to systematically help my neighborhood?"; "should I be patient with tyranny because it is god's verdict, or should I bring it down because god's mandate is justice here and now?" "how do I combat an evil that refuses to go away?"; and so on.

But since the whole exercise is an ongoing experiment with no termination date, and since the experiment is done in a social laboratory that is constantly changing its arrangement, the answers remain provisional. And it is the provisional character of an answer that sometimes suggests that the original question may have been improperly articulated. In that sense these social movements, like the science that seeks to study them, are unfinished experiments in assigning meaning to a world that, in crisis-laden times, threatens at every moment to disavow all meaning.

I

Islam as Social Movement

PRAGMATICS OF PARTICIPATION

From emergency to normal crisis

Islamic social movements are movements that mobilize Islam as a language of social activism. Two general environments, with distinct characteristics, appear conducive to mobilizing an old religion for new purposes: One is an environment of emergency conditions; another is an environment dominated by calls for profound social renewal. Movements responding to the former may be called "emergency movements," whereas those operating under and shaping the latter may be called "normal crisis movements." Emergency movements see themselves as reacting to an immediate danger. By contrast, normal crisis movements, which sometimes do have their roots in earlier emergency movements, see their goal as responding to a *long-term* cultural and social crisis that they identify to be the ultimate root of whatever emergency conditions they may also find themselves responding to.

Both types of movements are generally conservative, but in different ways: Whereas emergency movements do not aim to transform society as much as *preserve* it, as in the face of a common and immediate danger, normal movements aim to *transform* society by reminding it of its deep but forgotten cultural roots. In reality this means the opposite: *modernize* society, but with the aid of its own indigenous cultural resources (as interpreted, of course, by such movements).

1) Emergency movements: The movement is conceived as an urgent response to extreme, immediate, and collective danger. Such danger

amplifies the need for greatest social unity in its face. The sense of such danger tends to amplify the role of the *most common* (though not necessarily the most *deeply felt*) expression of collective identity, which then serves as a common language of struggle. In modern history, such sense of danger occasions early phases of Western colonial invasions of lands where Islam is a common faith. The earliest phases of Algerian struggle against French colonialism, especially between 1832 and 1847, but also intermittently afterward throughout the nineteenth century, relied on transforming Sufi orders and other social groups into militant fighting machines, and Islam served as a unifying discourse of otherwise fragmented society against a completely foreign, technologically advanced and brutal enemy. The early phase of Libyan struggle against Italian colonialism, between 1911 and 1931, was led by a recognized religious pedagogue and mobilized especially the *Sanusiyya*, the dominant Sufi order in Libya. Some similarities to these legendary struggles, pitting relatively resourceless people against a mighty Western empire, could also be seen in later times, such as the mobilization of the *mujahedeen* in Afghanistan following the Soviet invasion in 1979. In all these episodes, the greatest novelty insofar as "Islam" was concerned was that Islam was made to serve—at least temporarily—the role of collective anti-colonial nationalism. Indeed, in Islamic societies, emergency movements tended to use Islam as the language of their identity, usually wherever a common national identity was not yet solidly established. "Islam" meant in such cases not any particular practice, but rather a handy and quick reference to an urgent need for collective mobilization in the face of an extreme, sudden, and collective threat.

2) Normal crisis movements: These movements operate in environments where alternative movements exist, and where Islam enjoys less of a monopoly as a reference for translocal identity. The very pluralism of the cultural and political landscape compels some adherents to consider that Islam requires being revivified, even "updated," so as to retain a central role in social and political life, and in ways appropriate to modern needs. Unlike emergency conditions noted in point 1), these environments tend to be perceived as possessing an enduring feature, even though they may be experienced by their inhabitants to be crisis-laden. But the "crisis" here tends to be seen as deep-seated and to result from long-term processes of decay, rather than as an emergency condition that could be quickly corrected with a general mobilization.

Thus these movements tend to see themselves as responding to a profound crisis, but through a long-term project at social transformation. Normal crisis movements tend to be the most typical, most enduring, and most transformative Islamic social movements. The Muslim Brotherhood in Egypt, both Muhammadiyyah and Nahdatul Ulama in Indonesia, and Jamaat-e-Islami in the Indian subcontinent are some prominent examples of these types of normal Islamic movements.

Some movements may be considered a synthesis of both types. They tend, as would be expected, to be entrenched in areas where colonial struggles or foreign invasions remain endemic, but where strong non-religious national movements also exist and a sense of immediate collective threat is accompanied by dynamics calling forth long-term transformation in the role of religion in society. Hamas in occupied Palestine and Hizbullah in Lebanon are probably the clearest examples of this kind of synthesis: Both originated as militant anti-colonial or national liberation organizations, while at the same time regarding themselves as permanent movements for social renewal. While both are quite young movements relatively, dating only from the 1980s, they do possess roots in earlier forms of Islamic mobilization and, in the long run, tend to be more similar to the "normal crisis" type of Islamic social movements.

Normal crisis movements do not lack for militancy when they operate in environments that generate enough reasons for militancy, as evident in the Muslim Brothers' sporadic attacks on the British during their occupation of the Suez Canal. However, the long-term orientation of these movements is toward rejuvenating and reinterpreting the role of Islam in modern society, and not toward simply solving an immediate, large problem. Indeed, in the Arab World, the main difference in the anticolonial perspective between secular and religious forces has always been that whereas the secular forces saw colonialism to be the main *cause* of underdevelopment of colonized societies, the religious forces tended rather to see colonialism as a *symptom* of a deeper problem—namely of the accumulated weakness and degeneration of the *umma*. Both secular nationalist and religious movements opposed colonialism, but the religious forces in particular saw their task to consist of curing a deeper malaise, of which colonialism was no more than a symptom.

Normal Islamic movements are part of the cultural fabric of global modernity. By this I mean that while they may be seen and analyzed in terms of their local contexts, they may also be seen and analyzed in the larger context of modern conservatism globally. Specifically, they are part of the larger story of how traditional conservative sentiments everywhere have in modernity assumed the character of modern movements and political parties. This more general global trend has its roots in nineteenth-century Europe, which gave rise to Christian social democratic parties. In Europe, the rise of Christian social democracy is commonly understood in the context of competition with socialist movements, a competition in which traditional conservative forces found themselves compelled to offer an alternative, but modern enough, social perspective. That alternative perspective was based on the claim that it was rooted in established conservative social traditions, which now had to address modern social problems—notably inequality and mutual obligations—as meaningfully as the new socialist movements seemed to be doing. In many Muslim countries, parties that make a similar claim about mobilizing conservative social traditions for the purpose of ameliorating social inequalities and addressing modern problems have enjoyed significant electoral successes when the political theater was opened up. Examples abound, from the Justice and Development Party (AKP) in Turkey to its namesake party in Morocco to the former Freedom and Justice Party in Egypt to the *Nahda* movement in Tunisia, to mention just a few significant theaters. It is also noteworthy that these movements, too, saw the old local socialist left as their main nemesis in their earlier phases, even though both shared a common anti-colonial attitude.

Another global root of modern normal Islamic movements, also similar to European social democratic movements, can be traced to the enlightenment. This point becomes clear when we consider the roots of modern Islamic movements in nineteenth-century Islamic enlightenment, about which more will be said in the second chapter. Here it suffices to say that that enlightenment was both social and intellectual, in the sense that it was organized around the activities of globally interconnected Muslim public intellectuals. They became identified, at least partially, with constitutional revolutions and modernist reform movements in Iran, Egypt, Ottoman lands, India, and Indonesia, as well as Central Asia before the Bolshevik Revolution.

Nineteenth-century Islamic enlightenment—which was by no means the only variety of enlightenment thought in Muslim lands—represented, like European Christian social democracy, a conservative adaptation of enlightenment thought. In addition, the Islamic enlightenment also shared with other non-European modernist trends a project that Göran Therborn

(2003) has called "reactive modernization." Examples of the latter include the Chinese Self-Strengthening Movement and Japanese modernization (Hamed 1990). The latter in particular was explicitly cited by some Muslim intellectuals, notably Rashid Rida in 1931, as an inspiring example of how to mobilize social traditions so as to modernize, and by extension empower, society, especially against Western colonial threat.

In each modern society, the discourse of normal Islamic movements addresses both internal social problems and external threats and opportunities. The features of normal Islamic movements that are tied to internal projects of overall social renewal will be the focus of this chapter. Features associated with how external threats and opportunities are conceived, whether as anti-colonial mobilization or as "reactive modernization," will be addressed in later chapters. Suffice it here to mention that anti-colonialism and reactive modernization are those features of modern Islamist discourse that show most affinity to secular nationalism as it arose in response to European colonialism as well as the ineptitude of local despotism in the nineteenth and early twentieth centuries. In fact, the earlier phases of those struggles tend to show how much social consensus they generated, and consequently how little difference there needed to be expressed between an "Islamic" versus "non-Islamic" ways of fighting European colonialism or the increasingly ineffective local despotism. Early twentieth-century national revolts in Muslim societies, such as in Iran in 1906 or in Iraq in 1920, at best included "Islam" only as one of their slogans, and Muslim authorities tended to be one of their components rather than their defining agents. Those early resistance spectacles could hardly be seen as religious revolts. Other national revolts from the same period, as in Ottoman Turkey in 1908 or Egypt in 1919, had virtually no religious dimension. On the whole those movements addressed themselves to such modern questions as the colonial threat, popular participation, and national mobilization. *None* called for an Islamic state, even when religious authorities took part in them. Rather, they tended to express their aims in the language of national sovereignty, self-rule, and constitutionalism (Barut, in Alawi 126).

Social renewal: The long march into normal crisis

Eventually, modern, self-consciously Islamic movements came to express such general modern national goals in Islamic terms, although this task took several more decades of elaboration. The organized genealogies of modern Islamic movements in the Middle East and South Asia can be traced to the 1920s, while their intellectual genealogies can be traced to the latter part of the nineteenth century. The styles of action as well as public intellectual systems of the most effective of these movements have tended to disseminate globally. The longest lasting movements also tend to display common features that are associated with their more or less stable presence in social life, even under conditions of persecution. The social presence of Islamic movements is indicated by a wide range of institutions encompassing social services, media, political action groups, cultural and educational work, and in some cases a militia.

As many observers have noted, when it comes to Islamic social movements it makes little sense to distinguish clearly between formal organizations and informal networks (Singerman 1996), since formality and informality of organization are really two interchangeable ways of doing work in environments where state tolerance is uncertain and where constitutional life enjoys neither consistent adherence nor reliable future prospects. Indeed, it is often the case that when the openness of political institutions proves long-lasting, it is because normal Islamic movements had largely contributed to making them such. Examples of this process of normalizing politics due to Islamist mobilization already exist or are emerging in Turkey, where the AKP fostered the decline of military influence on politics during the first decade of the twenty-first century, as well as in Indonesia after Suharto.

Modern Islamic movements espouse religion as a worldly guide rather than as an orientation to the other world. Indeed, one of the most significant transformations of Islam in the twentieth century has involved the virtual disappearance—at least for the time being—of mystical religiosity in its old forms, so that even Sufi practices became over time either more worldly or subordinate to worldly struggles. (This transformation parallels earlier episodes of mobilization, in which Sufi orders became mobilized as worldly fighting machines against foreign invasions, as during the Crusades period, in nineteenth-century Algeria and Sudan, or in early-twentieth-century Libya). Although the process of that transformation is complex and there are some indications that a mystical revival now may be underway in the form of a new symbiosis with worldly religiosity, the story of modern Islamic movements shows a remarkable sobriety and worldliness in all of its dimensions. Hasan al-Banna, the founder of the Muslim Brotherhood and a key figure in elaborating modern Islamic approaches to mass organization and popular mobilization, came from a mixed Sufi-Hanbali background. That is, his early education fused together mysticism and orthodoxy in a way that had not been uncommon since al-Ghazali's (d. 1111 C.E.) popular synthesis of the two traditions. But the worldly struggles and organizational work that preoccupied al-Banna and successor generations of activists increasingly placed the accent on the more orthodox and sober part of the equation. In fact, as the twentieth century progressed, modernizing movements, both Islamic and secular, came to associate Sufi approaches with backwardness and insularity, and their earlier role in anti-colonial struggles was forgotten. The world of modern struggles seemed to encourage sober reflection and outward rather than inward attention.

Accounts of al-Banna's life locate him precisely in those demographics that would become the backbone of modern normal Islamic movements: close enough to lower-class life but not living in abject poverty; coming from a socially marginal and recently urbanized background; an organic intellectual whose ideas are elaborated in cafes and neighborhood study groups rather than universities or bourgeois clubs; and someone with the quality of a preacher yet doing his work outside the mosque, the latter no longer being regarded as adequate for teaching the people about their religion in modern times. The genesis of the movement that he founded are in fact directly traced by al-Banna himself to his dissatisfaction with mosques, which emphasized a highly ritualistic approach to Islam and seemed to have little to say about how an old religion may infuse modern life with active rather than passive spirituality. Thus the site of his early message was not a mosque or a religious gathering, but a cafe in Ismailiyya where he spent short intervals every day (Hathut 2000:34). His brother, Jamal, observed that the earliest nucleus of the Brotherhood consisted of Suez Canal workers, that is, the part of the modern working class that was in most contact with British colonial power, then in direct control of the Canal area.

This beginning needs to be understood in a proper context, however, since the Brotherhood never saw itself as simply a working-class movement nor, indeed, did the movement remain for long restricted to any particular class. From its early days, in fact, the movement stressed not any specific demands on behalf of any class, but rather the cultivation of a new personality that would be less alienated from its surrounding modern social reality. Thus a substantial part of time in early Brotherhood mobilization, as recounted by Hassan Hathut, an early leading figure in the Brotherhood who knew al-Banna personally, was devoted to spiritual study circles that would last all night long. Hathut highlights the enjoyable nature of that kind of study, which instilled in participants a new lively spiritual experience that differed profoundly from old but somewhat comparable Sufi circles: Whereas in Sufi orders adherents were expected to follow and obey the master, in al-Banna's nightly educational circles, members were free to disagree with him and express their opinion (Hathut 2000:21).

Throughout its history, members of the Brotherhood have recounted an empowering combination of spiritual enlightenment and social purpose as the main contributions of the movement to their lives. A typical combination of incentives to join, as recounted by a former member (Abdel-Samad 2010), included how the group provided a sense of community that was especially important for curing his feeling of isolation in Cairo, to which he had recently migrated from the Egyptian countryside; his dissatisfaction with mainstream, traditional Islam that respected existing corrupt authorities and discouraged revolutionary attitudes even as those appeared necessary; the group providing its members with both a sense of being recognized individually as part of god's plan and with an emancipation from the passive traditional Islam they had known in their villages or former lives; and its overall ability to provide individuals in modern settings with a solid sense of orientation in an otherwise disorienting world.

These psychological and social benefits seem to have been part of the Brotherhood's cumulative contribution to the lives of its members from its very beginning. While all of the benefits mentioned above appear worldly, members often mention a profound sense of spiritual elevation, sometimes of a mystical quality, that is associated with their activism and in a way that sets the Brotherhood clearly apart from secular movements that also strove to give modern individuals a different sense of orientation and purpose. For example, Abdel-Samad recounts a spiritual–physical exercise in the desert, in which after several hours of strenuous walking in the heat, the commander of the group asked the participants to peel the orange— the only food each was allowed to bring with him—and then bury the fruit in the sand but eat the peeling. One felt then, in a sort of mystical way as he recounts, as being part of god's plan and became confident of being a positive force for changing the world for the better.

Such deprivation exercises, which celebrated rather than rejected the already familiar deprivations in everyday life and gave them a deep spiritual meaning, appear to have been experienced as positive and elevating forms of self-discipline, planting better seeds of change in the world at large, while allowing individuals to live with their otherwise unsatisfactory social, political, and economic realities. The combination of spiritual, educational, and physical exercises consumed much of the idle time of members and gave them a sense of solidarity and unique purpose. "Being useful to oneself and others" was a mantra repeatedly stressed by al-Banna, as well as the importance of avoiding idleness and wasting time. These standpoints, couched as religious duties, gave the spiritual exercises that would otherwise have served an individual and escapist purpose a worldly and others-oriented purpose. This general attitude meant that socially useful parts of older religious practices could also be incorporated, but after being excised from the old schools that had generated them. For example, in spite of their rational and sober religiosity, the early Brothers actually maintained those aspects of mystic Sufi spirituality, such as wealth-sharing (Hathut 2000:21, 98), that were oriented to a collective social purpose of mutual help.

The Muslim Brotherhood quickly developed a reputation for being the most organized group wherever it operated, and its members were usually highly dedicated to its teachings. Their worldly religiosity was mobilized for a broad range of social activities about which more will be said later. But in general, in so far as "changing the world" is part of anyone's program, one would expect some sort of logically defensible method, since a variety of different methods could be proposed for that purpose. In the case of the Brothers, observers have long noted their gradualism as the preferred method. But it is important to note where this attitude itself comes from and becomes widely appealing, since alternative approaches (confrontation, militancy, coups, conspiracies, and so on) were always options and had indeed been practiced by other modern revolutionary groups operating in the same societies where the Brothers were operating, and indeed occasionally (but rarely strategically, except in Sudan) by the Brothers themselves. But gradualism in this case seems to have been associated with the very proposition that Muslim society has declined steeply in modern times and succumbed to colonial domination largely due to long-term cultural weaknesses. This meant that it would require a *long-term* process of rejuvenation.

Turning away from traditional institutions like the ancient mosque and centering one's modern religious vocation around cafes, schools, neighborhoods, and ordinary needs of especially the new urban poor also gave the Brothers a sense of horizontal engagement with society that suggested to them with every encounter the need to get to know their own societies better. Thus from an early point, gradualism as a strategy was associated with the notion that Islam, as the Brothers understood it, was in reality *not* deeply rooted in society, and that furthermore it could not be imposed on the people without persuasion. Thus in rejecting revolutionary change in favor of gradualism, al-Banna himself argued that one must first know the people and their needs before one may propose a revolution to them, and that furthermore no Islamic law could possibly be applied to them until they themselves have become proper Muslims again (Hathut 2000:17–18, 114).

The proposition that an activist Brother was educating society about the forgotten nature of religion also suggested reverse communication: That activist himself experienced being educated at the same time about the same religion, especially its relation to modernity. Hathut (2000:14) mentions an example of a question being raised to al-Banna about cinema, and whether it was *halal* (permissible) or *haram* (forbidden) according to Islam. After some uncertainty, he answered: "*halal* cinema is *halal*, and *haram* cinema is *haram*." One here confronts a modern invention, whose moral stature and potential for disrupting some traditional ways requires a religious verdict. The solution—typical of the whole approach of the Brothers to modernity—is not to reject or accept a new technology or instrument in its entirety, but to validate it on the basis of the use to which it is put. Implicit in this judgment is the assumption that all modern things are both beneficial and evil at the same time, and therefore can be neither rejected nor accepted in their entirety and without discernment as to what they are doing for the moral fabric of society. The principle that evil is always latent in that which is good meant that the proper attitude should be one of constant caution and self-discipline.

This attitude may be termed "discerning worldliness," in which new things are judged in terms of uses, and is in principle better suited for building a broad community of followers who come from a variety of cultural backgrounds, social classes, and professional interests. Yet, Islamic movements show at least at some point in their history an opposite tendency, which is to advocate total bans on entire categories of objects and practices, regardless of their use. While this standpoint is more typical of governing autocratic authorities, it is not uncommon especially in young movements. Especially where such total bans target pleasure, they may be regarded as "strategies for directing focus": ways by which all pleasure is directed at the movement itself and away from any competing habits, as those may take the person's attention away from a movement. That is especially the case when the movement sees itself to be a total world unto itself, and thus as the most legitimate outlet for all of its activists' energies, *including* pleasure.

Strategies for directing focus are evident in bans that affect items not clearly prohibited in the scriptures. In such cases, the tendency to extend total bans to cover more and more items suggests that prohibition is more geared in that case to directing the focus of pleasure into the movement, rather than following any religious rule. The Taliban prohibited music, for example, but downplayed the ban after it lost state power in Afghanistan and needed more recruits. Hizbullah prohibited smoking in areas it controlled in south Lebanon in its early days, but found itself forced to give up the ban given local resistance and the fact the ban seemed to interfere with the movement's real focus then, which was fighting the Israeli occupation of the region. More recently, Da'esh went above and beyond all previous prohibitions, banning both smoking and music, in addition to alcohol. What seems to support the proposition that in such cases the movement does not prohibit pleasure as much as seek to direct it to the movement itself is very evident particularly in the case of Da'esh. Here, the movement specifically prohibits instrumental music, but allows and even encourages poetry (*anashid*) that praises the movement (Haykel and Creswell 2015). Is this because music cannot be controlled as well as poetry? It is possible that instrumental music is more suspicious than poetry because the textuality of poetry suggests clarity of evidence in comparison to music: We are in a better position to know what poetry is saying than what emotions a piece of music may elicit. And thus the text of poetry may be useful for channeling pleasure toward the movement if that is what the poetic text seems to say. The same focusing of pleasure cannot be as guaranteed with music.

It is possible that all forms of religiosity involve some strategies of pleasure, including "prohibitions" that direct pleasure into objects or practices (for example, into fellow believers or piety) with such focus that requires eliminating competing pleasure outlets. Of course, the more extreme varieties of strategies of focus, such as Da'esh's, were not possible without effective control over territories and populations, since those strategies were unlikely to be accepted voluntarily. Without constant vigil and a great deal of control over members or populations, strategies of focus always run the risk of alienating potential supporters, or at least fail in directing their erotic energies toward the movement. Thus the alternative strategy, which is here called "discerning worldliness" and is evident in its broad outline in al-Banna's answer regarding cinema, seems to have furnished the basic common denominator of the broader variety of modern Islamic movements. In theory, "discerning worldliness," because of its acceptance of different results and situational tolerance of various sources of selfhood, is more compatible with a democratic culture than are the prohibitive and burdensome "strategies of focus" that require constant external vigilance.

Whereas strategies of focus highlight the individual's obligation to obey, discerning worldliness highlights the capacity of the individual to judge, select, justify, and reject—*and* also "obey," but within a larger matrix of options, not as the most basic rule. As such, discerning worldliness became associated with the emergence of *participatory ethics* (which are not exactly the same as "democratic culture") in Muslim societies in which modern Islamic movements have adopted it as an approach. The nature of those ethics is often missed in debates as to whether Islamic movements, or "Islam" in general, may be "democratic" or at least compatible with democracy (and also other presumably derivative principles, such as human rights, gender equality, social justice, and so on). The basic effect of discerning worldliness, and the situational activism tied to it, is to create spaces or opportunities for *everyday* social participation in local, national, or global life, and in ways that are personally felt.

These sorts of participatory ethics are not confined and typically are rarely oriented to electing parliaments. Rather, participatory ethics are discharged through means by which an otherwise lonely and ineffective modern individual may acquire capacity, or at least the feeling of a capacity, to participate in larger social issues on a daily basis and do so as a matter of ordinary life. In the pre-revolutionary (pre-2011) Arab world, opportunities for this participation preceded democracy and are still capable of being practiced independently of it. And in any case, forms of everyday participation facilitated by modern Islamic movements were premised not on any elaborate theory of democracy or pluralism, but in the more elementary proposition that the modern individual had a duty to discharge large social obligations directly rather than delegate them to a distant bureaucratic system, such as the modern state. After all, the modern state in most of the Muslim world was ruled throughout the twentieth century by a narrowly based secular elite. Such secular elites rarely demonstrated credible interest in broad popular participation, whether through formal democracy or otherwise.

While modern Islamic movements have frequently entered formal democratic contests when the stage was open to them, they have historically formed themselves outside of such a stage and have fostered ethics of so-cial participation that remained autonomous from state institutions. That has been their greatest accomplishment, and it clearly distinguishes them from more secular opponents who, while they may have been active in local civil societies, have not had access to a broadly based and *familiar* discourse through which participation may be motivated by a sense of binding ethical obligation.

Unlike episodic democratic participation, the everyday participa-tion fostered in modern Islamic activism assumes many practical forms depending on local need and ability—from building neighborhood schools to providing help with housing and marriage to fostering chari-table endowments to participating in outright political and in some cases militant activism. This variety of possibilities, which are dependent on the one hand on external opportunities and on the other on opportunities cre-ated by the previous activism of such movements themselves, offer a con-tinuum of participatory options, "participation" here being understood as discharging in a practical way one's ethical obligation in the world. This variety of possibilities of participation allows for a wide range of practical adjustments to a variety of local conditions, including political realities and levels of institutional development.

Three organizational models

The most established and successful Islamic social movements, therefore, are about participation—which, again, should not be confused with de-mocracy, and may in fact not require democracy at all. Certainly before the Arab Spring, but probably after as well, these movements tended to be more concerned with promoting the arts of participation than with either democracy, typically unavailable, or authoritarian rule over society, typi-cally unattainable.

The relative success of this emphasis on ordinary participation over rev-olutionary takeover of state power may be briefly illustrated by comparing the careers of two modern Islamic movements, the Muslim Brotherhood, founded in Egypt in 1928 and now in existence in almost every country where Muslims live, and *Hizb al-Tahrir* or "Party of Liberation," founded in Jerusalem in 1953, and now global, although operating largely un-derground and with much smaller membership than the Brotherhood. Modern jihadism may be considered as a third variety, and is closer to the *Hizb al-Tahrir* model, although with significant differences as will be discussed later. The first two types of movements in particular strive, at least in theory, for the establishment of an Islamic state. However, whereas the Brotherhood has usually posited that theoretical outcome as a product of the gradual Islamization of society as a whole, *Hizb al-Tahrir* adopted for much of its history a vanguardist approach similar to Marxist revolutionary models in the developing world, where the takeover of state power was deemed central for enacting social transformation.

The difference between the first two types of movements seems also to inform their organizational structure. Whereas the national branches of the Brotherhood operated independently and were free to choose any tactics that were appropriate for local conditions, *Hizb al-Tahrir* highlighted centralized global leadership and coordinated action. And whereas the Brotherhood members had a wide range of possible daily charitable and social tasks that could count as fulfillment of ethical obligations, the *Hizb al-Tahrir* members displayed an attitude similar to that of secular political parties, in which fulfillment meant establishing the caliphate (that is, capture the state) (Pankhurst 2016). That distant task made it difficult for members to find enough meaning in their little everyday accomplishments (e.g., Umm Mustafa 2008).

Consequently, it was the Brotherhood model rather than that of *Hizb al-Tahrir* that proved to be most successful in establishing large and lasting movements. By contrast, the *Tahrir* model, in spite of its global reach was always a minority party. And this in spite of the fact that the *Tahrir* movement could in some sense be said to be more politically developed than the Brothers—in the sense that it had from an early point in its history detailed ideas for a constitution, institutions of governance, and rights and duties under a hypothetical Islamic state. By contrast, the Brothers rarely bothered with elaborating any such details, and their simple yet undefined message before they came to power that Islam was "the solution" freed them from having to fight over distant details. Rather, they focused on practical and immediate action on a wide range of daily worries, but also capitalized on systemic opportunities whenever those emerged. With few exceptions, notably Rachid Ghannoushi of Tunisia's *Nahda*, the Brothers spent little intellectual energy on elaborating the exact nature or structure of the hypothetical Islamic state.

This brief contrast of two global models of Islamic activism clearly shows that a vague or very general, even underdeveloped, political program (Ayubi 1993; Roy 1994) may be an advantage, and that a more elaborate ideology is a handicap in situations that favor flexibility and adaptability.

And it was flexibility and adaptability that proved to be more necessary when members' shared religiosity, which in theory expressed their
common global commitments, nonetheless had to be discharged under
very different circumstances. That meant that local contexts posed to the
modern religious activists multiple and changing rather than standard
possibilities. They could therefore scarcely make good use of standard
global scripts.

The third model of modern Islamic movements is broadly captured
under the term "jihadism," a trend that before Da'esh consisted of a
cluster of small movements not exceeding a few hundred members each
(Kurzman 2011). While jihadism has recently been most associated with
violence, it should not be confused with all instances of violent conflict
involving Islamic groups; jihadism as commonly understood now was not
a factor in the Algerian civil war during the 1990s, since that war was pre-
cipitated not with prior jihadist ideology and agitation, but by the regime's
cancellation of elections, which turned a peaceful process of political
transformation into a bloodbath. Nor should national mass movements
like Hamas or Hizbullah be confused with modern jihadism, since their
ideology is substantially an outgrowth of local programs of national liberation rather than global jihadist agendas. The Taliban likewise were not,
strictly speaking, a jihadist organization, but a local national party with a
specific agenda focusing on ending the civil war in Afghanistan.

Modern jihadism, in contrast to all movements mentioned above,
tends now to operate through global networks, just like the first two types
of movements.[1] It is closer to *Hizb al-Tahrir* in world perspective, though
not in organizational structure. Charitable work is sometimes associated
with the origins of this type of movement, although the pattern here is less
consistent than in the case of other types of Islamic movements. Al-Qa'ida,
for example, began as a "database" (which is where its Arabic name comes
from), that is, as a tabulation of foreign fighters who took part in the fight
against the Soviets in Afghanistan, with the expressed intention being to
help in locating and supporting their families. Modern jihadism, therefore, did not precede modern wars but was itself created in their theaters.
Over time, jihadism gained vastly more energy from local wars (especially
in Iraq, Syria, Yemen, and Libya) being increasingly fought as *global* wars

---

1. There were of course varieties that acted substantially as national organizations, such as
the *Gama'a Islamiyyah* in Egypt during the 1990s, before it abandoned violence and exited
the jihadist camp.

in both senses of the term: as wars between outside states, and as means of mobilizing global networks. Therefore, those could scarcely be regarded simply as "local" wars, even though the theater of war *appeared* to be local.

What concerns us here is how global mobilization emerged out of otherwise local conflicts. In the case of al-Qa'ida, the fact that a mere database proved sufficient as a mobilizing tool suggests that these sorts of organizations come to a certain extent out of engaged informatics: Persuasion is expected to be minimal, as the energy is already there, and it only needs to be recorded and then mobilized. If this is true, it still explains little. The demographically miniscule size of early jihadism may not warrant treating it as a significant social fact, but the fact that Da'esh managed very quickly to recruit 30,000 foot soldiers once it declared the caliphate in 2014, and that in the preceding two years before al-Nusra in Syria already enlisted a few thousand fighters, suggest a *sudden* transformation rather than a long historical evolution as was the case with the earlier two models.

Based on the nature of evidence thus far, a number of propositions about the evolution and trajectory of jihadism may be proposed:

1. Jihadism as generic radicalism: The "Islamization of radicalism" thesis, proposed by Olivier Roy (2017), identifies in the sudden growth of Da'esh not so much a radicalization of Islamic politics, but rather the emergence of Islam as the newest venue for the discharge of radical energies that in previous decades would have been invested in some variety of Marxism or other forms of radical secular politics. The thesis shifts attention away from questions of ideology, since it proposes that in any age, radical energies will gravitate toward *any* ideology that expresses the seriousness of the struggle and its apocalyptic and global nature. This thesis may help explain, at least in part, the otherwise inexplicable lack of familiarity on the part of a large percentage of recruits to Da'esh with even basic Islamic practices, rituals, and teachings; their general lack of previous jihadi experience; and their disinterest in seeking guidance from traditional religious authorities (Rosenblatt 2016).

   What lends some credence to this thesis is the fact that recruitment to Da'esh seemed to be less based on theology than on apocalyptic success, which explains the sudden appeal of a previously obscure movement. Clearly, apocalyptic success appeals most in catastrophic or hopeless conditions, as will be addressed in the third hypothesis below. However, while the "Islamization of radicalism" thesis seems to be relevant to explaining a *part* of Da'esh in particular, it does not explain much about the earlier al-Qa'ida or older jihadist groups. Even with regards to Da'esh, the thesis seems to address only one-half of that phenomenon, that is, the half that is related to global youth cultures. This leads us to the second point.

2. Jihadism as convergence of two cultures: Da'esh in particular seems to have resulted from the fusion of two previously separate environments: local wars and global youth cultures. For almost a whole decade, the earlier version of Da'esh operated only in Iraq, making no more grandiose claims about itself than being the Iraqi branch of al-Qa'ida, and then only after the U.S. invasion in 2003 provided a uniquely hospitable environment for establishing such a branch that had never existed before. During the decade following the U.S. invasion, the organization was almost completely decimated on more than one occasion, only to regroup by capitalizing on increasing disaffection with hopelessly corrupt post-occupation Iraqi governments, their short-sighted sectarian politics, and their dominance by mediocre politicians lacking any capacity other than manipulating regional rivalries for short-term gains. That dismal political system reached its low point under Nouri al-Maliki, under whom Da'esh, still relatively small, defeated the already demoralized Iraqi army, captured all of northern Iraq except Kurdistan, and camped just outside of Bagdad. In addition to the local Iraqi calculus, Da'esh growth during that period benefited greatly from the dynamics of the Syrian civil war next door. There, Da'esh had established al-Nusra Front as a local franchise, before gradually advancing into the Syrian theater directly. Its capture in short order of two major cities in Syria (Raqqa) and Iraq (Mosul) were spectacular advances that laid down the foundation for declaring the caliphate, and also to absorb a large part of al-Nusra itself, whose leadership refused to rejoin the new organization. While a stream of global jihadists were already coming especially into Syria before 2014, it was the spectacular takeover of Mosul that opened a floodgate of global volunteers, who then could verify for themselves that they were witnesses to a world historical mission that gave a worthy direction to their otherwise aimless radical energies and grand meaning to their otherwise insignificant selves. The fusion of those two theaters—local wars and global youth cultures—meant that two cultures, vastly different in their motivating forces, found themselves on the same front, and could only be kept together by a dictatorship, whereby united purpose was built on a fabric of apocalyptic vision and expansionist energy. Iraqi–Syrian roots of Da'esh had little to do with

any global youth culture. Just as in the case of Afghanistan earlier, local wars in Syria and Iraq had destroyed local societies, along with their traditional capacities and mechanisms for conflict resolution and conflict avoidance.

3. Jihadism as Islamized traces of old regimes: It is noteworthy that in some cases, Da'esh established itself most easily in territories that had broad support for deposed *secular* regimes: north central Iraq, where Saddam Hussein had his strongest base of support, and Sirt in Libya, which had been the most favorable city to Qaddafi in Libya and the last to fall to forces opposing him. In the case of Iraq in particular, it is known that eight of the 12 top military commanders of Da'esh during the zenith of its military might in 2103–2015 had been high officers in Saddam's dissolved army. Further, territories most easily captured by Da'esh in Iraq and Libya had populations less known for any unusual religiosity than for their hostility to the new order, or at least lack of incorporation into it. Here we have a phenomenon that has nothing to do with any religiosity, but is comparable to the German *Freikorps* that formed after World War I out of disaffected military men, who neither could be incorporated into the new order nor longed for the return of the Kaiser. Uncertain about their future and realizing that their past order could not return, they adopted a *revanchist*, masculine ideology that ultimately morphed into fascism.

4. Jihadism as symptom of nihilism, brought on by impasse: The ideology of a group like Da'esh represents a nihilist position that has become mobilized. Here, nihilism is one position within a broad social rejection of the socio-political order. Nihilism is not simply an idea but also a sociological phenomenon: That is, it is a standpoint that, given certain conditions, can assume a more socially persuasive meaning and organizational shape. As such, we would need to construct its story: How, where and when did nihilism acquire persuasiveness and organization?

Nihilism is not a natural or inevitable development of conditions of closed possibilities, since other options can always be pursued—for example: fatalism, surrender, mysticism, art, depression, mind-altering substances, graduate study—depending on availability and inclination. Thus nihilism must not simply be regarded as an outcome of a certain environment. Rather, it is a chosen option among many others that such an environment provides. Nihilism may gain traction not in explicitly or predominantly nihilistic circles, but as a sporadic practice or idea that inhabits part of an organization. We see obvious elements of mobilized nihilism in al-Qa'ida, for example, but those elements did not define that organization, and certainly not in the way that seem to define some of its offshoots. We also see some nihilist practices in earlier *secular* organizations, in which the practice of suicide attacks on the enemy was used. Nihilism thus is not a specifically religious idea. It is also a matter of degree. Nihilism seems most associated with a sense of closed possibilities, and it could be measured in some meaningful ways: for example, by the degree to which suicide attacks become more frequent or are used as *strategy*, rather than as an emergency tactic.

Social analysts do in fact speak of "radicalization" as one possible reaction to conditions of closed possibilities, although they do not typically use the language of "nihilism." But whereas radicalism is a generic term, nihilism is a more specific approach: It is the radical approach that foregrounds *revenge* above all other considerations, including considerations of strategic success. Nihilism also seems to be associated with the devaluation of one's own life.

However, it is difficult to imagine *leaders* of nihilistic organizations to be themselves nihilist individuals, given that building a successful organization requires planning, fortitude, amassing resources, and patience, that is, anything but impulsive action. But as a sociological phenomenon, nihilism is not necessarily what leaders of nihilist organizations do. Rather, it is what *attracts* individuals who have become nihilist to join such organizations, and such organizations, in turn, provide other radicals who may not yet be nihilists with a new option to consider. Nihilism therefore resides not in the structure of the organization, which may be highly planned and even bureaucratic. Rather, it resides in the mobilizing capacity of the nihilist idea itself.

5. Jihadism as critical mimicry of government ideology: The chauvinist, exclusive, masculine teachings that tend to be associated with jihadi ideology have in some cases affinities to long-established discourses of those governments that have fostered earlier varieties of more complacent jihadism. Political modernity has given rise to many political theaters where this ideological game appears necessary for governments, such as when government wants to justify expanding its power over society beyond what had been customary, or as a way of mobilizing society against imagined or real external threats, or where the elimination of internal opposition appears necessary in order to establish a new order. Modern Wahhabism, the ideological source of especially the jihadist variety associated with al-Qa'ida and Da'esh, is also the

official government ideology of Saudi Arabia. Wahhabism as a movement, to be discussed in more details later, has typically relied on coercion and, especially in the latter part of the twentieth century, benefited from lavish oil wealth that the Saudi system invested in propagating a xenophobic, authoritarian, repressive religious ideology into previously more enlightened localities around the world.

Obviously it could not have been the intention of Saudi authorities to promote an ideology they could not control, but when ideology is associated with transborder mobilization, the result is anything but controllable. It is well-known that the jihadist mobilization for Afghanistan in the 1980s, financed substantially by the Saudi government, provided the ideal climate for the emergence of al-Qa'ida—a movement of a type previously unknown. But the impact of Saudi ideology is also evident in a number of other empirics, including the fact that more than three-quarters of the participants in the September 11 attacks came from Saudia Arabia, which at a later point also supplied the largest number of foreign recruits to Da'esh.

In fact, there is little in Da'esh's ideology and even practices that cannot be traced to official Saudi religious teaching and practices, including avowed sectarianism; animosity toward all Muslims of different persuasions; reliance on coercion and violence as the main vehicle for transmitting the true faith; beheadings as legal punishment; and complete disregard for cultural heritage, including in Mecca itself. The fact that Da'esh opposed the Saudi regime does not negate that the regime had taught it everything it knew. But in that process of learning, the jihadist movement learned one more thing: that the teacher was hypocritical, whereas the student was pure still. Da'esh could see itself to be morally superior to its teacher: It acquired all of Saudi official ideology, minus the corruption of its royal family.

The five hypotheses on jihadism above (see Table 1.1) were presented as distinct analytical propositions, although in all likelihood the resilience of jihadism depends on the degree to which they converge (and in the process speak to each other). Together, they suggest that modern jihadism should be seen less as a problem in its own right than as a *symptom* of other problems. In particular, the last four of above hypotheses suggest that jihadism is a symptom of bad governance, and that persistent, large-scale violence in a given territory tends to be produced by the same systems that claim to fight it. What needs to be done becomes then obvious: Just as the cure to

Table 1.1 Five hypotheses on the origins of modern jihadism

1. Generic radicalism camouflaged (for the moment) in religious language
2. Fusion of two previously distinct theaters (local wars and global youth culture)
3. Islamized traces of former (non-religious) regimes
4. Nihilism borne out of sense of impasse
5. Critical mimicry of government ideology

Table 1.2 Comparison of key attributes of three general models of modern Islamic activism

Model	Global Organizational Structure	Coordination of National Units	Political Theory
Muslim Brotherhood	Relatively loose	Local independence	General
Hizb al-Tahrir	Hierarchical, vanguard party style	Global coordination	Elaborate
Jihadism	Franchise model	Local "translation" of global calls	Rudimentary (when not nihilist)

illness means eliminating the disease rather than its symptoms, it follows that the cure to so-called terror requires eliminating the political systems that produce it. Focusing only on the symptom gives us in due time only a more virulent form of the illness. The rise of Da'esh illustrates this point abundantly, just as does its fall, which required a large international coalition, including both superpowers, staggering costs, and the destruction of entire cities.

Due to its noisy character, jihadism tends to divert attention away from older and more broadly established forms of modern Islamic activism, which may also be "militant" at points, though it has a broader social character and a wider range of social roles than jihadism. Retracing our steps to the beginning of this discussion, we can finally propose a comparison between three general models of modern Islamic activism (see Table 1.2).

In spite of the noisy character of jihadism, it remains a relatively small phenomenon, judged by the number of activists it has been able to enlist compared to other types of movements, and given its tendency to be concentrated especially in already existing war zones and its association with local conditions of closed possibilities. Jihadism may therefore grow and become a dominant feature of Islamic movements to the extent that those conditions that encourage it spread geographically or deepen locally. In the process, jihadism may also develop a more coherent political ideology and also attract energy away from the two other models of Islamic movements. Until such a scenario, the more ordinary, brotherhood-type movements continue to define the mainstream of Islamic activism. They are more aligned with the ethos of ordinary social conservatism, for which they offer one participatory outlet—something that in a liberal political system may take the form of an Islamic version of Christian social democracy.

Figure 1.1 sketches the general character of the role of Islam as a discourse of social movements. The overlaps between ordinary social conservatism and politically mobilized religiosity may be comparable to parts of the history of Christian social democracy in Europe. But the larger picture has to do with ethics of participation more generally, and not with the specifics of democracy as a political system. For example, part of what Figure 1.1 registers is modern Salafism as a distinct type of movement, which is often said to be apolitical and non-hierarchical, being focused more on individual ethics and salvation rather than political programs. Yet we also know that such trends could also become politically mobilized given the demands of the moment, as for instance in post-revolutionary Egypt since 2011, where a number of Salafist parties emerged to contest

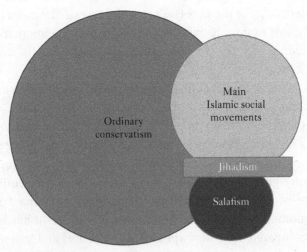

FIGURE 1.1 Islam and politics

elections, even though they had originally hesitated to take part in the revolution, in line with their overall apolitical doctrines. However, Salafism is also an approach to social participation, and usually not in ways that require the formation of political parties or contesting elections. If one can speak of a salafi approach to democracy, it would consist in the concern for an individual social role and the health of individual psyches, rather than in the takeover of political systems. On the other hand, salafism, like any other ideology, may also transform, as we see for example in the rise of salafi jihadism in recent years, or in the ascendance of what Lauzière (2015) describes as "purist" Salafism over a hundred years of experimentation.

In general, the most enduring style of religious activism over the past one hundred years was *not* one characterized by hierarchical control, centralized coordination, or even theoretical clarity. Rather, the preeminent style was one that used generic moral premises aligned with ordinary social conservatism, but in ways that foregrounded responsibility for other strangers in a larger society, a responsibility that was carried out in flexible formats adaptable to local situations. Religious activism, after all, is one way by which old religion acquires modern meaning. Now it acquires that by being put into social use, by being asked modern questions, which is the only way its continued relevance could be tested. And conversely, it slips out of modern times and dies out—unless entirely held up by a vigilant, coercive dictatorship—when it is held up as a book of esoteric doctrines, pure propositions, or arcane rules. If not associated with coercive government, modern religion lives on as a way of providing ethical justifications for activities that are deemed to be socially necessary and meaningful. A religion may be said to be living still, in a social sense, to the extent it informs earthly pursuits. When one lives in a modern society that calls on the individual to experiment with new ways of connecting to strangers and new communities in whose midst one increasingly lives, one option such an individual is offered is social participation in new formats but according to a familiar ethical discourse. Modern Islamic movements are born here, out of this modern condition, by modern individual wills.

What are the characteristics of religious movements associated with more general, modern participatory ethics? Bearing the above discussions in mind, we can identify five such features:

· Islamic movements tend to begin as mutual aid societies rather than as clearly defined political entities.

- Such movements offer themselves up as ways for society in general to organize itself outside the state (especially when the state offers little credible opportunities for effective participation).
- Islamic movements signify the increasing politicization of society itself, namely the entry into the political field of hitherto excluded demographics.
- The political success of religious movements is tied, ironically, to the fact religion is the only familiar discourse of participation that is not exclusively state-oriented.
- Religious movements tend to transform when they capture the state or become part of it. The nature of this transformation cannot be predicted on the basis of their former positions.

These features are intricately connected, but it helps to clarify things if they are discussed in the rough order in which they are listed above.

Mutual aid

The record of social services provided by Islamic social movements has been amply documented (Alterman and Hippel 2007; Clark 2003; Wickham 2002; Benthall and Bellion-Jourdan 2009; Cammett 2014; POMEPS 2014), and in fact it is impossible to identify any significant or even many small Islamic movements for which the provision of social services is not a central undertaking. It is easy, of course, to see how this propensity could naturally emerge out of a form of religiosity that had not initially been invested in any movement: Religious charity or ethics of mutual obligation, after all, are integral to historical religiosity and have formed a major feature of its public display (Faroqhi 1994; Hoexter 2002; Livezey 2000; Casanova 1994). But in so far as they are tied to the emergence of modern movements, the provision of services has tended to mold old charitable and mutual aid practices into the fabric of new networks, and it is those networks that formed over time the basis of lasting movements (see Figure 1.2).

Yet, there is no evidence that social services had, at least initially, been tied to any clear political program. Absence of evidence does not keep some "terrorism experts" from alleging that Islamic movements use charities to reach out to "impressionable youth" (e.g., Levitt 2007:17). This position has all the trappings of a paternalistic attitude toward which we are expected to be sensitized when it comes to analyzing historical minorities

Social Aid and Traditional Politics	*Social Aid and Modern Movements*
Patrimonial relations	Modern movements
Possible outcome: patrimonial loyalty	Possible outcome: ideological loyalty
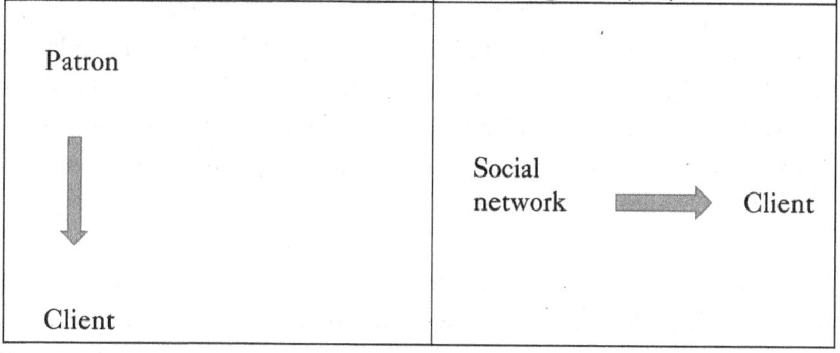 Patron ↓ Client	Social network ⟹ Client

FIGURE 1.2 Two models of mutual aid and loyalty

we are more familiar with, but seems to go unchallenged when it comes to Muslims or subaltern populations generally. It is unfortunate that often social analysis easily gives way to a presumption that people we do not actually know may still be understood as child-like entities, easily impressionable, deficient in intellect, and capable of being duped consistently and in large numbers.

There is in fact no evidence that a definite political program has ever motivated social services, although there is quite a bit of evidence that over time autonomous networks that came into being on the basis of providing such services *become* formally political when the social environments in which they live themselves become highly politicized. It is also important to distinguish the social service networks established by modern Islamic movements from older styles of patronage with which many poorer clients in the Muslim world had been historically familiar. Whereas older forms of patron-client relations (Khoury 1982) were hierarchical and helped consolidate the authority of traditional notables (who rarely required special religious credentials), the style of mutual aid established by modern Islamic movements bypassed the old elites and tended to form more horizontal and flexible networks. In tracing the organizational evolution of the early Muslim Brotherhood in Egypt, Ziad Munson (2001) identifies what would become a familiar pattern:

Probably the most important single feature of the society's [Brotherhood] expansion was its method of establishing new branches. After its founding in Isma'liya, the Muslim Brotherhood began construction of a mosque, using funds from membership dues and grants from local businesses. A boy's school, girl's school, and social club were subsequently added to the complex as the organization grew. Each new branch of the Society followed a similar pattern of growth. The organization would establish a branch headquarters and then immediately begin a public service project—the construction of a mosque, school, or clinic, the support of a local handicraft industry, or the organization of a sports program. (501)

This pattern would be repeated almost everywhere we find a successful and well-established Islamic social movement. The Lebanese Hizbullah, for example, which did not exist even as an idea until the 1980s, explicitly traces its origins to the mutual aid societies within Shi'a communities that coalesced in the 1960s and early 1970s as *Harakat al-Mahrumin*, "Movement of the Dispossessed," established by the legendary vanished Imam Musa Sadr. Just like the Muslim Brotherhood in its early days, *Harakat al-Mahrumin* had at best a vague political program. It resembled more a loose network of congregations focusing on local communal mutual aid than a clearly structured political party. Until it eventually transformed into the Amal movement in the mid 1970s (out of which Hizbullah broke away in the early 1980s), *Harakt al-Mahrumin* did little to systematically contest traditional leaderships even among the Lebanese Shi'a, and took no part in formal Lebanese politics, apart from mobilizing for a by-election for a single vacant parliamentary seat in 1974. But there is no evidence in either case that local individuals joined such local aid societies for anything other than in response to local needs and dynamics, and one is hard-pressed to find a clear political program expressed even by more leading members of such associations, including Musa Sadr himself. That of course would change over time for reasons that I will come to later. But explicit or direct political intentions are in short supply at the *foundational* period of these local societies.

The same tendency is apparent at the genesis of all other Islamic social movements. In Algeria, for example, where a sizable Islamic movement emerged in the late 1980s, more than a quarter of a century after independence, the genesis of Islamic activism likewise seems to have little to do with any political program. The networks that came to form the *Front Islamique du Salut* (FIS) did not define themselves initially in political or even Islamic terms, tending rather to be neighborhood groups coming together to solve practical urban problems (Vergès 1996). Similarly, Hamas in occupied Palestine was originally established as a charitable organization, and was so apolitical that it was originally regarded by Israel as a potential counterweight to what all Israeli governments until the late 1980s believed was their real nemesis, namely the secular Palestine Liberation Organization (PLO).

While formally established as a resistance movement only in 1987, Hamas's first recognizable nucleus of activism coalesced as early as 1973 in the Islamic Center of Gaza. The social institutions out of which that Center coalesced had developed earlier, immediately following the Israeli occupation of Gaza in 1967. For 20 years between 1967 and 1987, during which the Palestinian national movement was entirely secular, ordinary social needs were more and more being provided by various local civil society associations, which over time began to be more associated with religious segments. That was most clearly evident in Gaza, the poorest, most systematically deprived part of the Palestinian territories, and thus the part in which autonomous mutual aid societies were essential for the survival of the majority of the population. Even Hamas's enemies estimate that it spends about 80 to 85% of its budget on social programs (Levitt 2007: 237), and more friendly estimates are even higher. It is not incidental, therefore, that mosques tripled in number during those same two decades preceding the establishment of Hamas, from 200 mosques in 1967 to 600 in 1987 (Baroud 2010). This growth greatly outpaced the population increase of 1.6 times during the same period (Ennab 1994:64), reflecting the increasing importance of religion as a reference point for social solidarity and mutual aid under increasingly difficult and eventually hopeless conditions. Gaza today remains the heartland of Islamic activism in Palestine.

The range and size of services provided by Islamic groups may be quite impressive, even when compared to outlays of governments with superior resources and far higher budgets. In a country of less than four million inhabitants, for example, the Islamic Health Society of Hizbullah offered in 2005 alone medical services for free or nominal fees to nearly 450,000 individuals (HSI 2007). When the Muslim Brotherhood was banned in Egypt in 1954—by then it had an estimated membership of four million—the government was forced to continue to staff and fund its extensive range of services, since those had become so vast that sudden withdrawal would undermine social and political stability (Munson 501). When it was allowed to resume its social (but not political) role in the 1970s, the movement quickly reestablished a strong Islamic presence in the social welfare segment of civil society, claiming by 1993 about 43%

of all NGOs in the country, the largest of any category of NGOs (Kandil 1995). When a less competent government banned the Brotherhood again in Egypt in 2014 and confiscated its assets, hundreds of affiliated charities closed down or had their services greatly reduced, affecting primarily the poor. In the Palestinian territories, not only did Hamas's social services become over time essential for the survival of large numbers under conditions of occupations and pauperization, but they enormously accentuated the moral stature of Hamas. Compared to the secular Palestinian Authority, such services were offered more efficiently and untainted by the massive corruption with which the Palestinian Authority became identified in the lead-up to the 2006 elections, which Hamas won. In pre-Arab Spring Yemen, it is estimated that 70% of NGOs were religious in nature, while in Jordan the largest NGO has remained the Islamic Charity Society run by the Muslim Brotherhood (Clark 2003:12).

Apart from the range and size of social services, including everything from kindergarten, youth programs, health services to the poor, schools, marriage ceremonies, counseling, and housing construction, Islamic sources of social welfare tend to compare favorably with services provided through state bureaucratic means or by secular authorities, notably on account of the perceived corruption, unresponsiveness, and unaccountability of the latter. For example, an analysis of the Palestinian elections in 2006 shows clearly that the main issue that helped Hamas win those elections was its perceived lack of corruption in comparison to the ruling Fateh. Seventy-one percent of those who rated corruption as their prime concern voted for Hamas, as well as 56% of those who highlighted the inability of the Palestinian Authority to guarantee their personal safety (PCSR 2006). Hamas itself focused in its campaign literature on the corruption of its competitors and largely avoided the stalled peace process and the status of the conflict with Israel, which it had put on hold through its self-declared ceasefire for the year preceding the election.

More generally, this transfer of welfare responsibility seems to be, at least in the case of Islamic movements, an unplanned adjustment to what development agencies themselves have been suggesting in recent years as the normal path for much of the world, and which may be summed up by the following policy recommendation by a well-regarded source:

[A]s societies develop, the social contract is changing as well. The earlier paternalistic understanding of the responsibilities of the state has given way to a new type of social contract. Previously, social welfare was materialized in the form of handouts from the government to poor and needy recipients in society. Nowadays, governments act as the leaders and facilitators of concerted efforts made by a broad variety of stakeholders. (ESCWA 2009:4)

Of course, this statement describes not what governments always do, but what best government practices are from the point of view of contemporary development strategies. The actual attitude of Muslim individuals tends to be more nuanced. Tentative evidence from the World Values Survey, for example, seems to suggest that Muslims are not dissimilar to others, in the sense that while a large percentage of them expect government to assume some responsibility toward its society, opinion varies greatly as to whether it is capable of doing so alone, or even of being trusted.

As is evident in Table 1.3 and Table 1.4, such results vary widely from one country to another, demonstrating again what other quantitative researchers have found (Fattah 2006), namely that the "Muslim World" is really a number of different worlds when it comes to measures of values,

Table 1.3 Perception of government responsibility toward society in selected Muslim societies

Country	Turkey	Morocco	Iran	Jordan	Iraq	Malaysia	Mali
Percentage highlighting government responsibility	40.3	40.2	54.8	52	71.3	20	33.6
Percentage highlighting shared responsibility	43.9	24.7	28.8	37.5	25	46.9	36.8
Percentage highlighting personal responsibility	12.7	11.9	16.3	10.2	3.4	33.1	29.6

Source: World Values Survey

The figures are percentages in response to the statement (question 98 in WVS): "People should take more responsibility to provide for themselves vs The government should take more responsibility to ensure that everyone is provided for." Responses were given on a scale from 1 to 10, were 1 signified most agreement with government responsibility whereas 10 most agreement with personal responsibility. I simplified and recoded the results, with 1 to 3 as highlighting government responsibility, 4 to 7 highlighting shared responsibility, and 8 to 10 highlighting personal responsibility. As typical of WVS, the surveys were done in different years for different countries: Iran in 2005, Iraq 2013, Malaysia in 2011, Jordan in 2014, Morocco and Turkey in 2011, and Mali in 2007.

Table 1.4 Confidence in the same governments in Table 1.3

Confidence in	Yes	58.9	44.4	48.7	54.2	38.2	75.1	70.6
Government	No	38.6	48.7	51.2	43.4	57.9	24.8	29.4

Source: World Values Survey

The provided percentages are my simplified recoding into two answers (yes or no) of the original four possible answers. The original responses "a great deal" (of confidence) and "quite a lot" are combined here as "yes," whereas the original "not very much" and "not at all" are combined here as "no."

in spite of the fact that certain very general conservative patterns (Tausch 2009) may be identified. But in the final analysis such general measures do not really tell us much about what is happening on the ground. Further, the available measures suggest great changes in the same country over a period of time. For example, in Morocco the percentage of those highlighting government responsibility dropped significantly between 2007 and 2011, from 68.3% to 40.2%, while the small percentage of those highlighting personal responsibility more than doubled, from 5.6% to almost 12%. Interestingly as well, while almost everyone asked in 2007 had an opinion on the matter, we see much more hesitation four years later, when nearly one-quarter of those asked had no opinion. In Turkey, we see a trend in the opposite direction during the same period, with a sense of personal responsibility declining by almost one-third, while belief in the role of government rises by about 5%. In no case, however, can we say that these beliefs are tied to anything that governments may or may not be doing, since the question is really about what someone *should* be doing, rather than on what is actually being done. Only in isolated cases, such as in Iraq, can one explain the answers in terms of the habitual role of government, which as in other oil-producing countries has been the main employer and motor of development in the country since the second half of the twentieth century.

Why trust in expected agents of development—notably governments—has not become more solidly or uniformly established, and why over time it came to be invested in civic groups many of which eventually came to assume a religious nature, are impossible to appreciate if we do not hear directly from the people affected. Yildiz Atasoy, for example, relates a simple but telling story, in which an old village resident came to realize the superior ethics implanted in the youth by an Islamic hostel compared to pupils of the government public schools. A few days after mentioning to someone in a coffeehouse that he had noticed that someone had helped himself to his ripe cherry tree, two children from the Islamic hostel showed up to confess their guilt and ask for proper punishment. They had been told to do so by their teacher who investigated the matter on his own, even though no one pointed any suspicion to his pupils. After forgiving the two boys, the old man recounts how moved he was with such extraordinary ethics:

> After the children left, I was again moved to tears. I thought to my-self, the hostel is teaching them good moral values. And what is wrong with that? Do you think that the children of the state lycée would do the same thing? I don't think so. Quite the contrary, they most likely would have "talked back" to me, and called me a stingy old man. (Atasoy 2005:163)

Similar stories abound by researcher whose fieldwork has borne evidence of the remarkable moral effect that a few committed pious individuals disseminate in larger social environments around them. Alice Moscaritolo, for example, relates the story of two teachers in an Islamic school who traveled for 12 hours on tortuous roads in Kazakhstan in order to make sure that a student who in a public school system would have been abandoned is provided for so that he could continue to attend school (Moscaritolo 2009). Here, the school in question was built as part of the educational efforts of a global Islamic movement, notably the Hizmet movement identified with Fethullah Gülen (about whom more will be said in Chapter 2).

The basic dynamic does not vary from all other similar movements involved in welfare activities around the Muslim world. The "activists" live in and become part of a very local scene, even though they may be connected to a global movement. And the intense habitation of the local environment allows them to observe local and personal nuances, dynamics and problems that are otherwise missed in more macro-oriented development projects. And this lively and intense habitation of local environments means that a movement which may otherwise have political dimensions, or at least exercises an ideological impact on society as a whole, does so precisely because its more locally familiar dimensions, which do leave a felt impact on local life, are either apolitical or at best quasi-political.

One could hardly speak of a "conspiracy of activism" here, in which local people are "duped" into supporting an unrooted movement that has helped them for ulterior motives. There is simply no evidence to support the conspiratorial-paternalistic theory of Islamic activism in general. In any case the baseless assumption of conspiracy theorists that local people do not probe the motives of outsiders who help them has been invalidated time and again by anthropologists who did explore such situations (Scott 1977; Geertz 1985; Dahl and Megerssa 1992; Pottier et al. 2003). In the final analysis, local welfare projects that do consolidate the social basis of movements do so precisely because they are not too conspicuously oriented to establishing a movement. Rather, they introduce an ethic that sometimes appears in religious form though it is not essentially religious, an ethic that I have in a different context identified as a "new patriotism" (Bamyeh 2011). By that I meant then a feeling of personal responsibility for the welfare of a collective community, rather than (as in typical nationalism) a simple feeling of belonging to such a community. In general, the movements described here tend to take root to the extent that they form a solidly local, ethically rooted structure of mutual obligations. It is out of that structure that social movements may emerge in more discernible forms, although it is not a foregone conclusion that they should always emerge out of such dynamic. Rather, the structure of obligations laid down by local welfare activism forms a lasting basis for the *potential* of such movements to emerge, when other conditions call them forth.

Society organizing outside the state

Modern Islamic movements, therefore, may say something more about the nature of modern movements than the nature of modern religiosity. And more religiosity itself seems in almost all cases to be a product of the activities of the movement rather than its precondition. When Hassan al-Banna lost his campaign for a seat in the Egyptian parliament in 1945, one of his supporters sought to comfort others with the traditional adage that the outcome of the elections was a will of god, only to be reprimanded by another member who admonished him to refrain from mentioning the will of god (Hathut 2000:36). That standpoint was itself an original product of that campaign itself and noteworthy enough to be recorded by a chronicler. The originality here consisted not in rejecting the will of god, which was not possible from a religious point of view. Rather, divine will was now manifest in active effort to change reality, rather than as a command to resign to it.

"Changing reality" here means not simply following a long-term program but, more practically, also participating in ongoing daily activities that provide activists and sympathizers with a sense of social rootedness, self-discipline, and being part of a worthy world historical mission, in environments that otherwise provide them only with anomie, disconnection, and aimlessness. In this sense, most modern Islamic movements signify less inherent religiosity or conservatism among Muslims than the growing capacity for *society to organize itself outside the state*. As this happens, actors begin to seek any common or readily available ethical language. This kind of language is most suitable for the self-organization of an otherwise apolitical mass, because of its two related properties: It is widely rather than narrowly accepted, loosely rather than clearly defined.

That Islamic movements do not emerge out of an *inherent* or ancient religiosity is evident in the eclipse of traditional Islam throughout the twentieth century, a process that will be discussed in more detail in subsequent chapters. That eclipse was evident for several decades preceding the late 1970s to all social scientists who had studied Muslim societies, as well as to all significant political actors in such societies. During the Cold War, when almost the entire Muslim world was dominated by secular governments, and the credible political opposition were likewise secular, governments and opposition parties alike tended to ignore religious movements, which for them were echoes of a past or passing traditional society. Daniel Lerner's (1958) classic study of this passing away of traditional society, published in 1958 and largely forgotten today, represented for a long time not just an academic but also a political modernist consensus worldwide. The passing of traditionalism was understood to include the gradual replacement of religious sentiments by modern secular ethos (Stark 1999).

Until the late 1970s, therefore, few authorities and few scholars worried about religious revivalism. The illustrations are by now familiar. Israel was worried most about the secular nationalist PLO rather than any Islamic activism, and in fact it favored the latter since it seemed to be completely innocuous and apolitical. Anwar Sadat, the Egyptian president eventually assassinated by Islamist militants, likewise had initially in his reign little worry about Islamic groups, and thought it wise to allow them to operate again soon after taking office in 1970, as a potential counterweight to the left–Nasserite opposition that he believed posed the real threat to his regime. Indeed, it was the perceived secular threat that he diligently pursued for most of his term in office, through show trials, imprisonment, defamation campaigns, dismissals from office, and the usual fraudulent elections. The same could be said of Ja'far Numeiry in Sudan, a ruthless dictator by any measure, fully secular for most of his rule, who only toward the end of his regime in the 1980s came to the idea of using Islam as a political weapon, namely by allying himself with Islamist forces as he struggled against opposition from a largely secular opposition. The transformation of Zia ul-Haq in Pakistan, from the same period, is also similar. Coming to office through a military coup against an elected secular government, he vacillated for years before adopting Islamic credentials and allying himself with Maududi's *Jamaat-e-Islami,* which while an old party with obvious political aspirations, had rarely won more than 6% in any free elections previously. In less than two decades later, Pakistan, a state that had initially been founded by a secular elite and intended not as an *Islamic* state but as a home for the Muslims of India, experienced an increasing Islamization of its character and "shariatization" of its law (Ahmad 1998:23).

The regimes listed above were all Cold War era regimes with oscillating prospects internationally and a weak popular base domestically. Before as well as after the Cold War, regime survival remained as their main and constant obsession (Akbarzadeh and Saeed 2007; Hudson 1977). For our purposes, what needs explaining is how uncertainty of state purpose and regime calculations at the top construct an unwitting space for the emergence of popular movements possessing religious character. It is easy enough to understand how governments, being caught up in the short-term perspective of regime survival, may "miscalculate" and in so doing create space for a social mobilization that undermines them in the long run. But it is a different story to account for the resilience of the Islamic movements that had taken advantage of such miscalculations—especially given the dearth of evidence (Bayat 2007:16–48) for significant religious awakening previously and the abundance of contrary evidence of declining religiosity.

Explanations of the prospects of social movements in terms of political opportunity highlight the advantage Islamic forces had in cases where secular governments repressed all secular opposition, thereby undermining the natural leftist competition to Islamic activism and clearing the ground for the latter. A commonly cited concrete example of this phenomenon is the repression of civil society under the Shah of Iran. According to an influential thesis, the repression of all alternatives tended to make mosques into natural convergence venues for all opposition (Parsa 1989; Rasler 1996). This pattern would be repeated three decades later in the early phases of the Arab Spring in 2011: The absence of alternative mobilizing mechanisms insured that every Friday following the sermon, without any prior plan by any organized opposition, became the generally expected timing for collective protest for all regime opponents, even though those uprisings made virtually no religious demands and followed no religious leadership.

If we follow this thesis a little further, it would seem to suggest that as the discourse of modern social movements, "Islam" came into use due less to a religious awakening than to its demonstrated usefulness as a generic means for the gathering of large spectrums of social opposition. But one would expect this purely opportune structure to become filled over time with more religious *meaning*, especially (as in the case of Iran) when the generic opposition movement, in which the most organized (though not necessarily largest) segments are Islamists in ideology, succeeds in capturing state power. In other words, we would expect the discourse or frame used ("Islam") to acquire more meaning if it appears practically successful in guiding a movement or a revolution. Yet, several decades of experience with broad-based Islamic activism have delivered no developed Islamic political theory, which remains lacking, as many critics have pointed out, a detailed enough description of what makes certain politics or government particularly "Islamic," and in general modern Islamic political philosophy remains underdeveloped (Roy 1998; Affendi 2008).

One may of course respond by noting that a modern Islamic political philosophy is gradually emerging, and in ways that seek to communicate seriously with such modern conceptions as human rights, democracy, and the status of minorities. It is formulated not by academics but by political activists while they were out of power and had no prospects for it—for example Rachid Ghannoushi, who composed his political theory largely in prison and exile; Tariq Ramadan, who did so as a member of a minority in Europe; or Muhammad Shahrur, an independent scholar with no political affiliation. But it is still true that the longest-used slogan of the most established Islamic movements, such as the Brotherhood's long-running motto "Islam is the solution," was striking in its lack of specificity and even meaning, and it is remarkable that so many Islamic movements have not only sustained themselves for long periods without elaborating any political program in any detail, but even succeeded in capturing institutions and even governments without having to say much about how they were going to govern. Even in the case of Iran, where the revolution was led by someone who had actually written a book on the nature of Islamic government, his most dedicated adherents on the eve of the revolution were unaware of that book (Bayat 2007:29). It does not appear that the details of any religious *program* had inspired popular support for Islamic movements. Other factors seem to be more important, such as perception of lack of corruption—evidently important in Hamas's victory in Palestine in 2005; rootedness of the social aid networks in neighborhoods; and the apparent elitism or unrooted vanguardism of the alternative secular opposition.

At first glance it would appear therefore that as a language of politics, Islam was more of an afterthought than a product of prior intellectual elaboration. However, the earlier history of modern secular movements—whether nationalist or leftist—in much of the Muslim world shows that apart from certain exceptions like *early* republican Turkey, where secularism became explicitly anti-religious (or the even more exceptional case of communist Albania), Islam remained throughout the twentieth century as at least one element of collective cultural identity in society, and thus continued to be often seen as an ingredient within national consciousness (including in Turkey itself after 1950). Likewise, in the heyday of socialism, Islam was often seen to be hospitable to socialism (though typically not in those Islamic countries directly dominated by the Soviet Union). Even before the Iranian Revolution, theses could be easily found that sought to claim Muhammad, Ali, Abu Dharr al-Ghafari, or some of the early companions to the cause of socialism or Marxism.

In general, therefore, it seems that Islam as employed in the discourse of Islamic movements tends to parallel the prevailing character of the larger social environment in which they operate. Reflecting on the history of the Muslim Brotherhood in Egypt, Jamal al-Banna, the group founder's brother, notes how the Brotherhood was liberal in its outlook during the times of its founder because it lived in a liberal period, and only later adopted a militarized ideology after living under a military rule that undermined liberal society. Another chronicler who knew the founder personally noted how he came to change the meaning of the traditional Islamic canon of practices to avoid sinful acts known as *sadd al-a'thar* (or *sadd al-thara'i*, whereby sin is eliminated by eliminating the conditions that make it possible). Al-Banna then opined that elimination of conditions that produce sin now meant broad socio-economic justice, not the simple imposition of traditional prohibitions (Hathut 2000:114). That reinterpretation of a central religious canon was apparently possible only because al-Banna lived in an era in which demands for socio-economic justice were broadly shared in society.

Modern Islamic political mobilization, therefore, was based on social conservatism, but in reality entailed the opposite of conservatism: It was always part of larger processes of mobilization for the cause of social *trans-formation*. In addition, modern Islamic movements expressed one facet of a broad social sentiment of resistance to unfamiliar, unrooted, or imperial forces. And while they may have called in theory for a return to an imagined past, in reality they highlighted catering to pressing social needs, and sought to show how they communicated with a revolutionary *zeitgeist* that was larger than Islam. In the parts of today's Beirut dominated by Hizbullah, for example, one can see posters of sh'ia martyrs and contemporary religious leaders side by side with those of Nasser and the Arab nationalist secular leaders, as well as those of non-Islamic anti-imperial symbols as the late Hugo Chavez of Venezuela or the ubiquitous Che Guevara. Wherever it was broad-based, modern Islamic mobilization took root in part because it was *not* simply Islamic. Rather, it was because it had the capacity to be seen as another manifestation of a global struggle for justice and self-determination. And in these struggles, one distinctive feature of Islamic mobilization was that it combined rather than set as opposites the economic grievances of the *mustad'afun*, the "meek of the earth," and the political participation grievances of professional and middle classes (see Figure 1.3).

Part of the Islamic political program, therefore, is implicit in older cross-class grievances, although it is noteworthy how long it took for such grievances to be expressed in a religious language, eventually delivering revolutions and mass movements. Yet, the apparent absence of a specifically *Islamic* solution to national and social problems in *most* of the Muslim world was notable even in the case of the Iranian Revolution, which would become more clearly "Islamic" only in its final phases. The first president of post-revolutionary Iran, Abolhassan Banisadr, was hardly alone in being at a loss on the eve of the revolution to define the frame of reference of an "Islamic government," which either had never existed before, in which case one had to be explicitly inventive, or had existed throughout several historical epochs in very different forms, in which case one had to justify choosing one model over another. But the nature of an Islamic government was an afterthought; in Banisadr's words, "we had to formulate an ideology worthy of a revolution" (*al-Ahram Weekly*, October 26, 1995, 5) while the revolution was underway, rather than in preparation for it.

In a detailed study, Asef Bayat has argued that Iran experienced neither increased religiosity nor an Islamic social movement before the revolution, and if anything, the revolution only interrupted a different form of religiosity that may have been in ascendance before the revolution. According to

تقدمة مركز بيروت الوطن للتنمية الحضرية

الطريق الجديدة ـ بيروت ـ لبنان

رمز الممانعة العالمية   الوعد الذي صدق   أوقد شعلة التحرر

FIGURE 1.3 Symbols of global struggle, contemporary Beirut street poster

his thesis, the Iranian Revolution took an Islamic turn not because it was based on Islamic ideals, but because of the superior networking capacity of the clergy (2007:23–24). They operated in a rapidly changing environment in which perceptions of likely success appear to have played a more decisive role than any objective conditions (Kurzman 1996). Less than a decade before the revolution, Khomeini himself thought that it would take two centuries to get rid of the monarchy in Iran (Bayat 2007:32).

Unforeseen success creates an environment in which Islamic movements often appear to be unsure as to how to govern afterwards. Tentative evidence from pronouncements of the leaders of Hamas following the stunning victory of their group at the Palestinian elections of 2006, including their initial attempt to form a national unity government they did not need, given their large majority, suggests that they had not expected nor were prepared for such a decisive victory. Rather, by entering electoral politics (Hamas had boycotted those previously) the group may have aimed only to strengthen its status as the main opposition. The sequence of unplanned conflicts associated with such self-understanding of the movement's role in a political system it did not expect to control paralleled what we saw six years later in Egypt as a sister movement, the Brotherhood, had to decide how to govern after Mubarak when it had only planned to be his main opposition.

The apparent uncertainty of purpose or unpreparedness for the challenges when these movements capture state institutions seems to verify the proposition that the more pervasive character of Islamic social movements is that of society organizing itself outside the state or, more accurately, building a *parallel* political theater to the state. This development appears typical under conditions in which parliamentary structures are weak or are designed to serve an authoritarian system—under which Islamic movements have often spent most of their lives. Under such conditions, political life tends to migrate to other parts of civil society, since little of it is allowed in the parliament or state institutions. This is why studies of democratization that focus largely on formal politics under authoritarianism provide inadequate measures of the vitality and diversity of political life in such societies. And these theaters of civil society—most notably in professional associations and unions—were usually the most heavily and seriously contested spaces of organized politics (Norton 2005; Carapico 2007; Wiktorowicz 2003) before the Arab Spring, and they have continued to be very important since.

This structure of the political theater, namely its concentration in civil society rather than formal politics, was already in place before the rise of modern Islamic movements. Under authoritarian or partially open political regimes, professional associations and unions have provided political parties (both legal and clandestine) with a felt measure of their strength in places ranging from Egypt to Jordan to Mauritania. (In some cases, municipal elections could also be taken as good measures of political strength of parties, since sometimes (though not always) they were less interfered with by central governments than national elections.) The case of Egypt, which is the most studied in the literature, is illustrative here. As the Muslim Brotherhood was building its social service institutions, it also began to take over Egypt's 24 professional associations through elections beginning in the 1980s. By 1992 it had won impressive majorities on the councils of five of the wealthiest and most influential of those associations, namely the doctors, engineers, lawyers, scientists, and pharmacists (Kassem 2004:112). The latter in particular was an illustrative victory, since over 30% of the members of the pharmacists syndicate were Coptic Christians. The fact that such victories had little to do with a "religious awakening" is clearly evident from statements made by both ordinary members and triumphant Brotherhood members alike. Describing their democratic takeover of the Doctor's Syndicate, the Muslim Brotherhood

activist Ibrahim Za'farani describes a dynamic that would be repeated at
other associations:

> When we ran for elections in the professional syndicates, we never
> dreamed we would score land-slide victories. We were only hoping
> for a few seats, not the majority. A chief reason for our victory was
> the situation in the syndicates before the Islamists entered the pic-
> ture, rather than real support. Before the Islamists took over, the
> syndicate boards rarely convened and the election turnover was al-
> ways very meager.
>
> We offered a model for a good agenda, organized work and fair,
> free elections. People did not elect us because we pray more than
> others or have beards but because we manage to get things done
> efficiently.
>
> . . . We were playing a social, professional and political role.
> These three dimensions of the professional syndicates cannot be
> separated from one another. (Abdel-Latif 1999)

This perspective is confirmed by that of an ordinary member of the
Pharmacists Syndicate:

> I didn't want the syndicate to become a front for the Muslim
> brothers. But after a while you see that they help any member,
> whether he is a Coptic or a Muslim. Before the Islamists came,
> there was no one to meet you at the syndicate. If you had a problem
> with the tax authority, there was no one [to help]. Once the Islamists
> came, there were people in the syndicate headquarters waiting to
> help at all times of the day. My feeling now is that their performance
> has been excellent. (Abdo 2002:101)

Such opinions suggest that before the sudden growth of jihadist fervor
in 2014, most successful Islamic movements tended to focus on practical
campaigns aiming at providing tangible benefits rather than millenarian
politics. The few works that highlighted millenarian Islamic politics before then, such David Cook's (2005) *Contemporary Muslim Apocalyptic
Literature* or Joel Richardson's (2009) *The Islamic Antichrist*, did little to
measure the social impact of the apocalyptic literature they analyzed, nor
was there any evidence then, or after, that millenarian politics energized
significant Muslim publics. It is noteworthy that successful movements

whose discourse involved some measure of millenarianism, such as Hizbullah, managed on a daily basis extensive and tangible social services rather than provided abstract slogans of struggle. The latter tended to be reserved for war times and also for annual commemorations, such as the martyrdom of Husayn. But on a daily basis the movement was *felt* most through its social presence. Indeed, throughout the world the most widespread interpretations by Muslims of an appropriate political role for Islam seem to cluster less around any specific religious doctrine and more around an almost universal association of "Islam" as a generic concept (rather than as the program of any particular Islamic group) with clean and efficient governing. This was evident even in the central Asian republics, where Islamic learning had been so fully suppressed during the seven decades of Soviet rule that Muslims reportedly celebrate their religious holidays by drinking vodka. However, even in such environments of lackluster or unorthodox religiosity (Hassan 2002; Hilgers 2009), the concept of "Islamic government" was perceived as signifying an entity that is responsible and free of corruption (Khalid 2007:116–167).

In such cases, when "Islam" is understood as a generic template for "good governance," it tends to be associated not necessarily with a group that has an Islamic political program or even with any clear model of politics, but rather with an undefined condition of ethical purity. This ethical purity, in turn, is most in demand when it is felt to be unavailable *anywhere* in the world. This is partially evident in Moataz Fattah's (Fattah 2006:107–109) global survey, where over 40% of the respondents who were asked to identify an ideal political system responded by "none of the above," even though the choices they were given represented every imaginable type of current political system, ranging from pluralist secular democracy to authoritarian religious theocracy, and where the choices included Iran, Afghanistan, Saudi Arabia, Turkey, the United States of America, the United Kingdom, and a number of other model countries. Fattah's results also show that those who were most ambivalent about any of the available choices, including "real existing Islamic" systems, tended to be traditionalists, whereas those whom he classified as "modernist" or "pluralist" Muslims had an easier time identifying an existing system as closer to their ideal conception. On closer inspection, however, these categories themselves seem to not predict any particular orientation. For example, in the same sample, the most popular choice of those classified as "modernist" Muslims were two countries with very different political systems: Turkey (under the earlier, more democratic Erdoğan) and Iran, selected by 18 and 17% or the respondents, respectively. Furthermore, even where there seemed to be some preference for a "real existing Islamic" system, the choice was made mostly by those who had no experience with the system they had selected, and that same system was in fact overwhelmingly rejected by its own citizens. For example, of the 14% of the traditionalists who chose Saudi Arabia as their model, only 2% were Saudis.

These results also correspond to some extent with others obtained through global opinion surveys among Muslims, including Gallup and Pew surveys. It is not uncommon for Muslims to cite a non-Islamic system (such as the US, UK, or French system) as embodying some of the best virtues of Islam, as some respondents told Fattah, and it is even more common to define Islam not as a religion with definite doctrines but as a general namesake for justice, as one Iranian respondent aptly captured it: "Islam is justice. Whatever achieves justice is Islamic" (Fattah 2007:113). The same attitude can in fact be found long ago in the writings of Rifaʿa al-Tahtawi, one of the most renowned of the early modernist Muslim intellectuals in the nineteenth century, who in his commentary on the meaning of "freedom" in the French Constitution equated it with his own interpretation of the Islamic dictum of "justice." According to that already old interpretation, the Islamic notion of justice was introduced precisely in order to restrict claims of the state on people and property (Tahtawi 1993:148). In that sense, a modern concept of freedom appeared to be simply the most recent manifestation of an ancient concept of justice—since "justice" signified for Tahtawi freedom from state encroachment upon life, civil society, and property. Again, this discussion will be elaborated in more detail in Chapter 3, which explores the historical structure of self-organized Muslim societies.

How and why would an old religion be invoked as the best argument on behalf of one modern value or another? There is evidence to suggest that modern religiosity simply adapts to rather than dictates imperatives, whether organizational or communicative. What this means is that the apparent religiosity of ordinary individuals helps cement organizational and networking needs of modern groups or classes. In other words, "Islam" here signifies nothing other than a commonly available cultural frame being used to facilitate the networking of new classes or groups. This presumed cultural commonality tends to be more apparent to all participants than any specific religious practice, especially in the case of the countless modern enterprises that possess an Islamic face but no clear Islamic political program. Nazih Ayubi remarked that modern Islamic institutions, such as banks, companies, or charities, signify no necessary political goals. More importantly, they establish networks that could become political in times of acute crisis. This theme is also demonstrated by Janine Clark (2003:1–41,146–161) who, building on Marion Boulby's (1999) thesis that Islamic institutions represent the hopes of an emergent middle class for political power, argued that Islamic social institutions consolidate more than anything else middle-class ties, and were run by and for the emerging middle classes.

Such arguments need to be placed in a proper context, however. While there is clear evidence that much of the founding leadership of many Islamic organizations consists of middle-class professionals, this is not universally the case and even when it is, Islamic social institutions tend to cater to several publics, even though such publics may remain spatially segregated. For example, the fact that 38% of the founding members of the Islamic Action Front in Jordan may be considered "middle-class professionals" does not explain its electoral appeal to poor voters, neither does the observation that Muslim "publics" are themselves divided across class lines. Islamic organizations generally espouse a universalist, egalitarian discourse of faith, and seek to address real social inequalities through their charitable work, although they do not challenge such inequalities systematically. Describing Islamic social services in different neighborhoods of Cairo, Ayubi remarks:

> It is difficult for me to believe that the luxurious Mustafa Mahmud health centre in the prosperous Muhandisin suburb and the drab Fath Islamic clinic in the shabby suburb of Matariyya are really concerned about the same Muslim public. (Ayubi 1996:199–200)

Yet, there are two innovations that go unnoticed in this otherwise accurate observation. One is rooted in the history of civil society, another in modern politics of cross-class alliance. First, modern Islamic charitable activism has done something similar to what modern states have done (whether intentionally or not): putting themselves in the place once occupied by old patronage networks. Before modern Islamic charitable activism, welfare tended to be the domain of patronage networks led by local notable families that had also provided society with locally rooted political leadership (Batatu 1978; Batatu 1999; Khoury 1983), as well as extensive private endowments (*waqf*), that had been built up over centuries before being largely taken over by modern governments. (The

social role of such endowments will be discussed in Chapter 3.) In either case, the more lasting legacy of such old networks and institutions,
which had been replaced in one part by Islamic charity activism and
in another by modern states, is the consolidation of a reality that few
governments have been able to change, which is that civil society in
Muslim countries tends today to be what it has always been, which is
society organized outside of and parallel to the state (Bamyeh 2005,
2009). While one of the greatest transformations in the Muslim world
in the twentieth century has consisted of persistent attempts of modern
states to organize power around themselves and inculcate a complete
etatisation of society, modern Muslim organizations, *including* those that
have contested state power before the Iranian Revolution and the Arab
Spring, were busy building parallel societies to the state so long that
they did not control it.

In addition, while Islamic institutions establish new networks that con-
nect modern classes and groups, they also expand the networked presence
of Islam beyond the old authority channels of traditional clergy. In either
case, the emerging network establishes a society parallel to the state and
outside of it. And society organized outside the state itself consists of different classes linked through a system of alliances, whose ethical orientation is not toward equality but toward *reliability of obligations and loyalties*,
exactly as had been the case under the old patrimonial systems. And this
perception of "reliability" not only compares favorably to the impersonality, unaccountability, and distant and invented nature of modern states.
It also clarifies for those networked one important social meaning of religion as a namesake of self-organized society. In this fashion, modern
Islamic movements, embodied in their social and economic institutions,
link up to that old patrimonial heritage in ways that they themselves may
be unaware of.

The politicization of new demographics

If modern religious activism signifies a form of "cross-class alliance," the
previous two sections suggest that they do so in a more *tangible* and *participatory* way than has been possible for modern state nationalism. Thus
in reality modern Islamic activism may be said to embody a rooted form
of nationalism, even though on its surface modern Islamism usually rejects the ideology of secular nationalism. This becomes evident when we
consider how there is more to the story of Islamic activism than tangible

benefits to participants and beneficiaries: It has also established social networks through which parallel societies to the state have come to experience themselves as real social bodies in non-traditional ways, i.e., beyond tribal, familial, clannish, or other primordial solidarities.

The increasing significance of religious perspective within a socially networked life signifies the growth of a specific kind of *participatory ethics*, especially on the part of otherwise apolitical or disengaged segments. The religious character of such ethics allows them to have a broad meaning, in the sense that they are not necessarily oriented to formal politics, which in any case remains inaccessible to most inhabitants of Muslim lands. The notion of a "society organized outside the state" introduced earlier becomes one type of response to this restriction. Here one does not demand inclusion in a political system controlled by an unaccountable and non-transparent state, but instead does what is possible: partakes in other styles of participation in community life at local levels, and in ways that are more immediately gratifying and assured of results than the campaigns of formal politics.

Responsible factors for the emergence of such ethics include the rapidly increasing urban character of Muslim societies. Rapid urbanization has helped undermine the role of old countryside-based traditional leaderships, and concomitantly led to the growth of new networks of solidarity and mutualism not beholden to old loyalties. In itself urbanization does not necessarily lead to specifically Islamic forms of participation. But the Islamic character of these new networks seems to be helped most by Islam being the only familiar discourse that allows large numbers of people to express participatory ethics beyond the village or other local levels, and in a language they understand and are relatively free to modify in practice. This transformation is particularly evident in the second phase of the growth of Muslim Brotherhood in Egypt, that is, following the assassination of al-Banna and the debacle in Palestine that led to a broad popular questioning of the legitimacy of the whole political system. During that phase, when the group was already well-established, local *a'yan* and *'umada* (traditional lower notables and local mayors) offered to form new chapters of the groups and became their heads (Hathut 2000:93–94). In that way the group, while modern in other respects, grafts itself onto existing local authorities, but in the process also changes the nature of their traditional leadership, making it more contingent on a new national organizational framework as well as on a new ideology (whose advantage is that it *appears* to be old).

Table 1.5 Municipal elections in Shi'a-majority districts, 1998, 2004

	1998				2004**			
	Hizbullah		Amal		Hizbullah		Amal	
	Seats	Councils	Seats	Councils	Seats	Councils	Seats	Councils
Beirut and Mount Lebanon districts	90	5	0	0	98	6	10	0
South Lebanon* districts	219	22	325	39	1,163	87	613	55
Biqa' districts	224	18	158	9	490	36	30	2
Total	533	45	483	48	1751	129	653	57

* In 1998, 12 councils were split, and one was won by communist-Nasserite coalition.

** Includes additional councils where no elections took place in 1998.

Source: Hamzeh 2004:128–134.

But in general, the notion that modern Islamic mobilization is as-sociated to some extent with urbanization is evident from its earlier periods. For example, in its early years most of the membership of the Muslim Brotherhood in Egypt years was recruited from recent urban mi-grants or their sons (Ayubi 1980; Ibrahim 1982). By contrast, the Muslim Brotherhood fared less well in its recruitment efforts in the Egyptian coun-tryside (Starrett 1998:76). Evidence from later periods and elsewhere also confirms this pattern. In its municipal elections campaigns, for example, the Lebanese Hizbullah swept *all* councils in the Shi'a-majority urban dis-tricts of Beirut and neighboring Mount Lebanon in 1998 and again in 2004, but won "only" 40 out of 88 such districts in the more rural South Lebanon and Beqa' valley in 1998, and 129 out of a new total of 186 rural districts in 2004 (see Table 1.5).[2] While it had an almost complete electoral monopoly in the urban shi'a districts, in the countryside Hizbullah had to compete with or ally itself with groups tied to more traditional rural authorities.

2. Much of the increase in the number of contested rural districts in 2004 was due to the Israeli withdrawal from occupied parts of Lebanon in 2000.

However, the urban character of this mobilization needs to be seen with a little more nuance. In the first round of the presidential elections in post-revolutionary Egypt, for example, the two main candidates associated with Islamic politics (Mohamed Morsi and Abdel Moneim Abou al-Fotouh) scored their best results in the more urbanized parts of upper Egypt closest to Cairo, notably the provinces of Fayoum and Bani Suef, garnering nearly three-quarters of the votes in the former and over 60% in the latter. They did well likewise in the urban parts of Giza, where they won nearly half of the votes, but only about one-third of the votes in the major urban centers of Cairo and Alexandria. This suggests, as with the case in Beirut's southern *dahiya*, that this mobilization seems strongest in new rather than old urban neighborhoods and new rather than old cities.

The urban dimension of Islamic social movements seems to be associated with the effort of new classes, excluded from political power, to create new forums in which they could practice some form of participation. That we are speaking of new classes is most illustrated in the history of the Muslim Brotherhood. Prior to its banning in 1954, only 22 of the Brotherhood's 1,950 Consultative Assembly members did not belong to the new class of modern, "European" professionals (Ayubi 1980). This astounding statistic suggests that Islamic mobilization was initiated most fervently by new (urban and professional) rather than old traditional classes. Ziad Munson shows that the bulk of the movement's support then came from the most modernized segments of society, being disproportionately represented among students, engineers, doctors, and government bureaucrats (Munson 2001:492).

It is a mistake, however, to think of Islamic activism in simple class terms, or to highlight only the role of new classes, since there are situations of modern Islamic activism that do not exactly correspond to these restricted claims, thus causing us to look for the motor of participation at a more general level. The fact that Islamic institutions serve different classes also means that Islamic activism can be understood as a claim to entitlement to participate by all groups that either are excluded from power or were not traditionally thought of as "proper materials" for politics. Illustrative here is the case of *Hizb al-Islah*, the largest Islamic party in Yemen before the recent war. Unlike other Muslim countries, where the modern secular governing elites displaced or at least sought to displace more traditional authorities in society during the postcolonial period, Yemen, having always had a relatively weak government, experienced a semi-democratic evolution and a negotiated power system even before

joining the throngs of the Arab Spring in 2011. There, participatory demands of both new *and* old classes did not require and in principle could
not cancel each other out, and the popular uprising that resulted in the
removal of President Saleh in 2012 was largely aimed at contesting his effort to concentrate power. What concerns us here however is how, under
a political system that never managed to become as closed to participatory
demands as other Arab republics before 2011, we see the emergence of an
Islamic party that consists of almost equal components of modern professionals on the one hand and traditional tribal elements on the other. Here,
it is noteworthy that the survey cited by Janine Clark (2003:17) of the electoral candidates of *Hizb al-Islah* in 1993 directly contradicts her thesis that
the party represents middle-class aspirations. Of 190 candidates surveyed,
81 had a university degree. Most of the other 109 candidates who did not
have such a degree came from the tribal stream of the party. The party
seemed in fact to be jointly run by university-educated and tribal members, two distinct social groups that had "Islam" as a common reference
point. In this case, therefore, it is easy to see how Islamic activism incorporates traditional leaders into a new movement rather than expresses entitlement to replacing them (as would be the case elsewhere in the Muslim
world). In other words, "Islam" here appears as a language that allows
two otherwise conflicting segments, namely traditional elites and new educated classes, to continue to communicate with one another rather than
see each other as alternatives.

Modern Islamic politics thus provided *new* modes of participation that
circumvented closed or preset channels of authority, such as authoritarian
state politics, traditional tribal politics, or kin networks. They also added
to it a universal meritocratic quality, so that upward mobility in the movement was not based on traditional lineage, *wasta* [preferential personal
referral], or bureaucratic rank, but rather on the basis of dedication and
service to the movement, and in a way that was open to any dedicated
individual regardless of background. The model of Hasan al-Banna continues to serve as a template for this meritocratic model of participation.
He came from no notable traditional background, worked as an ordinary
school teacher, and is said to have travelled the tram in third class, and
jumped out of it like all others as it barely halted at its designated stop
(Hathut 2000:31). The model of al-Banna highlighted non-traditional
source of merit, making the organization itself, rather than the leader, the
ultimate reference point, so much so that the organization could go on
living after him and regardless of charisma. For instance, the victory of

Morsi in the Egyptian presidential campaign in 2012 was a testimony not simply to the organizational muscle of the Brotherhood, but also to meritocratic qualities that it shared with no other party: No other party could have nominated so uncharismatic, ineloquent a candidate and had any realistic hopes of winning.

Elections, however, are not the only venues of participation, even though they are episodes in which it could be measured. But the participatory ethics of modern Islamic movement exceed electoral politics and in fact are conducted most of the time away from them. This is significant especially for new demographics that have little in the way of regular access to formal political channels or whose informal networks may still be underdeveloped—new professional classes, urban migrants, and dislocated individuals. Together, these new demographics may be taken as a measure of anomic isolation, since they stand for new social categories consisting of individuals who are increasingly detached from older networks and loyalties. One means to dramatically resolve this anomie is through attaching oneself, formally or informally, to an Islamic movement that has a generic enough quality to absorb all newcomers or meet them wherever they happen to be. Along these lines, Said Arjomand argues that those drawn to Islamist groups tend to be among the most socially connected individuals in society (1984:22). What this suggests is that social connectedness and participatory ethics reinforce each other, although what still needs to be explained is why participatory ethics here take specifically religious forms.

A Weberian answer may consist of understanding how Islam itself calls for social engagement. But that cannot be a satisfactory approach if we begin from the proposition that it is the believer who makes Islam say something or another; that we already know that different Muslims stress very different aspects of Islam, including aspects that call for withdrawal and resignation to fate rather than activism and engagement; and when a believer thinks that Islam calls for his social engagement, there is no standard answer as to how such engagement should be discharged. The answer therefore has to do with how "Islam" comes to be understood as supplying specific participatory ethics that are more adequate to new social realities than those supplied by competing discourses—for example, socialism, liberalism, nationalism, and so on.

What we know about modern Islamic activism, especially in terms of how it expresses participatory ethics, suggests that its resilience stems from the flexibility of a message, moral focus, few entry obstacles, and a serious orientation to mundane everyday life. The notion of a "flexible" message seems at odds with the received wisdom about religious movements, but it is in fact what makes them attractive across different social environments. As Munson describes the appeal of the Muslim Brotherhood to different demographics, a member may be a "fighter for the poor in poverty-stricken rural areas, or voice of democracy within educated urban areas" (2001:498). This stands in sharp contrast to potential alternative modernist movements, for example the Communist Party, which required common adherence to centrally determined policies and doctrines, and also years of training and testing before one may become a member. By contrast, Islamic mobilization made action possible in a variety of immediate ways, notably by allowing members and sympathizers to attach themselves to tangible causes in their own lives and neighborhoods (Munson 2001:506).

This flexibility is sometimes sustained by organizational features that resemble familiar religious practices. Hizbullah, for example, has a relatively small core of dedicated officials and an ebbing and flowing circle of supporters and followers. Hala Jaber notes that this structure closely mimics that of a congregation and allows the party to maintain both internal cohesion and constant communication with its fluid constituency. One advantage of such a structure is that it combines two otherwise contradictory qualities, namely maximum flexibility with a clear definition of goals and slogans (Jaber 1997:64–68). The party's relation to its former supreme theologian, the late Sheikh Fadlallah, was governed by this dual practice. Fadlallah served more as a spiritual guide than a policymaker for the party, lending it his considerable clerical pedigree without getting entangled in its governance and daily business. In its earlier history, that structure was particularly well-suited to an environment typified by fluidity and requiring preparedness for quick action. It was also suited to the needs of the followers themselves, who belonged to lower-class backgrounds and had usually little time or inclination for long periods of full-time commitment.

In an important sense, therefore, modern religious politics are the politics of the apolitical. It is the politics of an average worshipper or someone with a spiritual moral compass, ordinarily disgruntled with some trouble in society but has otherwise no political language by which to express grievances. If approached by some religious activist who argues this grievance in a familiar language, he might be persuaded if he is disgruntled enough. That is because in environments in which religiosity is common, a religious attitude to social or communal participation should not pre-suppose the same level of organizational commitment or ideological elab-oration as secular ideologies may seem to require. Rather, a call to social action couched in religious terms, often simply allows participants—for instance modern women (Mahmoud 2005; Macleod 1993)—to express both protest and adjustment to new realities in a way that is familiar to them and acceptable to others.

Along these lines, Ayatollah Muhammad Taqi al-Madrasi sums up the main contributions of modern Islamic movements not so much in terms of their ideology—although he seeks to elaborate that—but more in its *personalization* of large themes of modern struggle that had been misman-aged by distant or irresponsible secular authorities that owe their power, according to him, entirely to colonial machinations and foreign patronage. In contrast to those, the "Islamic trend" begins from below, and with the individual rather than with the group, even though it may be motivated by some group or another. But the elaboration of an Islamist trend remains a personal *choice*:

> Personal initiatives and self-motivation . . . is what contributes to developing the Islamic movement ... it is behavioral disposition that imbues the Islamic movement with a civilizational character. It is possible for one person, a progeny of the Islamic movement, to take a practical initiative or develop his thought, in any field, so that he may change the course of history. (Madrasi 1998:48)

This grand language belies the more ordinary, personal nature of religion in modern politics. The personalization of the world means that national and local struggles are governed less by a centrally commanded and uni-versally agreed upon program, and more by participatory ethics that flow in the final analysis out of personal choice. So long, of course, that the movement has not developed a coercive apparatus or captured the insti-tutions of the state. Otherwise, religion serves largely as a means of en-tering politics by those who may or may not wish to remain there. Stated otherwise, political religion expresses the expansion of the political field to encompass all otherwise apolitical individuals.

Islamic social movements have not arisen out of conversions from secular ideologies—although these do happen—but primarily out of politicizing *new* strata and demographics. If Islam is a default common reference point for substantial social demographics that had not pre-viously regarded politics to be their business, then "Islam" would be expected to offer them the least complex and immediate claim to a right-eous message, even though of course they may completely disagree as to what Islam should mean here. But the point is that Islam as a discourse has offered large enough strata an immediate way to participate when they never did before; Egypt's first post-revolutionary parliamentary elections in 2012, which saw vastly more participation by hitherto non-participating citizens, saw the Islamic parties garnering together more than two-thirds of the votes, even though that percentage would have cer-tainly altered over time had the democratic experiment been allowed to continue. But "participation" as discussed here is not confined to voting and usually takes other formats in most places. Social action in a neigh-borhood may not always look like politics. But it represents both social ingathering in the symbolic language of religion, and personalization of collective tasks performed through a practical immersion in local or any other accessible levels.

This may mean that Islamic movements do begin with, and for a long time maintain, amateurish political outlook and slogans, since politics is only part of their business, and only so in times of opportunities. Their resilience resides not so much in the effectiveness of their politics, for which the available theaters in formal politics—apart from Pakistan and Bangladesh—were usually restricted until the Iranian Revolution, and almost everywhere else for long afterwards until the fall of Suharto in Indonesia, the rise of the AKP in Turkey in 2002, and the Arab Spring in 2011. Formal politics were not therefore where modern Islamic move-ments acquired their taste for participation.

Rather, they drew sustenance from the end of the era of postcolonial populism—where great hopes were invested in savior national leaders with heroic attributes—as well as in vanguardist cliques (such as the Ba'th Party) that relied more on conspiratorial or designated elite group rule than popular participation. Eventually, those postcolonial systems became exhausted as they delivered little to their populations. Not only was their promise discredited, but along with that apparently also their mode of op-eration, which constituted of substituting populism for participation and symbolic mobilization for systematic social mobilization. In those envir-onments, Islamic movements appeared as logical alternatives, especially where their discourse seemed to express not so much specific doctrines but more diffuse yet socially shared ethical symbolism. That allowed for constant and varied styles of participation, and outside of the institutions and discourse of the postcolonial state.

As such, these movements may herald a widely shared feeling that "society," which had previously been delegated to other saviors to worry about, has no savior other than itself, and thus it must act *as society*. However, religious symbolism ends here, precisely where it begins, since the core point is not religion as such, but religion as a *familiar starting point* in addressing an enduring problem: How may I, as an ordinary, apolitical individual, translate an otherwise abstract standpoint, namely my own responsibility to "my" society, into everyday personal practice and everyday local commitment?

Partial politics

This approach to politics, which views it only as a possible extension of other tasks, has made Islamic movements so resilient. Islam as a social movement was helped most by the fact that of all available modernist ideologies of mobilization, Islam was the only one that was not exclusively or even primarily oriented to the state. Rather, Islam tended to be employed most frequently as a means to give guidance to personal and local life as needed. In some sense this may be seen as a creative adjustment to limited possibilities, when a person or a group is legally or practically prohibited from assuming a political role. The electoral behavior of Islamic movements in the pre-Arab Spring era does suggest that "winning" meant something quite different than it did for other parties, since elections served for them the role of consolidating their social presence, rather than as a way to actually share in governing a state.

For example, the Muslim Brotherhood's performance in the Egyptian parliamentary elections of 2005—the least manipulated elections before the revolution of 2011—was considered by all observers as well as the movement itself as an astonishing success, certifying its status as a viable and popular alternative to the ruling party. Yet, in reality the group won only 19.4% of the seats, and in any case had contested only 32% of the total seats in the parliament, thus clearly sending a signal to a government that barely tolerated it that it was not aiming at winning a majority. In the Lebanese parliamentary elections of 2009, where Hizbullah faced no legal restrictions as did the Brotherhood in Egypt but a complex national demography, the party was seen as a strong contender to win, even though it had nominated only 14 candidates for the 128-member chamber.

After "losing" those elections (in which *all* of Hizbullah nominees actually won their contests), a supporter saw the loss to be a good thing, since
it saved Hizbullah's reputation, in comparison to Hamas's in Palestine,
from being tarnished by being associated with governing.[3]

That observation spells out one attraction Islamic movements hold to
many individuals: The appeal of the movement resides in its superior ethical aura. Yet it is precisely ethical purity that is the quality most difficult
to sustain when it becomes involved in the practical, complex and profane business of governing. An aura of superior ethics provides part of the
reason for this relative aloofness and halting orientation to the state, since
practical calculations are clearly involved: Most modern Islamic movements have to some extent experienced life underground and the sustained hostility of national governments not keen to see their entrenched
powers challenged by any social movements with wide popular appeal.
Thus an Islamic movement could oscillate between an impressive electoral performance one season, and a complete or partial boycott of the elections the next—as, for example, was the response of the Egyptian Muslim
Brotherhood when the government changed election rules to make it difficult for its members to compete in 2010, or as the Jordanian Muslim
Brotherhood did in 2007 when the government simply told the group how
many seats it would be allowed to win, or again in 2013 when the Jordanian
government refused to change a blatantly inequitable election law.

A fuller understanding of the attitude toward the state must therefore involve considering both the significance for the movement of its
ethical appeal and its realistic calculations. Most existing Islamic movements, including ones calling for an Islamic state, have in fact ignored
the state for most of their lifespan. Rather, they have tended to emphasize the more cultural goal of Islamizing modern society. Both Banna
and Maududi, working in two different environments from early periods
of modern Islamic activism (first half of the twentieth century), argued
that Islamizing the state would not be possible if society itself were not
Islamized first. That standpoint essentially meant disseminating a specifically Islamic enlightenment, whose main features would be social solidarity and ideological conservatism.

One of the best examples of how this has worked was Fethullah Gülen
Nur movement, which originated in Turkey but eventually developed a

---

3. See http://www.aljazeera.net/Portal, accessed June 9, 2009.

global presence and renown (Wood and Keskin 2014). In spite of vigorous accusations by its detractors, the movement always stated that it was not "political," which meant that it did not run or endorse candidates for office, nor did it train its members for careers in politics. This did not protect the movement from being accused of being a tool of US policies, and it did not help matters that Gülen himself eventually moved to the United States, nor did the fact that some of his positions—including his questioning of the Marmara Flotilla sent in 2010 to help besieged Gaza—do indeed align with US policies in the Middle East.

Before being accused by the AKP of seeking to topple its government via a coup in 2016, Gülen himself had been occasionally at odds with older Islamic political parties in Turkey, including the Refah Party that had briefly ruled Turkey before being removed from office due to pressure from the military in 1997 and eventually banned. However, this apparently apolitical stand belies the undeniable fact that the vast social networks, schools, and media established by the *Nur* movement have contributed to eroding the secular stranglehold on power in Turkey and paved the way for the triumph of modern Islamic conservatism across Turkish society *and* politics during the first decade of 2000s.

The specific "Turkishness" of the Gülen movement tends to be over-emphasized (e.g., Yavuz and Esposito 2003; Yavuz 2013). This national overemphasis, as I hope to show in Chapter 2, results from a convenient tendency to compare the *Nur* movement to Islamic movements outside of Turkey that are very dissimilar to it rather to those that are more similar. One can see basic similarities here even with something like the Muslim Brotherhood. The similarity in this case resides in the basic proposition that improving the spiritual quality of society is the only *constant* goal of all modern Islamic social movements. Such a goal may or may not involve political work; the same movement may at times be highly political and at others less so or not at all. This is true of the Gülen movement just as well. Its leader has not shied away from making comments on elections, parties, and military coups (incidentally, he endorsed the coup of 1980 in the name of restoring order). His forerunner, Said Nursi, asked his followers to vote for the friendlier secular leader Adnan Menderes in 1950, so that the *Nur* movement could breathe easier than was possible under the harsh secular climate of early Kemalism.

Improving the spiritual quality of society as a constant, basic goal of all Islamic movements meant that they could always be active at some level, regardless of the political climate surrounding them. The basic strategy for such an improvement does not vary much across the span of Islamic movements from the basic outline of Hasan al-Banna, founder of the Muslim brotherhood, or Abu Ala' Maududi, founder of Jamaat e-Islami, both of whom elaborated the modern Islamization project in the form of successive levels of struggle, beginning with the individual and leading up to the world (see Figure 1.4).

Such a program is striking for its simplicity, but also for its capacity for immediate implementation: The clearest elaborations as to what an "Islamic" attribute might be are to be found at the level of the individual. The further away we move from that foundation, the less clarity and less description there is in the writings of modern Islamic thinkers as to what it means for a "society" or "state," for example, to be Islamic. The underlying assumption seems to be that a state or a society becomes Islamic simply by virtue of its consisting of properly Muslim *individuals*. Sayyid Qutb, one of the most renowned figures among the founders of modern Islamism, wrote actually little on the Islamic state even though he is identified with the struggle for one. When describing higher levels of struggle above the individual, Qutb preferred to speak of a general condition of "social justice" in Islam, rather than the structure of an Islamic state. The few thinkers who sought to define an Islamic state in more clearly constitutional ways, like Rachid Ghannushi, Hasan al-Turabi, or Muhammad Shahrur, represent exceptions in the spectrum of modern

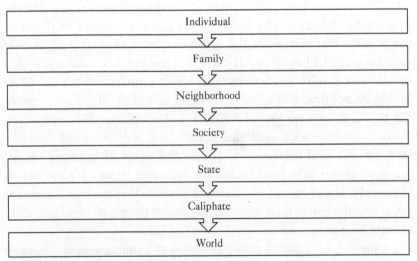

FIGURE 1.4 Levels of struggle according to Banna, Maududi

Islamic thought.[4] More common is the simple notion that an Islamic state is one that "applies" the *shari'a*. But that proposition itself only masks the vastly indefinite nature of which it speaks, since the *shari'a* has historically never been actually "applied" by *any* state, including Islamic states. First, the *shari'a* does not consist simply of legal rules, which provide only a small part of that corpus. Second, it has never been a uniform body of laws, and in any case cannot be translated as is into the form of modern state law without being altered so that it could actually look like "law" as we understand it today. Neither the nature nor the details of such law are presupplied in any self-evident fashion in the *shari'a*, and certainly not in a way around which there is a consensus among Muslim jurists (more on the historical character of the *shari'a* in Chapter 3).

This lack of a definite program of politics, noted by critics of Islamic movements, has rarely bothered those attracted to them. For them, much of the appeal of this modern religiosity resided in the greater attention it gave to the micro-levels of action (individual or neighborhood), where religiosity spelled tasks most clearly. By contrast, tasks at the macro-levels (including the state) were vague and could remain such since they were not usually open to initiatives from below. This was the case even for Islamic movements with a more developed political program, but which otherwise emerged out of the dynamics discussed previously. For example, until 2006, Hamas in Palestine experienced great difficulties in figuring out how to use opportunities for inclusion in the larger Palestinian political institutions (al-Madbouh 2011). Until then, the movement seemed unprepared to assume political responsibilities that transcended its constituency of loyalists, even though it *did* have a political program and politics had been part of its usual business since 1987.

It is not evident that the clarity or even coherence of the Islamic program as a whole and at all levels matters that much for the prospects of the movement. That nonchalant attitude is made possible by the very conception of *levels* of struggle; all levels are fields of struggle, in theory, but not all are reachable or relevant at any given time. Thus one needs no elaborate plans for how to deal with prohibitions, limits, or opportunities at a higher level when that is inaccessible or too distant from daily life. One could always seek to cultivate oneself as a Muslim individual,

---

4. The first two belong to the Tunisian and Sudanese branches of the Brotherhood, respectively, and Turabi's own commitment to the democratic values he ascribes to Islam in his writings may be questioned given his former opportunistic alliance with the military dictatorship. The third is a popular independent thinker who will be discussed in the next chapter.

and the instructions as to what that should mean are the most abundant types of instruction in the Muslim world today. These include countless religious manuals on daily manners, relationship issues, finances, psychic health, and so on (Watson 2005; Tütüncü 2012). And this voluminous literature corresponds precisely to the pragmatic program outlined already by Banna, in which the modern individual is the *locus* of the fundamental struggle.

That is because it is out of the programmatic cultivation of the *person* as a Muslim individual that a foundation is laid for the building of a Muslim family; out of that a Muslim neighborhood emerges, and then a Muslim society. In theory one could keep on going up to higher levels of struggles, until one hits a limit—for example, a legal license for social work but not for political action, or tolerance for religious upbringing within the family but not for religious education outside of it, or permission for religious rituals but not for proselytization, and so on. In such cases, one occupies the social level one is allowed to occupy, filling it up with spiritual quality, until one is able to go beyond it. It is hard to see a more apt and flexible application of Antonio Gramsci's strategy of hegemony.

A program of this kind thus gives one something to do on an ongoing basis. Unlike the Marxist, for example, the Muslim activist does not need to languish in impotence in wait for a revolutionary moment; nor constantly eye the capture of the state as a necessity for putting into effect one's own political, social, or economic program; nor read too many complex books on the science of history and the dialectics of political economy, before one may understand the world "scientifically." One *already* has the science one needs in one's own pocket, and the ability to act in one's own hands. Far from being the opium of the masses, here religiosity means immediate action whose goal is to create spiritual spaces at any available level of struggle, including one's own person when all else is barred. The sum total of millions of such individual daily acts may result in political opportunities, which then lead to outcomes, whose exact nature can remain vague and general until they materialize.

Yet, both eventual opportunities and current limits are not necessarily interesting as "real" conditions, in at least two senses of the word. First, there is a crucial difference, apparently more evident in revolutionary climates, between actual and perceived opportunities, as Charles Kurzman (1996, 2005) shows us in the case of Iran in 1979. Second, the discourse of religious activism, or more particularly *struggle* (jihad), is geared to

Table 1.6 Levels of jihad according to Khomeini, Sheikh Qasem

Level	Target	Goal	Precondition
Greater jihad	Self	Improve one's spiritual quality	Mandatory, permanent
Lesser jihad (elementary)	World	Establish the hegemony of the true faith	Presence of divinely guided authority (prophet, infallible imam)
Lesser jihad (defensive)	Aggressive enemies	Defend the faith (including social communities)	Mandatory when needed (authorized by legitimate clerical authority)

activating human agency and not simply to the art of assessing opportunities. "Jihad" is not a uniform style of struggle, but a concept that encompasses a vast repertoire of possibilities that one may select from as needed for any battle. In most cases this will be personal struggle, as that is the most familiar and immediate level, and as Muslim theologians have long argued. Even the most hardline modern Muslim revolutionaries, including Khomeini, have highlighted the concept of jihad precisely in a way suited for constant action on the self and immediate environment, and only occasionally and given rare conditions, on larger environments. (see Table 1.6.)

How reaching state power transforms the movement

Why did Islamic movements initially appear to be so well-positioned to capture power in the first free elections in Egypt and Tunisia following the 2011 uprisings, only to lose popularity shortly afterwards to secular political forces that were initially very weak in comparison? The traditional explanation is that the Islamic movements were better organized, and that their opponents needed time to get their act together. This explanation is broadly accepted, even though it accepts as a fact what needs to be *explained*: It is of course important to know how organizations emerge and collapse. But more important is to know how *ideas*, notably those that provide modern organizations with their life force, become more or less popular. The problem of modern Islamism was that it governed. And by governing, it became like any other political party, that is

to say, it no longer appeared as a generic custodian of a collective heritage, and as such, as the ultimate guarantor of social cohesion. Rather,
Islamism in power appeared as simply the project of just another political party. This was not necessarily a "mistake," since ruling parties
behave as parties, that is to say, they cannot represent society: They generate opposition because of the simple reason that they govern. Thus
Islamism in power ensured social *division*, just as any other party would
be expected to. Whenever that happened, Islamism lost the greatest asset
it had, which had always been its aura as generic custodian of a collective
heritage—and in some cases it also lost its other aura of ethical purity, as
the most non-corrupt force in society. In other words, it took only a democratic experiment to reveal Islamism to be an ordinary political force,
like any other.

More generally, the character of any social movement may transform
at any time, as a result of misadventures, experiments, or changing
context. Any of these factors can come into play before the movement
has experienced anything like state power. For example, evidence from
the study of militant groups suggests that they can be transformed
through a combination of external and internal factors, including state
repression, selective inducements, and socialization. This was the case
with the Egyptian Muslim Brotherhood between 1951 and 1973, the
once-feared Gama'a Islamiyya in the same country between 1997 and
2002, and the Algerian armed Islamist groups between 1997 and 2000
(Ashour 2009). This applies to some extent even to *Jabhat Fath al-Sham*
(formerly known as *Jabhat al-Nusra*, al-Qa'ida's affiliate in Syria during
the civil war), which modified its approach and message on the bases
of valuable lessons from the earlier misfortunes of the Iraqi branch and
the special demands of the Syrian theater. (We are speaking of modifi-
cation, an analytical term, not "moderation," which would be an evalu-
ative term. In any case, neither the movement nor its detractors would
likely accept the latter term.)

But the question here is what happens when a movement that has all
the characteristics described previously is able to act upon higher levels of
struggle and larger social environments? Much has been made of the specter
of Islamic movements capturing the state apparatus, whether through an
insurrection or popular elections. Evidence suggests that Islamic movements tend to transform or even fail when they capture the state or at least
when they become part of it. Cases of Islamic movements becoming part
of governing coalitions or assuming power outright include—apart from

the exceptional case of revolutionary Iran—Indonesia, Turkey, Pakistan, Bangladesh, Jordan, Iraq, Egypt, Tunisia, and Morocco.[5]

The dynamics associated with state power are quite different from those confronting the more militant groups that typically do not participate in formal politics. The electoral success of the Muslim Brotherhood in Jordan in the early 1990s, which led to its participation in the government, also led to a decline in its votes in following rounds of elections, as a result of both changes in election law as well as dissatisfaction with the movement's performance in the cabinet. It boycotted the elections for one round afterwards in 1997, returning to parliament with a strong contingent of 17 deputies out of 110 in 2003, only to dwindle to a record low representation of six deputies in 2007, after which it again boycotted the subsequent elections due to an unfavorable election law. These cycles are associated with a number of factors other than the popularity of the movement at any particular point. Such factors include geopolitical regime priorities, manipulation of elections, legal changes, and the degree to which the support base of religious candidates intersects with other loyalties, including tribal and kin loyalties. But the rough numbers may still serve as a rudimentary guide for the fortunes of a movement whose relationship to formal politics must be seen in the context of the degree to which such politics are controlled by an unfriendly state apparatus. One must also consider the nature of the political field in uncertain environments, whose openness and inclusivity are typically perceived by all actors, religious or otherwise, to be temporary until proven otherwise.

At any rate, once part of formal power structures, Islamic parties tend to be evaluated on the same basis as all other parties, namely their success in delivering public goods and resolving social problems. Judging by the massive popular mobilization against it in 2013, the Muslim Brotherhood in Egypt appears to have lost popularity rapidly after its successive victories in parliamentary and presidential elections in 2012. That may be an extreme case tied to the revolutionary climate in the country then, but the basic lesson is the same everywhere: Governing is experiential learning,

---

5. One may also mention the aborted case of Algeria, where FIS (Islamic Salvation Front) was on the verge of winning the elections of 1991–1992 outright, when intervention by the Algerian army shelved the democratic experiment and sank the country into a decade of civil war resulting in at least 100,000 deaths. The already discussed case of the Da'esh caliphate is too exceptional thus far to be counted as part of this pattern. The case of Afghanistan is likewise exceptional but for different reasons. Its dynamics will to be discussed in Chapter 3 in the context of puritanical experiments.

particularly for new movements that were not previously oriented to the state. This reality does not always entail a disaster for the movement as was the Egyptian case. Experiential learning as a factor in transforming the movement may lead to adjustment and continued survival, as in the case of an-Nahda movement in Tunisia or the Justice and Development Party in Morocco in the aftermath of the Arab Spring.

The same could be said of the AKP in Turkey during its first decade of rule (but not since the beginning of its second decade in 2013, by which point the party had acquired enough monopoly on power to give its authoritarian faction more confidence). The AKP emerged out of decades of experiential learning—in government or formal politics generally—that had resulted in the banning of several predecessors. After several regroupings, each with its own record of electoral success and subsequent repression by the secular elite and the army, the politically organized segment of the Islamic movement finally coalesced around a program of "traditional conservatism" of the AKP—hitherto the most successful mass-based party in the history of modern Turkey. That story showed an adjustment to the reality or demands of state power, an approach that has been called "passive revolution" (Tuğal 2009). But it also showed a more general dynamic, which is that some kind of reorientation of perspective cannot be avoided once Islamic movements have acquired some experience with governing at some level, before reaching the national level.

Transformation affected by the prospect of state power may follow substantially different trajectories. It appears that the availability of a democratic path to *some* power is likely to alter the program of a movement away from authoritarian inclinations, since a movement then has to adjust to the real diversity of the political field, and since its own prospects within a democratic game require that it accepts pluralism as a rule of political life. This was the case, it must be recalled, even with a group as militant as Hizbullah, which, once it agreed to enter the parliamentary game, found it imperative to put aside previously expressed central goals, notably establishing an Islamic republic in Lebanon.

The same logic could be applied to the aborted Muslim Brotherhood rule in Egypt in 2013. The movement arrived at power in 2012 through elections, only to lose it in a military coup a year later. The coup was welcomed as expressing "popular will" by opponents of the Brotherhood. Those opponents never considered that, given mounting popular opposition, the Brotherhood would have likely lost the next elections in any case, without a coup, the resulting bloodshed, the poisoned social fabric, and the slaughter of the infant Egyptian democratic experiment. All of the above was possible because of the myopia of even educated observers (e.g., Kandil 2014; Ghitani 2012), who could not see the Brotherhood as anything but a monolithic society, mobilized by an unchangeable ideology and immune to experiential learning. It is true that the Egyptian Brotherhood then had the misfortune of being led by a leadership that was poorly suited for revolutionary times. But that did not mean that it was immune to experiential learning—certainly no more than any other liberal political party in the country, each of which was *learning* how to behave for the first time in an open environment.

Similarly, democratic experiential learning may not be apparent in the case of groups that had won elections but were prevented from exercising governmental power, such as FIS in Algeria or Hamas in Palestine. In Algeria and Palestine, the democratic path was undermined by local secular opponents who had lost out, and who were explicitly encouraged to undermine democracy by prominent external actors such as the United States and the European Union and, in the case of Hamas, also by Israel. (Obviously in such cases, democratic experiential learning was not available to *any* political group, and not just to the Islamists.)

A second path leads to power through a non-democratic trajectory. Here, one would expect any transformation to be immediately more authoritarian in nature. The clearest case of such a transformation is the Sudan, which Gallab (2008) argues must be seen as the first Islamist republic. There, the local branch of the Muslim Brotherhood was led by Hasan al-Turabi, a man whose earlier writings reveal remarkably progressive ideas concerning independent reason in religion, the role of women, support for civil liberties, and minority rights. However, al-Turabi appears to have seen no problems and only opportunities in his movement being used by two successive authoritarian regimes that had come to power through military coups. Nor, curiously enough, did he see a contradiction between his liberal views and the idea of Islamizing society in an authoritarian way by using governmental power acquired through a marriage of convenience with military leaders of state. Of course, seeking a shortcut to power is hardly unique to Islamic movements, including ones like the Muslim Brotherhood that otherwise emphasize grass-roots activism. But it is apparent that the method by which power is acquired predicts to a great extent how such power is likely to be exercised.

This also suggests that the prior record of opinions and writings of leaders of Islamic movements may not by itself be a good predictor of how

Table 1.7 Experiential Learning of Islamic Social Movements: Two Influencing
Factors

Path to power	Prospect for monopoly	Experiential learning
Democratic—liberal (e.g., Turkey 2002–2013, Tunisia since 2011)	No	Pluralist
Democratic—illiberal (e.g., Turkey since 2013)	Yes	Semi-authoritarian, semi-pluralist
Democratic—partial or aborted (e.g., Jordan, Algeria, Palestine)	No	Semi-pluralist, semi-authoritarian
Conspiratorial (e.g., Sudan)	Yes	Authoritarian
Revolutionary (e.g., Iran)	Yes	Semi-pluralist

they would behave once in power. In Tunisia, Rachid Ghannushi's writings while out of power reveal a highly developed conception of Islamic liberalism, one that lives well within a pluralist field. A decisive factor seems to be that the movement came to power through elections rather than a military coup (and furthermore by winning a plurality rather than a majority of the votes, meaning that it could not govern alone). That reality delivered a political landscape in which expressed earlier opinions could be translated into negotiated politics, willingness to share power with secular forces, and an acceptance of the reality that the movement could not alone control a pluralist society, no matter how rightly guided it might be. Thus here we have two leader-intellectuals, Ghannushi and al-Turabi, whose earlier writings are quite similar, yet whose political behavior so opposite. The main difference appears to be the *method* of acquiring power (see Table 1.7).

There is nothing specifically "Islamic" about the basic principles of experiential learning. But it is clear that religiosity provides no immunity from behavioral transformation—only a different way of justifying it. There seems to be a certain path-dependency, namely the method of arriving at power, that greatly affects whether a movement would switch from pluralist convictions to authoritarian practices once in power or vice versa.[6] In addition to this path-dependency, there seems to be another

---

6. However, some literature, which does not focus specifically on Islam, suggests that the quality of leadership, rather than any objective conditions, makes the most difference in the final analysis (see, e.g., Samatar 2002).

important factor, namely the capacity to monopolize power. The fact that here we are identifying what looks like "structural factors" over ideology or expressed opinions is probably justified by the fact that conditions of political fluidity and institutional uncertainty in much of the Muslim world over the past century did not contribute much to ensuring continuity of convictions of *any* movement that contests state power. This applies to secular movements as well. What is to be noted here is that now we know that religious movements are not immune from those dynamics either. The nature of the path to power, coupled with the prospects of pluralism, seem to have a greater impact on whether one's prior convictions will survive once one is in power. (This does not mean that there can never be exceptions. But those will require "heroic" personalities, which is another way of saying that they will not be delivered by the circumstances alone.)

Apart from the democratic and conspiratorial pathways, one may also consider the pathway of revolutionary insurrection. This offers a most interesting learning process since popular revolutions tend to engage large numbers in an intense collective process, thereby laying ground for a broad sense of entitlement to define the revolution. In the Arab Spring, no single political force has been able to define the revolutions in its own ideological color. This may be contrasted with the Iranian Revolution more than three decades before, which did result in an Islamic republic and came to acquire an Islamic imprimatur, in spite of the original ideological variety of participants. Thus Iran continues to house the only example of a popular revolution that acquired Islamic terms and resulted in a political system that claims to be based on Islam[7].

There are, however, important studies that suggest that the Islamic revolution in Iran was hardly "Islamic" (Bayat 2007; Kurzman 2005; Ghamari-Tabrizi 2016), in the sense of being *inspired* by the need to establish an Islamic system. According to this view, only at the very last moment did divergent sentiments, all having in common an opposition to the Shah, converge on a vaguely defined Islamic core. Bayat in particular shows that there was hardly anything like an Islamic "movement" preceding the revolution, and therefore the other common features of

---

7. But it is a mistake to assume that this unique case has something to do with the nature of Islam. After all, the same region did witness at least two other successful popular revolutions before the Arab Spring, namely those of Algeria and South Yemen against colonial rule. In both cases violence played a role, and the organizations that led the anti-colonial struggle (and in both cases they happened to be secular) did have an opportunity to define the revolution, and consequently the postcolonial political system, on their own terms.

Islamic social movements outlined here do not apply in this case. The Islamic identity of the new system required at least two more years of post-revolutionary struggle to become more consolidated, and that process required eliminating the more secular wings of the revolution that had briefly become partners in the new power structure. Eight more subsequent years of mass mobilization in the Iran-Iraq war further cemented both the role of the clergy and their identification with Khomeini.

Yet, the closure of political space in Iran for all non-religious opposition only made it more natural for all subsequent opposition to express itself in the language of religion. Ironically, that happened precisely for the same reason as under the Shah, but with a twist. Whereas under the Shah religion was the only common language of opposition that could not be prohibited outright, under the Islamic Republic religion became the only common language of political life. In either case, religion became *more* political because all alternatives were crushed—in the earlier case by a secular regime, and in the latter case by a religious regime.

But this amplification of the political role of religion also transforms its meaning. An important source of this kind of transformation is tied to participatory claims made by mobilized populations, since those could in principle always regard their own activity to be the real source of revolutionary change. This would be the case even as "the people" regard "god" to be the source of their collective action—as I saw in Cairo in 2011 amidst an otherwise secular revolution. But the conclusion is the same, regardless as to whether the mobilization of millions of participants is credited to god's will or to "the people" acting directly on their own behalf. Either claim must then compete with or be reconciled with the claims of the more organized wings of the popular movement, clerical or otherwise, who would be expected to claim some level of guardianship over any large-scale popular mobilization. In Iran, the compromise was found in a system combining elements of both popular sovereignty and clerical rule. This formula, while reconciling competing claims, also set the stage for perpetual if controlled conflict. It expressed itself in the form of a controlled democracy. The limits to that democracy could be expanded or restricted further on occasions, so as to accommodate either clerical divisions or tame a particularly strong opposition.

As we know, various degrees of controlled democracy are typical of its long global history, since "democracy" is not a standard global system but an arrangement of power distribution whose shape depends on the capacities of local actors at any given time and place (Bamyeh 2009:71–117). The post-revolutionary Iranian arrangement included regular elections and an institutional balance between elected and unelected bodies. The system does include the notorious mechanism for disqualifying candidates, but it also runs on the basis of institutional regularity—with only one major irregularity in over three decades: the apparent fraud during the tenth presidential elections of 2009. The removal of Abolhassan Banisadr, the first president during the tumultuous early years of the new system, may be regarded as another interruption of institutional regularity, but even that extraordinary event was done according to the already established procedures of the new system.

In such a system, the "religious field" becomes coextensive with the "political field," to use Sami Zubaida's terms (1993:150–151). This is precisely what Abdolkarim Soroush, one of the reform intellectuals of the new system, came to realize as he argued that in a "religious society," all political issues will tend to be discussed in religious terms. But we may restate the same thesis without having to assume the innate religiosity of society: Since a religious standing is *required* for participation in formal politics in Iran, and anyone with such a standing has in theory a valid claim to the right to participate, religion parallels political life completely. This does not simply mean that religion dominates political life. Rather, religion itself becomes *as multiple as the political field*. Thus *all* interests and expectations expressed in the political field, whether economic, social, cultural, or intellectual, come to be expressed in religious language.

The split that emerged in Iran over the first two decades of the Islamic Republic between "conservatives" and "reformers" expressed precisely the most general features of that reality. Both camps used Islamic discourse, and the revolution was their common reference point. That was not simply a question of rhetoric or framing, since the system itself developed institutional accommodations that adjusted to the plurality of the revolution—so long, of course, as all claims and counter-claims could be expressed somehow in the language of Islam. For example, in spite of the conservative dominance in the judiciary, the system could not exclude the "reformers," who assumed the presidency for two terms under Khatami, and enjoyed significant influence under two other presidents (Rafsanjani and Rouhani), and also a majority of the parliament for a while. The fact that Khatami's program was frustrated by various machinations and that his camp was held back from holding a subsequent majority must be seen in a larger context, in which reformers' popular mobilization could not be outlawed and where the public sphere, especially during the Khatami period, became one of the most open of such spheres in the Middle East. The language of a common revolutionary heritage itself became the weapon of the reformers, just as it was for the conservatives. As the country was galvanized again following the 2009 elections, both claimed Khomeini and accused the other camp of betraying his spirit.

Thus by providing a different wing within revolutionary Islam with a common theater of formal politics, the Iranian Revolution also provided it with quasi-organizational shape. This development could not have been predicted from the point of view of the early years of the Revolution. In those years, advocates of the different camps were not so clearly distinguished from each other. For example, one of the main groups identified with the reform movement, the Association for Combatant Clerics (*majma'-e rowhaniyun-e mobarez*), founded in 1987, was known in its early years more for its radicalism and call for state control over the economy, and not for its defense of democracy or free thought (Brumberg 2001: 152–184). Abdolkarim Soroush, a leading reform intellectual, took part in the project of re-Islamicizing the universities in the early 1980s, and many accuse him of having had a role in closing the universities then. Saeed Hajjarian, another leading reformer under Khatami, was most known until then for his contribution to building the intelligence apparatus of the new regime. And so on.

But while the experience with state power in Iran gave birth to what is now identified as a reform or progressive wing in political Islam, even more interesting is how it also transformed the so-called conservative approach to political Islam, in ways that were mandated by the imperatives of governing and legitimized by Khomeini himself. The clearest expression of this shift was represented in a remarkable *fatwa* issued shortly before his death, in which Khomeini exempted the Islamic government from the requirement of referring to the *shari'a* in justifying its actions, and in fact allowed government to suspend *shari'a* provisions if its interests warranted such action. He then *explicitly* placed the pursuit of government interests above the fulfillment of any religious obligations (Zubaida 1989:63–66, Eickelman and Piscatori 2004:50). That meant that the actions of an Islamic government no longer required being *constantly* justified as being "Islamic." More directly put, a verdict of this kind, evidently novel since it had to be spelled out (and there is in fact nothing similar to it in Islamic history), entailed removing religious justification for *any* governmental action.

There were of course practical reasons for that kind of *fatwa*, reasons that would have never materialized had there been no Islamic republic. For historically the *shari'a*, as will be discussed in more details in Chapter 3, has in fact never been applied systematically as a guide to any government in Islamic history. As Tarif Khalidi (1996:193–200) effectively shows, it was *siyasa* (a medieval genre devoted to the secular science of politics, that in Europe would later be identified with Machiavelli), and not *shari'a*, that had formed the source of political behavior of Muslim governors, especially since the tenth century. The *shari'a* itself had already become a multiple practice elaborated by multiple scholarly traditions (and *not* by governments) even before then. But *shari'a*-based *fatwas* were sought and given as needed, that is, as learned opinions to facilitate a specific governmental practice, but never on an everyday basis or continuously.

Thus the coming into being of an Islamic Republic in the late twentieth century revealed, quite inadvertently, that the *shari'a* had never actually been used as a consistent source of political guidance. This fact became very evident *only* when the *shari'a* was called upon to authorize thousands of government decisions annually. It was thus only an Islamic government that could finally confront as a pure fiction the proposition that government could be guided by a body of sacred edicts that has never had anything to do with governing. That the *shari'a* had nothing to do with governing could thus only be discovered by the one government that sought to follow the proposition to its ultimate conclusion. Thus from a conservative perspective, one evidences a consolidation of a specific form of religious knowledge: Proper religious guidance of political behavior cannot be derived from detailed religious instructions. Rather, it consists of claiming a pious identity, while doing what is *practically necessary* to keep running a system that one regards to be virtuous overall. In other words, a religious behavior is what a religious entity does.

It is in this sense that we can say that the Iranian Revolution does not have an essence, in the sense that it is impossible, for example, to verify the statement often made about or by each subsequent camp that its movement represents the true revivification of the Revolution. The Revolution, as Daniel Brumberg aptly puts it, produces in the final analysis many children even though it may have had just one father. And those many children themselves are changed, each in their own way, by their experience in running or observing a revolutionary system in practice.

If such a transformation occasioned the most complete takeover of a government by an Islamic program, what could one expect in systems where the takeover is either partial or requires being negotiated across multiple movements and actors not unified around an Islamic program? Lebanon, Palestine, and Tunisia are good examples, thus far, of this more likely scenario. In Lebanon, Hizbullah found itself compelled to accept the multi-confessional character of the country and abandon its goal of establishing an Islamic republic as soon as it entered parliamentary elections—even though it remained "militant" in other respects. In Palestine, Hamas began its transformation already when it agreed to contest elections, observing a cease-fire with Israel, focusing its campaign on issues of corruption in government, and seeking a national unity government with its opponents as it realized the difficulties it would face in case it governed alone—a belated realization that saved it neither from governing alone nor from the subsequent difficulties. In Tunisia, al-Nahda had to negotiate a new constitution in a crowded political field, and in the process found itself compelled to abandon reference to the *shari'a* and agree to broad liberal principles advocated by its secular partners.

Transformation and learning, therefore, are natural dimensions of Islamic social movements, especially to the extent that they succeed in acquiring state power or become in some ways partners in it. The most meaningful transformation entails giving concrete meaning to the vacuous old slogan "Islam is the solution." The degree and nature of transformation seems thus far dependent on the nature of the path to power and the pluralist quality of the political field. A particular path to power presupposes a particular style of organizing and mobilizing, and the pluralism of the political theater supplies opportunities and limits whose magnitude depends on the quality of such pluralism.

Whatever form it takes, each process of mobilization enlists and exposes to experiential learning social strata that, already infused with participatory ethics at local or interpersonal levels, eventually come to regard the political system as "theirs" in a particular way, depending on how they arrived there. As mentioned before, the very fact that one sees mass protests in Iran after a fraudulent election in 2009 is to be seen in the larger context of the *absence* of protest following more massively and routinely rigged elections elsewhere in the same region.

Even when a movement does not reach state power, it transforms as it transforms society, but in ways that are less obviously political in nature. Here we are talking about ways that are more oriented to spreading ethics that consolidate the status of religion as a reference point in everyday culture and commerce. In recent literature this orientation to issues of everyday life and culture, where the political program is abandoned or downplayed, is often noted as "post-Islamism" by many commentators, including Asef Bayat (2007), Nilüfer Göle (2000), Amel Boubekeur (2007), Ihsan Dagi (2004) and Husnul Amin (2010), among others. In this case, religious mobilization no longer takes the form of call to arms against political targets. Rather religion becomes part of an everyday social ethic, which may or may not lead to an obvious political outcome. But in such a case, the arena is already prepared for political involvement when and as needed. The Arab Spring, again, illustrates this dynamic: In no country did Islamic movements initiate the uprising, but they found it natural to join it once it was already underway.

In either case, whether one is speaking of political or cultural fields, transformation as a product of experiential learning is connected to the nature of religious movements as *movements* in the first place. In one sense, a social movement is an art of exploring the social world in which it moves. But if the movement is based on religious consciousness, that consciousness may through the movement assume both dynamism and stability: One is moving and thus already transforming, but feels oneself to already possess a familiar interpretive structure. In learning about limits and possibilities through social action, a religious person could always say that he has just discovered a deeper truth that had always been integral to religion, although he could not see it before. The complexity of "god's wisdom" (which for sociologists may be expressed as the "complexity of the social world"), can always be cited as the reason for a prior myopia.

This dynamic is readily evident in ethnographic studies of modern Islamic consciousness. That a woman preacher becomes popular because she made people "like their religion" (Mahmood 2005: 86) illustrates this conservative dynamism. Her statement assumes that religion exists naturally in society, that it is already "ours." That does not mean that "we" as believers necessarily understand or appreciate it properly. But it means that the believer is capable of infusing more sense into it and, in the process, "liking" it more, that is to say, aligning it with a new perspective that had been acquired through social action. Evidently the learning process here is not about making religion say what one wants it to say. Rather, one learns something more about divine intention as one seeks to make religion say what one thinks should be true. Experiential learning, therefore, means in the modern world that one meets god halfway, so to speak, rather than simply applies god's incomprehensible rules mechanically or out of thoughtless obedience.

In the case of political success of a movement, there seems to be a number of basic dynamics that influence the path of experiential learning, apart from the specific nature of the path to power or the pluralism of the theater in which it moves. First, there is the vagueness and poor definition of the Islamic political program itself, which makes possible the exploration of a myriad of possible directions. This vagueness may be a valuable asset to a movement, although what one does with this vagueness depends on whether one is governing or is sitting in an opposition. But a vagueness of this kind is evident in general slogans, typical of being in the opposition, like the old "Islam is the solution." That very general slogan meant nothing concrete and appealed precisely because nothing concrete was associated with it. But vagueness is also useful in cases of political success, for example when religion is established as the common language of the entire political field, as in the case of Iran. In the former case, Islam as "the solution" expressed the generality of all social problems and the lack of trusted secular custodianship over such problems, whereas in the latter case all worldviews came to be expressed in a common language, even though specific and detailed interpretations became more important. In either case, experiential learning became unavoidable precisely because of the generality and openness of the message. In other words, vagueness rather than clarity lent legitimacy to experiential learning.

Second, political success means contamination of the sacred with the profane. Hasan al-Turabi—angel in opposition, devil in government—is a clear example of the worst outcome of this contamination. In general, when they rule a political system directly, religious authorities find it difficult to maintain detached moral prestige and an aura of ethical purity, that is, the very elements that had historically given them so much authority in civil society. This danger appears to be more known to traditional religious authorities, but less so to those invested in social movements. Ayatollah Sistani in Iraq, for example, saw a clear danger to shi'ism itself in the establishment of Khomeini's Islamic republic, since the traditional authority of the clergy had relied on an indirect influence on political life rather than on governing.

Overall, however, modern Islamic movements must be considered as broad experiments of social engagement. Sayyid Qutb, for example, revised his outline of social justice in Islam no less than seven times while he was alive, and likely he would have continued to do so had he lived longer. Islamic movements are not finished products, and usually they fare poorly if designed as such and with a clear program, as in the case of *Hizb al-Tahrir*, for example, or *al-Gama'a al-Islamiyyah*—the latter, facing political irrelevance and the prospect of complete annihilation, spent years completely revising its earlier radical program. The more common type of Islamic movement corresponds to broad participatory demands for which venues may be lacking in formal and institutional politics.

In an important sense, these movements evidence not a "revival" of an old religion but rather the politicization of the entire society, and the attempt to enter into the political and cultural field by hitherto excluded demographics, through whatever door may be open, however slightly. And "participation" here can also be felt in a very direct and concrete sense, namely through social engagement with one's immediate surroundings. A modern individual does not seek religion for no reason, and given other opportunities and outlooks may not seek religion at all. But she will always seek some relief from a sense of personal impotence or closure and unresponsiveness of her world. This should only mean that the world requires being made responsive and open, and that the person should feel that the world is hers. The quest to "participate" signifies only this longing, even though it may take countless other expressions, as the specific environment may be willing to accommodate.

Finally, there is the question of whether Islamic social democracy as a long-term project is comparable to European Christian social democracy, where ordinary conservatism was mobilized to combat modern problems and offer an alternative to liberal and socialist solutions. The Islamic project however has not appeared comparable to the European experience, likely because it has less experience with governing. In addition, the project has not been conscious as "social democracy," only as "Islamic." In this connection, if we allude to social "democracy," it is not because Islamic movements are naturally "democratic." Just as in European history, a democratic program is simply the ultimate result of an awakening, perhaps after several wars and revolutions, to the fact that no movement can monopolize control over society. Like Christianity, like Judaism, like any other religion, Islam becomes "democratic" not because it is essentially so, but because it ultimately reveals itself to the believers to not be the universal ideology of their own society. Al-Nahda in Tunisia was the latest of these types of movements to understand this reality. And we should also keep in mind that since democracy can always be abandoned by any force— religious or not—that feels that it has enough power or license to fully

control any society, no democratic transformation of any movement—
religious or not—could be *guaranteed* to be permanent. Once established
as a principle, pluralism is something that can only survive if constantly
defended. It is not guaranteed solely by texts, ideologies, or constitutions.
It survives only when it is a social fact.

2

Islam as Public Philosophy

PRAGMATICS OF KNOWLEDGE

LIKE ALL PERSISTENT social phenomena, Islamic movements and Islamic consciousness do not exist without being intellectually justified and debated in the public sphere (Salvatore 2007). Public intellectual work is especially informed by the very nature of *modern* Islamic consciousness, in which Islam becomes a social program rather than followed as a "tradition." (In the case of "tradition," there is generally less need for public intellectual justification, since one can simply mechanically follow old rituals that may satisfy spiritual needs of personal life, but are devoid of larger social purpose.) It is difficult to imagine any ideology that becomes the substance of a broad social program to not invite constant public debates about its meaning.

In this case, the relevant public questions include the social intentions of Islam; the character of any social order that make it particularly Islamic (or not); what social justice may mean from a religious perspective in a modern society; the extent to which religion justifies struggle, and in what ways, against unjust authorities; the proper analytics by which we figure out god's social intentions; and so on. Modern Islam has therefore been intellectually elaborated throughout the twentieth century. This elaboration was typically directed at some public sphere, meaning that it was intended to offer a "guide to the perplexed"—as Maimonides long ago thought of the role of intellectuals when their communities became disoriented due to the inapplicability of a literal understanding of their old traditions in changing times.

While it is impossible in one chapter to cover the full range of a hundred years of public debates across the vast range of the Muslim world, it is possible to identify two basic, competing approaches to a modern Islam, as outlined by public intellectuals as well as by movements expressing variants of their public philosophy. One approach saw Islam as a "solution," that is, an *instrument* for solving modern problems. A competing approach placed more emphasis on the way by which Islam gave *meaning* to the world. The former trend manifested what might be called an instrumental approach to Islam, whereas the latter a more hermeneutic approach. As in all social philosophies with broad popular appeal, each school included several varieties and there were also overlaps across them, and it is possible to see them coexisting in the same mind. The main difference lies in the expressed goals of each style of thinking.

One condition that seems to orient the mind to one framework or the other is state power: Islam tends to be more philosophical when distant from state power, more instrumental when it is close to it. The same applies to *opposition* to state power: Islam tends to be more philosophical when its direct relevance to oppositional programs is not obvious, more instrumental when the ethical character of the state or its accountability to constituents, having become suspect, seems to require (what is then assumed to be a forgotten) religiosity.

Of course, hermeneutics too can be associated with certain political standpoints, as we will see shortly. Generally it is aligned with what we call "liberalism," but is less organized politically than its instrumental counterpart, and in any case its "liberal" program is something that is inferred from its theory of knowledge, rather than enunciated as a systematic and explicit commitment to a political ideology. Hermeneutics, therefore, may generate different types of liberal politics, whereas instrumentalism, if allowed to take full course in a political theater free of dictatorial threats, would likely develop in the direction of conservative Islamic social democracy.

The other difference between the two programs in so far as politics are concerned has to do with how public philosophy is aligned with organizational tendencies. Thus far it seems that whereas instrumentalism gravitates by its nature toward political organization in one form of another, hermeneutics seems to provide grounds for politics but is not as well-equipped to generate its own political party.

Generally, the two approaches form distinct paradigms, in the sense that each approach is founded upon starting points that define the scope of what is possible to ask of religion in modern times. In either case, both paradigms signal a departure from traditional Islam as it had been approached for centuries. By "traditional" I mean a taken-for-granted, self-evident compass of everyday intellectual reflections. Old tradition-alism meant neither lack of intellectual activity nor uniformity. It implied only a common agreement on basic reference points in public intellec-tual life, safeguarded by a learned elite that was institutionally stable and within which there existed an agreement on what "standards of judgment" may be valid (but not necessarily an agreement on what *judgments* may be valid). That form of tradition disappeared from public intellectual life throughout the twentieth century, as is evident from the fact that Islam it-self required being justified in new ways as a reference point for modern social, political, cultural, and economic life. It is also evident from the fact that Islam no longer exercised a monopoly as an ultimate intellectual reference in Muslim societies, even though it came back to occupying a prominent role (but with new justifications) by the late twentieth century.

For our purposes, it is important to distinguish this conception of tra-dition from the way Talal Asad defines it, namely as a discursive relation to the past governed by the requirement of engagement with a defined set of foundational texts (Asad 1986:14). I find this definition unsatisfac-tory, since it applies to almost all varieties of modern Islam, rather than simply to traditional Islam. Tradition is uncontested immediacy. If we apply this perspective, we see the decline of traditionalism, for example, in what Eickelman and Piscatori (2004:37–45) describe as the modern "objectification" of Islam. By this they mean that Islam itself becomes an object of active knowledge; it needs to be discovered by the faithful, who now wish to learn what it may tell them about how to conduct their lives. Objectification here means that the social meaning of religion is no longer self-evident: While it may be old, the object exists now at a remove from the immediate knowledge of an inquiring person, and only in being so distant does it invite contemplation.

A non-traditional religion, therefore, has a complex relationship to one's *identity* as a religious person. In one sense it may mean that reli-gious identity exists in a state of psychic nervousness. That is, religious *identity* is the only portion of religiosity that is taken for granted. If that is the case, then this identity requires completion and certification by ac-tive inquiry: One needs to know what else is in religion besides its being "mine." In another sense, it could mean that a religious identity is un-derstood as the *goal* of inquiry and activism, rather than as a self-evident, already existing reality.

The historical point of departure away from traditional Islam is often thought to be associated with the need to respond to colonial challenges from Europe, although the reform program upon which both varieties are based may be traced to earlier movements (Dallal 1993). Wherever the point of departure may lie, a globally interconnected Islamic Enlightenment became visible as a public intellectual movement in the later part of nineteenth century, especially in the Middle East, and South and Central Asia.

Instrumental Islam, as will become more apparent shortly, formed an earlier basis of Islamic social movements. The founding of the Muslim Brotherhood in Egypt in 1928 was an organizational crystallization of an intellectual movement that had been gathering distinct public momentum for half century prior. Hermeneutic Islam, by contrast, formed the basis of later movements, whose earliest organizational expressions may be found in the *Nur* movement in Turkey and other variants that have emerged in several Muslim countries since the 1960s, evidently independently of each other. The intellectual genealogy of the hermeneutic approach is quite complex—its roots lie less clearly in nineteenth-century Islamic Enlightenment. Rather, modern hermeneutics have emerged out of a fusion of modern philosophies of science, classical Islamic hermeneutics, and modernized forms of Sufism. (See Figure 2.1.)

Intellectuals   Theaters of operation

Instrumental Islam

Afghani   → India → Maududi → jama'at-e-islami   {

→ Istanbul   {

→ Persia   {

→ Egypt → 'Abduh → Rida→Banna/MB→   {world MB
(70+countries)

→ Paris

Hermeneutic Islam

Nursi   → Turkey → Gülen → 30+ countries   {

Shariati   → Iran → Soroush   {hermeneutic
convergence

Taha   → Sudan   {

Shahrur   → Syria → Arab World   {

FIGURE 2.1 Intellectual genealogies of hermeneutics and instrumentalism

I would like to suggest that this dichotomous division of public intellectual Islam into instrumental and hermeneutic varieties makes more sociological sense than more popular divisions that highlight attitudes toward modernity and, by implication, also political attitudes. Representative of those include John Voll's (1994a) distinction of modern Islam into three varieties (liberal, conservative, and fundamentalist), or Akbar Ahmed's (2008) also triadic division of modern Islam into three paradigms represented by the scholarly traditions of the Indian cities of Ajmer (mystic), Deoband (orthodox), and Aligarth (modernizing).

Such triads are constructed on the basis of presumed distance from or closeness to something called "modernity." But the history of Islamic social movements, even over a short period, shows experimentations with all these attitudes, as we saw in Chapter 1. For example, it is not at all clear that "fundamentalism" presupposes any particular social or political attitude by necessity. After all, the most self-conscious modernizers among Muslim intellectuals in the nineteenth century called themselves "fundamentalists" (*salafi*), in the sense that they were trying to show the modernity of religion by going back to its *fundamentals*—and in doing so, disregarding existing *tradition*.

Thus in so far as it allows one to reject a common tradition, fundamentalist attitudes are just as "modern" as any other attitude, and even modern liberal Muslims can be shown to exercise a fundamentalist critique, in so far as they go back to the "fundamentals" in trying to prove the liberalism of Islam. A good example from recent decades is the pioneering approach of Fatima Mernissi (1992), who illustrated how founding texts of Islam may be read from a feminist perspective. Her critique, which other advocates of gender equality have used as well, was based on the proposition that original Islam (if properly understood) has advocated women's emancipation, and in a way that is compatible with (but much earlier than) modern attitudes. But in order to see that old truth, one had to reject "tradition," that is, the unreflexive approach in which religion is made to correspond to taken-for-granted cultural attitudes. In other words, here one uses a fundamentalist method to arrive at a liberal conclusion.

Similarly, it is unclear the extent to which terms like "mystic" or "modern" explain actual differences, since all mystics now live in modern times, use modern communication technologies, and use mysticism as one among many ways of handling the complexity of modern life. Unlike such terms, the instrumental/hermeneutic divide appears more helpful, since this dichotomy describes how a believer *approaches* the very idea of religion, rather than what *outcome* may be served by one standpoint or another. In other words, an instrumental/hermeneutic basic divide of modern Islam takes as the starting point how Muslims themselves approach the very idea of religiosity. This is a more fruitful approach, I think, than starting out from a grand abstraction called "modernity" (or assumed value subsets of it, like democracy, individualism, or gender equality), and then try to figure out how Muslims relate to a problematic that is presumed to have come to them from without.

Another facet of the assumption that Muslims are simply responding to problems that come to them from without emerges out of the otherwise legitimate and now profuse critique of orientalism. The most sophisticated outline of the argument here is perhaps that of Reinhard Schulze, whose voluminous contribution highlights how one develops a vision of one's history and makes it speak to a present. Schulze (2016) criticizes European ways of seeing Muslims as people defined by their culture, rather than by a *weltgeist* of modernity, as well as the European tendency to see every other modernity as simply "Westernization." Once those views are appropriated by Muslim intellectuals, they become the real source of fundamentalism.

This critique is of course partially true, but we know now (e.g., Dallal 1993, 2018) that Islamic reform movements preceded significant encounters with Europe. And as we shall see, it is not true that Muslims could not make use of Western historiographic terms like nation, state, or capitalism, since in fact they did just that—though they often did so by blending those terms with a trans-Islamic ethos that allowed them to see no contradiction in what they were doing. And what they were doing—this mixing of elements—during this *weltgeist* of modernity followed the already familiar process of mixing perspectives and loyalties (e.g., Bamyeh 2000:1–58), depending on the conditions of the moment.

In the final analysis, however, it may prove not very meaningful to insist that everyone in the world defines herself in relation to a "modernity," when reality is much simpler. An ordinary person would be expected to be foremost interested in giving one's own empirical life a sense of meaning and direction with the aid of whatever repertoire of knowledge that happens to be available. So the question for everyone is not an abstract puzzle called "modernity," but the method of ascertaining and verifying any truth claim in or concerning concrete social life. Thus the question of method is everyone's question, and not simply that of the scientist.

If we understand that, then we understand how instrumental reason and hermeneutics provide the basic, but opposing, elements of a *method*: In

Table 2.1 Main features of an instrumental versus a hermeneutic approach

	Instrumental Religion	Hermeneutic Religion
Social purpose of religion	Solve problems	Enhance knowledge
Knowability of god's mandate	Knowable with certainty	Knowable without certainty
Character of proper religious knowledge	Authoritative	Interpretative
Source of religious instruction	External (*I apply* god's law)	Dialectic (*I interpret* god's intention)

the former instance, god's mandate is comprehensible and the role of humanity is to apply it, whereas in the latter instance god's mandate remains aloof from human understanding, precisely because he is god and we are humans. In either case one may be active in the world as a religious person. But an instrumentalist wants to solve social problems with the assistance of god's mandate, whereas a hermeneut wants to cultivate a practical philosophy of life that synthesizes god's infinite wisdom with finite human reason. (See Table 2.1 for a summary.)

It is of course quite possible that one approach—for example hermeneutics—correlates better with other attitudes or programs like liberalism, mysticism, or democracy. But that determination, along with an explanation as to why it should be interesting, belongs to a different study. What is unfortunately missing still from the voluminous literature on modern Islam is how Muslims themselves develop a religious reason in one form or another out of the basic working materials of religion. Instrumental reason, for example, may or may not be correlated with "fundamentalism," even in the life-course of the same movement or the same person. In the final analysis, the salience of instrumental reason tells us little about the nature of religion itself. Rather, it tells us how the *existence of problems* to begin with calls forth or highlights the problem-solving aspect of religiosity.

The secular question

One way to understand the salience of modern religiosity and its role in intellectual debates in the public sphere is to ask why we are asking this question to begin with. As a "tradition," religiosity requires explaining from only a secular rather than religious perspective. But in its post-traditional form, religiosity requires *justification* from a religious perspective, and *explanation* from a secular perspective. Justification gives rise to instrumental and hermeneutic approaches, both of which involve thinking aloud in the public sphere about the question as to why religion may still be needed in the first place. Explanation, which has generated an endless literature on the secularization thesis and why it has failed (or not) (Berger 1999; Stark 1999; Inglehart 1997; Norris and Inglehart 2004; Casanova 1994), also asks the same question, but without a religious motivation. And it is often the case that what needs explaining here is less the rise of religion than the failure of secularism. However, as I will try to show shortly, instrumental religious reason is in fact analogous to secularism and in some important respects modeled after it.

By way of getting to this point, I want to briefly suggest the limits of the view of secular reasons as inherently more open than religious reason. A presumably excellent example of a secular society is the Netherlands, a "one nation without god" (Achterberg and Waal 2011). The country exemplifies in some sense one of the classic expectations of the secularization thesis, namely that over time, secularization leads to more tolerance of diversity. In this case, however, it apparently leads to an intolerance of religion itself, that is, everyone in society being *required* to abide by some core (liberal) values, regardless of one's religious belief (Vollaard 2013). However, the counterargument in defense of this secular intolerance is that there is no intolerance here, since what is not being tolerated is the presumed intolerance (of religious people, in this case migrant Muslims) toward liberal values (homosexuality, gender equality, individualism, and so on) (Bohemen and Kemmers 2011).

Obviously, an ideology based on tolerance (such as liberalism) can regard its own intolerance only as furthering the requirement of universal tolerance (Popper [1945] 2013:581, n.4). The point here does not concern whether such a standpoint is philosophically defensible or not. Rather, all social ideologies, including all varieties of religious and secular thought, must define in some way what does not belong to them. But in the final analysis, tolerance is a sociological and not simply a philosophical theme. This means that social struggles involving ideals (including tolerance) ensure that such ideals cannot remain as unadulterated philosophical propositions, independently of how we *experience* them. An example of the purely philosophical attitude is the quite common presumption that Muslims are incapable of tolerating a principle or behavior (for example gender equality or homosexuality) because of something that is essential to Islam. Yet, there is nothing less illuminating than assuming that we know what people would tolerate, without knowing who those people are to begin with. Typically, those who make grand claims about the unfit nature of "Islam" in Europe have no Muslim friends, know no Muslims as individuals, and are generally interested in knowing them only as grand categories, not as persons.

Roots of the secular question: The modern state

This more sociological task was in fact the foundation of one of the earliest, and now forgotten, critiques of secularism in classical sociological theory, to be found in Karl Marx's early essay "On the Jewish Question." There, Marx criticized the project of a secular state even as he maintained his view of religion as an expression of social defect. Marx saw clearly that secularizing the state does not remove religion from politics: It only makes the state appear to society as heaven to earth. Whether modeled after the US separation of church and state or French *laïcité*, the modern state only does what god had always done, namely, police social imperfection and, like Jesus, mediate between man and his freedom. Marx rejected such secularism because it was liberal rather than communist in character. That liberal secularism did not, for Marx, solve the fundamental problem, namely *the state*. That early Marxist critique of religion thus recognized the basic *similarity* of religious society to one envisioned under a liberal secular state. Neither had an interest in human emancipation, only in calculated political licenses. Both posited themselves, in the place of civil society, as the only viable embodiment of all that was good (and hence missing) from earth.

Though apparently addressing the persistence of religion in political life in the United States after the separation of church and state, Marx's 1843 critique aimed at a deeper problem, one that remains unresolved to this day. While there are still endless squabbles in the United States over purely symbolic issues (the state's use of the word "god," the state's display of the Ten Commandments, or prayer in public schools), nothing is mentioned of the *ordinary political fact* that successful politicians are expected to have a religious affiliation, attend church, express their faith in their speeches, ally themselves with religious groups, swear their oath of office

on the Bible, and include in their platforms policies that flow directly out
of the religious beliefs of some constituency or another.[1]

Though contemporary European discussions of secularism, heavily
laced with anxiety about immigrants, appear different, one can detect a
similar pattern of defending secularism on the *symbolic* terrain—against
headscarves or religious symbols in public places.[2] An enormous amount
of political capital and media coverage, for example, were spent in France
(and eventually other countries) on passing a law in 2011 banning the
full face female cover presumably associated with Islam, even though it
was worn by less than 400 women among France's more than 4 million
Muslims. In this political circus little was made of the fact that a common
agreement existed, including amongst immigrants themselves, that they
should be more integrated into host societies, that their children should
learn modern school curricula, and that it was advisable for religious authorities to take part in such processes.

The contemporary resurgence of religion, which appears as a coordinated assault on the secular state on its (supposed) home turf in the
West, to say nothing of the Muslim or even Hindu worlds, must be
reconceptualized as a problem of the modern state, rather than as one of
religious consciousness. For example, the fact that religious parties may
contest elections has to be understood in the context of the fact that *all*
parties contest elections when they can. All do so because they understand
the modern state as a vehicle for their own programs, which corresponds
exactly to how the modern state sells itself to its people: The state itself
says that it is a good vehicle for the implementation of *any* political program that manages to take it over. The problem, thus, is the nature of the
modern state, which encourages all political aspirants to treat it as a natural depository of their campaigns for any kind of social good. There is

---

1. The saturation of US politics with a variety of religious expressions, *both* liberal and fundamentalist, has become more obvious over the past three decades. Jimmy Carter was the first
"born-again" president in the contemporary period. For an overview, see Diamond (2000)
and Aikman (2012).

2. The larger (and by now very old) issue of Turkey's accession to the European Union casts
a wider net around these debates, as it becomes a question of integrating an entire Muslim
country rather than small immigrant communities. For an excellent collection on this issue,
see Leggewie (2004). The cultural side of the debate in this collection clusters around inherently murky and insoluble issues concerning "the identity of Europe." When the debate
moves to *practical* matters, however, such as specific economic, political, and legal reforms
that Turkey must undertake in order to join the EU, the debate becomes clearer, focusing
only on Turkey's ability to follow through on what is required.

nothing particularly exceptional about the role of politicized religion here. It only appears as a problem because of a secular assumption that religion will become political if not expressly prohibited from doing so.

However, a sociological approach to religion would be more nuanced: A religious perspective serves as a sanctuary of various conceptions of personal or social order. These conceptions may or may not lead to political action, depending on the circumstances of the moment.

Ample evidence from both Muslim and non-Muslim countries suggests that when there is enough reason for religious conceptions of society to be mobilized politically, legislative prohibition alone is unlikely to stop their incursion into the public sphere or public policy. They become political when influential groups advance the case that certain social problems can be addressed more meaningfully in religious terms. This avenue is usually wide open given that religion—whether understood as an intellectual system, a spiritual relation to the world, or a communal identity—can always appear to be larger than ordinary politics. The extent to which religious conceptions of social order eventually take on a political form may be a function of persistent failure of secular discourses to address, and in broadly felt ways, concrete and widely shared social problems. What follows will illustrate the point by highlighting specific junctures in the history of public, intellectual Islam over the past century.

Religious consciousness, modernist orientation, and feelings of national belonging were a closely interconnected triad in the emergence of the modern world, and they were not always clearly separated. The early, instrumental Islamic thought systems sought to infuse the twin projects of social modernization and anti-colonial nationalism with a religious character. In doing so, they shared a field in which both of those projects were also being advocated from a secular point of view. ("Secular" in this case means non-religious rather than anti-religious framing of social issues.)

Islam was increasingly marginalized in the public sphere in most of the Muslim World for most of the twentieth century, until the late 1970s. Until then, an apparently secular era held sway, defined socially and economically by the pursuit of global modernization and politically by the rhetoric of national sovereignty and independence from colonialism. Yet the marginalization of Islam did not indicate its disappearance, only a transitional period in which traditional Islam slowly gave way to new forms of modern religious reason that eventually became highly influential in the public sphere.

The two public intellectual systems of Islamic modernity addressed the questions of modernity and national liberation through one of two major frameworks: an earlier, largely instrumental and a later, more hermeneutic approach. The instrumental pathway, which is more familiar to us due to its dramatic history and appearances, sought to defend Islam by presenting it in a form that was closely compatible with modernist national goals. Instrumental Islam in effect responded to secular consciousness in kind: It was immediate and results-oriented; it highlighted purpose and reflexivity over ritual in religious life; it emphasized action in the world, including political action; it was more attuned to the dialectics of combat than to the inner qualities and even meaning of spiritual life; and its paradigmatic public slogan "Islam is the solution" clearly specified the role of religion as an instrument for solving pressing social and political problems.

In this sense, instrumental Islam did not reject secular nationalism so much as seek to "improve" it. That was to be done precisely by combining a developmental, modernizing project with a principle of sovereignty grounded on a definition of collective identity that was assumed to be more solid, historically and culturally, than secular nationalism, but also compatible with it. Already in the nineteenth century advocates of instrumental Islam, rather than challenging nationalism, tended to blur the distinction between nationalism and religion and, more generally, between local or national identity and Islamic cosmopolitanism. The prominent thinkers of nineteenth-century Islamic modernity, such as Rifa'a al-Tahtawi and Jamal al-Din al-Afghani, were also early defenders of nationalism. The former defended Egyptian nationalism even as his arguments were couched in terms of Islam, while the latter defended Arabism and outlined a distinct Arab history (in a way remarkably similar to the arguments of nationalist Christian Arab intellectuals of the period), even as he elaborated a larger modernist message intended for a universal Muslim audience. Such fusion tendencies continued to be visible well into the twentieth century: Ismail Ragi al-Faruqi (1921–1986) moved back and forth between the two frames of identity seamlessly. In the early 1930s in Egypt, Rashid Rida, then the foremost public intellectual of instrumental Islam, pointed to Japan as his model for nationalism: modernizing while maintaining a strong sense of cultural identity and indigenous heritage (modernization without westernization). That would be precisely what instrumental Islam hoped to accomplish for Muslim societies.

During its early phase, advocates of instrumental Islam sought less to challenge secular nationalism than to expand and deepen its meaning, and to rejuvenate Islam so that it maintained a strong presence in the public sphere. But in the process they also altered the meaning of religion itself, as well as the role it had historically played in social life. The meaning and role of religion changed yet again in the hermeneutic pathway. Hermeneutics presents Islam in ways that are closely compatible with postnational (Bamyeh 2001) and neoliberal, even post-state, guides for life in a global civil society. In the case of hermeneutics, Islam becomes realigned as a framework of a cosmopolitan spirituality, and becomes less understood in terms of identitarian religiosity.

In the same way that these intellectual developments altered the meaning and role of religion, they likewise altered the meaning of other terms of debate, such as "development" or "heritage." Both appear from a hermeneutic point of view as outcomes of spiritual experience, rather than as elements of political programs. Hermeneutically conceived, social "development" is an element of the eternal dialectics of progress and change in the movement of an imperfect and limited humanity toward an infinite and perfect god.

Likewise, hermeneutics generalizes the idea of "heritage" beyond the parameters of identity: "Our" heritage as Muslims is not the property of Muslims, nor is it evident in what Muslims themselves do (and this is already an old point, noted just as well by Afghani in Paris, where he observed that there was Islam without Muslims). A Muslim culture is immanent in the world, without it always being expressed as such, and Islamic mores are universally present, beyond self-identified Muslim communities.

The state, the original problem, also fades as a concern from a hermeneutic perspective; its manifold modernist failures inspire a desire for distance from it, not a quest to take it over. In either case, both the instrumental and hermeneutic pathways lead to the building of societies that are parallel to the state or that substitute for it in ordinary life; the one key difference is that from an instrumental perspective the state may remain an object of a potential battle, whereas from a hermeneutic perspective the state fades from view and is replaced by society.

Exploring the long path toward these ways of thinking will be the goal of the rest of this chapter, which will begin by charting the trajectory of the secular nationalist program in terms of its unruly relation with instrumental Islam, especially in various countries in the Middle East, and end by describing the rise and limits of the hermeneutic alternative.

The national question and religion

Two well-known events of modern Middle Eastern history bespoke forms of secular consciousness quite distinct from instrumental Islam, even though one of them was argued from a religious perspective: the 1924 abolition of the caliphate in Turkey under Atatürk, and the publication in 1925 in Egypt of Ali Abd al-Raziq's *Al-Islam wa Usul al-Hukm* (Islam and the Foundations of Governance), which argued that Islam never supplied a system of government.

These two epic battle cries of secularism in two largely Muslim societies, the work of two very different types of authorities, also differed in their outcome, their prehistory, and their surrounding contexts. Atatürk was a political leader and national hero of almost mythic proportions. Abd al-Raziq was a public intellectual besieged by enemies in the public sphere. Atatürk got his way because he was the state, while Abd al-Raziq seemed to have lost the battle when al-Azhar, the most prestigious Islamic institution of higher learning, issued a *fatwa* against his book and reasserted the union of religion and state in Islam.

It would appear that we have here, in two comparable Muslim societies around the same time, contrasting stories of secular success and secular failure. Further, it would seem that the state's being on the side of the secular idea determined success or failure; traditional authorities alone would not reject an idea that gave them claim to some power. (Even though that idea itself was not contested before precisely, because it never corresponded to the way any Islamic political system actually operated.[3]) But, there is a puzzle here—in fact two. First, the success of Atatürk and the failure of Abd al-Raziq seemed to matter little in the long term. From the 1920s until relatively recently, the political field in *both* Turkey and Egypt was effectively dominated by secular forces, and by the 1960s politicized religion (though certainly not religious sentiment) had in fact dwindled almost out of existence in both countries. Second, in both societies, secular intellectuals were caught unawares toward the end of the century by the substantial advance of religion *back* into the center of the public sphere and political life. The puzzle here—roughly similar paths and outcomes in the long term in spite of apparently greatly different starting

---

3. Charles Kurzman argues that Abd al-Raziq's thesis would have been perfectly acceptable just a few years before its appearance. A more accurate reading of the affair is that a few years earlier such a thesis would not have needed to be proposed.

points—suggests that the dynamics of secularism and religiosity originated outside the visible theaters of state politics or public debates.

To add to the puzzle, the prehistory of each event seemed to suggest that secularism was more poised for success in Egypt than in Turkey. Shortly before the final collapse of the Ottoman Empire, Egypt, and not the Turkish center of the empire, had sustained century-long modernist reforms in education, politics, and economy, backed by government effort almost uninterruptedly since the reign of Muhammad Ali in the early nineteenth century. The Egyptian reforms had begun about quarter of a century before the comparable Ottoman *Tanzimat*, had been more comprehensive, and had met less resistance than in the Ottoman Empire.

By the beginning of the twentieth century, reformist triumphs in Egypt stood in contrast to the difficulties of reform in the Ottoman Empire. In Egypt the clergy, de-privileged but also co-opted since Muhammad Ali, posed a far lesser challenge to reformed government, education, and law[4] than did the entrenched and institutionalized Ottoman clergy, which saw itself as a pillar of the old system and formed a formidable power bloc. Whereas in Egypt the title of the most important religious officer, the *Mufti*, came to be held by the famous reformer Muhammad Abduh, the highest religious office in Istanbul, the *Sheyhulislam*, continued to be held by compulsive anti-modernists out of touch with their time.[5] In short, throughout the nineteenth century, Egypt seemed to showcase successful modernization whereas the Ottoman Empire, weighed down by long tradition and institutional inertia, moved only slowly or in uncoordinated steps toward them.

By the 1920s, therefore, a state builder in Turkey and a public intellectual in Egypt were confronting contrasting histories. Yet in both situations, the question of Islam's relation to the state had become secondary, notwithstanding the intense debates over the dissolution of the caliphate and the tumult around Abd al-Raziq's thesis. In both Turkey and Egypt, the most urgent issue now was colonialism, not what to do with Islam. Egypt had been under direct British domination since 1882, and the massive revolt in

---

4. Family law is an exception, evolving more conservatively than other branches and still viewed by the religious establishment as its proper domain.

5. Even after the dissolution of the Empire, its very last *Sheyhulislam* simply continued, in exile, to write arcane commentaries on medieval Muslim philosophers with no apparent relevance to contemporary realities, much less to the needs of the high office he had assumed (see Rahman 1984).

1919 voiced a full-throated anti-colonial nationalism. In the Turkish center of the Ottoman system, the gradual disintegration of the Empire, combined with internal revolts and defeat at WW1, likewise highlighted the national question–the very survival of a sovereign Turkish territory at all from the planned dismemberment by Western powers.

In both societies, therefore, questions of religion and secularism were overshadowed by those of imperialism and nationalism such that the differential record of a century of modernist reforms became secondary.[6] Rather than interminable abstract debates over which mode of thought was more proper for modernity and how, the immediate question to be decided in the court of instrumental reason was which form of thought provided the more *effective* vehicle of resistance against colonialism.

But even this question was in some sense superfluous. Especially in its anti-colonial phase, national consciousness could easily house both religious and secular expressions. Everywhere in the Muslim world, up to and including the Algerian war of independence, nationalist movements combined secular and religious identities seamlessly. The emergence of a distinction between the two in nationalist thought required something other than pure logic: a material demonstration that one style of thought led to defeat and another to victory. That religious and secular thought lead to different *outcomes* was what needed to be demonstrated, before they could be regarded as distinct enough paradigms of social thought.

In Turkey, the failure of religion seemed evidenced in the defeat of the Empire in which the most conservative elements of the religious establishment were implicated.[7] And the success of secularism, likewise, was inseparable from the success of the old Ottoman/Young Turk elite by 1922 in a direct war against the colonial plan for Turkey, *after* the defeat of

---

6. The reforms in Egypt were directly motivated by the failure of the old Mamluk system to defend Egypt against occupation by Napoleon's forces in 1798–1801. In the Ottoman Empire, the reforms were also directly related to successive military losses against European powers over a longer period. The military institutions of the Ottomans were modernized at a faster pace than other parts of the system, which may partially explain why Turkish modernity following World War I tended to be led by the military with an authoritarianism combined with the notion of the military as a guardian institution supplementing the mythical status of Atatürk.

7. I am using "conservative" here as a term of convenience to refer to institutional rigidity and reluctance to change patterns of behavior embedded in institutions, and not as reference to any specific doctrines. For example, the Ottoman Empire officially subscribed to the Hanafi School of Islamic jurisprudence, which is usually regarded as the least conservative of legal schools within Sunni Islam.

the Empire. Thus, secularism and religion became clearly separated only when they produced *different results* in the national struggle. By the 1920s, this difference was far more obvious in Turkey than in Egypt. In Egypt, until Nasser and especially the Suez Crisis in 1956, no single force could definitively dislodge British colonial presence and domination. Egypt's ideological story thus continued to unfold as an ongoing symbiosis of and mutual accommodations between various local voices, including the religious and the secular.

In this, the story of Egypt is the more familiar one on the world stage. As in most of the colonial world, the debate in Egypt rarely posited secularism and religion as mutually exclusive ideas. Abd al-Raziq's own argument for the separation of religion and state itself relied on classical Islamic sources rather than on secular reason. The founding figures of Arab nationalism in the nineteenth century rarely saw a contradiction between the secular idea of Arab nationalism and universal Islamic identity. Similar symbiosis between secular nationalism and religious identity also reemerged to some extent in Turkey itself with the rise of Adnan Menderes in 1950, and became especially more pronounced during the period of prime minister Turgut Özal following the 1980 coup. Islam then became increasingly viewed as an inseparable element of Turkish national identity, but also as an important source of personal moral discipline.

Indeed, practically everywhere, the secular and the religious remained so deeply intertwined in social and intellectual practice that their strict separation would be analytically misleading. Keeping this point in mind also helps us appraise the religious renaissance of our times, whether we are speaking of present-day Turkey, Egypt, or even the United States. It suggests that the epic battles of secularism against religion, whether led by state builders with a sense of historical mission or well-intentioned public intellectuals, expressed programs that were far more problematic and difficult to achieve than initially imagined.

From religion to nationalism and back

The dissolution of the caliphate in 1924 only formalized the long-term disintegration of the material foundations of that institution, and its practical irrelevance in light of the dismemberment of the Ottoman system after World War I. Husayn ben Ali, the Sherif of Mecca, laid a short-lived claim to the caliphate after its dissolution in Istanbul, but found himself forced to withdraw it after losing his battle over Hijaz with the Saudis.

The Sherif's case was not helped by the fact that he was operating in a demographically and economically marginal corner of the old Empire. His Hashemite family had then to resign itself to less glamorous deals for dynastic rule over Iraq and Jordan, and then only under British tutelage.

The fact that such an old and symbolically significant office as that of the caliph could no longer, unlike the Vatican for example, survive or even be claimed without some material basis reveals the importance of the modern principle of national sovereignty for any political claims, including claims that on their face seem to suggest aloof spirituality. After all, the same person who sought to claim the caliph title, Husayn ben Ali, was also the leader of the explicitly *Arab* (and *not* "Islamic") revolt against the Ottoman empire. The Sherif obviously recognized no contradiction between his version of Arab nationalism and a claim to a universal Islamic office. The only factor that mattered was sovereignty, which was already an inescapable component of nationalist thought worldwide and which was carried over, as in this case, to a caliph's office that in earlier historical periods would not have required it.[8]

Thus everywhere in the Muslim world (with the exception of Turkey which had escaped direct colonial control), the primary issue continued to be colonial domination, not the fate of the caliphate. In British India, one of the anti-British movements among Muslims was known as the Khilafat movement. Although ostensibly aiming to prevent the disappearance of the caliphate, in reality it had little religious pedigree and its slogans were by and large anti-colonial (Alavi 1997; Enayet 1982). The most important intellectual spokesperson of Muslim India, Muhammad Iqbal, in fact praised the Turkish experiment and supported the dissolution of the caliphate. A decade later, when the extremely secular nature of the Kemalist project must have been obvious, Iqbal (1934) was still nonchalant: Even if the doctrine of caliphate was mandated in Islam—a debatable proposition in any case (Gibb 1955)—an elected modern parliament, embodying god's trusteeship of the earth to its people, could just as well fulfill that role.

Iqbal was hardly alone among Indian Muslims. It may seem stunning from today's vantage point that most intellectual and political founders of Pakistan thought of their project as a *secular* experiment. In his inaugural speech to the Constituent Assembly of Pakistan, president Mohammad

---

8. The point may become more apparent if we were to compare it to the situation in the Muslim middle ages, where the Abbasid caliph was maintained for centuries as a rallying focal point of cosmopolitan Muslim loyalties, long after he had lost effective power.

Ali Jinnah formulated this vision of the future of his polity: "You will find that in the course of time, Hindus will cease to be Hindus and Muslims will cease to be Muslims, not in the religious sense because that is the personal faith of each individual, but in the political sense as citizens of the state" (Pandey 1999:612). For about half a century—from at least the 1920s until Zia ul-Haq's regime in the 1970s—the idea of an "Islamic state" in the Indian subcontinent had meant for most of its advocates not an Islamic theocracy and not even a state based on Islamic law. Rather, it simply meant a state for British India's Muslims, that is, a sphere in which they would be free from possible discrimination as a minority group.[9]

In the half century between the dissolution of the Ottoman Empire and the first signs of Islamic political revival, secular authorities that ruled most of the Muslim world tended to regard leftist movements rather than Islamic groups as their main threat, repressing the latter only when they appeared to pose a challenge to the state, as in Egypt after 1954. When no such threat was perceived, there was little reason from a secular point of view to actively repress a version of national sentiment just because it was expressed in a religious language. Even in Turkey, that perspective became established with Menderes in 1950, and became even more entrenched after the coup of 1980. Very likely, the basis of this view was the reigning modernization thesis during the immediate post-independence period. According to that view, there was no compelling reason to actively repress religion, since social modernization would itself lead to religion's gradually becoming less relevant to the public sphere and public issues.

The problem with this perspective, as should now be obvious, was that when secular authorities were increasingly perceived to have failed the developmental test of modernity—to bring about a sovereign, prosperous, and participatory society in which religion would become less relevant for maintaining social cohesion and thus less credible as a source of social critique—the secular order entered a critical period. Such a failure did not necessarily signify a fatal crisis, especially given that, initially at least, the failure could be blamed on external conditions requiring no paradigmatic shifts in ideology, only pragmatist adjustments in planning and policy (for instance a shift from import-substitution industrialization to export-oriented economics; obviously such a shift alone requires rejecting

---

9. That was indeed Maududi's and the JI's main complaint about the Pakistan project. Though well-entrenched in social networks, they nonetheless exercised little influence over the state or in parliamentary politics until the late 1970s.

neither secularism nor modernization). But wherever such failures were compounded with catastrophic defeats, and a sense of malaise, stasis, increasingly closed systems and closed horizons, as in the pre-revolutionary Arab World, a social consensus emerged that saw a need for a radical rearrangement of the entire political order, including its ideological basis. In the Arab world, elements of that consensus clustered around a number of pivotal issues, including the demonstrated impotence of the ruling regimes regarding the galvanizing agony of Palestine; the failure to undo the colonial division of the region; the extreme and unusual uniformity of postcolonial authoritarianism; endemic corruption and the transformation of virtually all governments into unaccountable kleptocracies; and, with the decline of Nasserism, the subservience of many postcolonial governments to powerful foreign patrons.

Anticipating as well as responding to such catastrophic failures, intellectual Islam in the public sphere now embarked upon a second path in society and politics. The earlier path, as mentioned earlier, had opened up in the late 1920s out of the heritage of the Islamic enlightenment and spread worldwide. Dominated by instrumental reason, it sought to add a specific cultural dimension to a national developmental and sovereignty-oriented project it endorsed. The second path began to take shape in the 1960s in different countries, forging itself out of a combination of Sufi traditions, Islamic hermeneutics, and modern science. Dominated by a hermeneutic approach to Islam, this latter trend moved away from the instrumental approach. While endorsing democratic participation and pluralism, and diagnosing the same modernist failures of the secular order around which there existed a national consensus, it also developed a critical perspective toward instrumental Islam. The latter had by then accumulated enough of an intellectual record and political experiences to be assessed from another religious perspective, and not simply from the point of view of secular critics.

Instrumental reason versus hermeneutics

In general, religious revivalism in any period seems to include some basic, recurrent impulses. In the Reformation, for example, revivalism involved a call to go back to the ancient roots of the faith as a way of removing sediments of obscurantism, making religion more relevant to the times, and providing the faithful with a claim to a right to direct access to the spiritual realm in a way that challenged the prerogatives of traditional religious authorities. In its earlier version, Islamic modernity was regarded by its proponents as *salafi* in spirit, that is, it espoused good and forgotten traditions of early Islam. But there was a global context for this consciousness: Modernizing Muslim intellectuals in the nineteenth century were deeply mindful of what they regarded as the backwardness of Muslim societies compared to Europe.

While the term *salafi* today is frequently a term of abuse, connoting retrograde, fundamentalist anti-modernity, 100 years ago it had meant just the opposite. In British India, Muhammad Iqbal still favored this conception of revival in the 1930s: Fundamentalism was a necessary, recurrent, and creative historical force, shaking us out of customary inertia and reminding us of the forgotten but elementary questions of the faith, and forcing us to ask those questions again in the context of the time in which we live. For pioneers of Islamic modernity such as Jamal al-Din al-Afghani and Muhammad Abduh, being *salafi* meant being modern. They argued that their contemporaries had become disconnected from global modernity only because they forgot, rather than adhered to, the (always already modern) early traditions of Islam.

Afghani was a well-known public persona in various circles crisscrossing the Muslim world—in Persia, Egypt, Istanbul, and India as well as in Paris, where he engaged Ernest Renan in a famous debate on modernity. He was intimately involved in the Ottoman *Tanzimat*, in a similar attempt at reform in Persia under Shah Naser al-Din, and in anti-British agitation in Egypt. His close associate Muhammad Abduh enjoyed an equal renown and led an educational and legal reform effort in his capacity as the Grand Mufti of Egypt. Their student Rashid Rida further expanded the public intellectual presence of revivalist modern Islam, lecturing widely and establishing *al-Manar*, the renowned journal of Islamic modernist thought.

The Muslim Brotherhood (*Al-Ikhwan al-Muslimun*) was founded in 1928 in Egypt by Hasan al-Banna partially in response to the failure of the nationalist revolt of 1919 to dislodge the British from the country. Al-Banna was influenced by Rida, who by that time had taken the modernist Islamic message in a socially conservative direction. By combining social conservatism, advocacy of an independent modernity, and anti-colonialism, the Brotherhood expanded prolifically over the past nine decades. Loose models or "branches" of the organization exist currently in about 70 different countries. By the 1950s it claimed some four million members in Egypt alone, though such size did not save it from Nasser's ban. After the

2011 revolution, it generated the best organized and largest party in Egypt, which went on to win the first free parliamentary and presidential elections in the history of the country. Earlier that year, its Tunisian branch, known as the al-Nahda movement, emerged as the largest party in the first free elections in the history of that country, following a popular revolution that had culminated in the overthrow of president Ben Ali on January 14, 2011. Its Libyan branch emerged as a credible force in the first free elections in the history of the country, again following the revolution of 2011. Its Sudanese and Jordanian branches sat in national government in the 1990s, as did its Algerian branch later. Its Palestinian branch, Hamas, won the national elections of 2006, and its Syrian branch was kept away from power in the early 1980s with the aid of a horrific bloodbath that cost an estimated 20,000 lives in the massacre of Hama. This did not prevent the group from reemerging as one of the components of the Syrian rebellion beginning in 2011.

The Brotherhood emphasized the idea of Islam as a "total way of life," to be practiced through the ethical cultivation of the free but responsible individual, a modern being who had rights but not apart from social responsibilities. Such ethical individuals, one at a time, would restructure society at large, linking small, daily, individual tasks to large, future-oriented, social goals. Consequently, the Brotherhood's program could at any moment result in political action, but did not require such action on an ongoing basis. This flexibility accounts for the survival of the Brotherhood in different social and political contexts and through various periods of repression and toleration.

The fundamental objective of the Brotherhood was and remains to re-Islamize society through an incremental educational and cultural process, and when possible through direct political action.[10] The project unfolds in concentric circles beginning with the individual, then the family, then society, then the state, then a caliphate unifying Muslim states, then the world (see Figure 1.4). Tasks are most defined at the center of that circle, at the individual level, gradually losing clarity outwards. The Muslim individual, whether male or female, strives to remain healthy; cultivates good manners and thoughts; leads daily life in an organized and efficient way; and is always eager to learn and strengthen faith. Such an individual possesses a self-struggling or self-critical ("jihadist") character, observes the proper manner of worship, and remains conscious of the value of time

10. As condensed on its semi-official web site, http://www.ummah.net/ikhwan.

and of being of benefit to others (Banna 1978). His daily life, in other words, is driven by instrumental reason, by the calculus of benefit and loss and the measurement of accomplishments and setbacks. At the next level, the family, the primary tasks include judicious choice of one's life partner, educating the children in the faith, and inviting other families to it. Then follows society, which is conceived as an ensemble of families. At that point the task is oriented to solving common social problems. Out of that project a Muslim state takes shape, and an ensemble of such states on the world stage provides the realistic basis of some sort of caliphate. Somehow out of that accomplishment the whole world gradually becomes Islamized.

The Brotherhood has often claimed in its long history that it strove not necessarily to rule society directly, but was prepared to accept any ruler it regarded as a "good Muslim." It advocated the liberation of Muslim lands from foreign control. Most consistently, however, it sought to foster social ties and learning about the faith on a daily basis. Though the Brotherhood came to include various prominent intellectuals and spiritual leaders who differed in their approaches to social and political life and lived in different countries, it gained tract and resilience through its grass-roots emphasis and broad platform, spanning both solidary social action and individual cultivation.

The notion of Islam as a "total way of life" possesses at least two per-spectivist advantages in modern society, the first of which is shared across the two paradigms, while the second distinguishes instrumental reason from hermeneutics. First, the notion of Islam as a total way of life gives all incidents in otherwise anomic individual life a relational meaning. Thus, this principle provides a sense of overall orientation, increasingly important in modern society given the decay of attributes such as certainty and predictability that had been associated with old traditional religiosity. Second—and here the paradigms part ways—for the instrumentalists, this overall orientation suggests that all action should be guided by a unified ethical system, the validity of which is based precisely on its being *external*: to society as well as the believer. Only in being so may such ethics remain untainted by the evident injustices and myopias of error-prone, man-made (rather than divinely ordained) social systems. Further, the idea of an external ethical authority serves to distinguish proper ethics more clearly from mere personal desires. In the process it provides individual psyches with a source of self-discipline that they presumably do not pos-sess otherwise.

For the hermeneuts one cannot but live in man-made systems. These, in the final analysis, can only be human rather than of divine construction. Even if we use god's instructions to construct them, we would simply be *interpreting* god's instructions. And interpretation is a human, not divine, act. From a hermeneutic perspective, all interpretations are probabilistic rather than exact renditions, given god's infinite wisdom and our finite one. Thus while in instrumental reason god is the author of a law that requires being obeyed, in hermeneutic reason the very idea of a law is an outcome of a human interpretation of god's mandate. And interpretation is never absolute: It is valid only with a view to the limits of knowledge that happen to be available in the environment in which it is produced.

Both paradigms have eloquent proponents, testifying not simply to the resilience of intellectual thought in Muslim public spheres. Both also correspond to different social attitudes, and thus require being propagated and defended as pubic rather than scholastic philosophies. In both cases, the public presentation of ideas often follows a simple format, exemplifying to a public how one should think about the world, rather than as learned instructions to be followed as is. For example, when Khurram Murad, a modern Islamic educator, author and a member of Jamaat-e-Islami, explains the basic form of relation of god to man, he puts it in these simple yet evocative words:

> [Y]our heart beats 72 times a minute. Every time it beats, it does so with the permission of Allah. The moment He withdraws that permission, the heart will stop beating and your life will certainly come to an end. (2010:23)

Murad's approach, which is spelled out in several easy-to-read, pedagogical manuals filled with selected Qur'anic citations, is typical of the public philosophy of instrumental Islam. The point above delivers religion at the most basic level, that is, as a foundation of life itself. Whatever political or social leanings that may result remain derivative. In the same way that one cannot really become a Marxist before one is persuaded of the centrality of class analysis, one cannot entertain any religious program in political or social life before being persuaded of the centrality of god's role in the world. That is what needs to be established first and continuously reaffirmed, so that doubt may be expunged and replaced with certainty, confidence, and a sense of empowerment.

But social and political attitudes remain in the final analysis derivative affairs and can change with circumstances. What distinguishes instrumentalism most from hermeneutics is not that one paradigm is more or less "liberal" than the other, but rather the very style of religious thought. Religious people generally worry less about whether they are "liberal" or "conservative" than about whether their way of approaching a religious consciousness is appropriate and to what extent. The instrumental approach is characterized above all by a strong sense of external authority, including authority over one's own body. Yet rather than being haunting or simply oppressive, this external authority is ultimately highly useful, since it becomes the aid with which one could solve modern problems at all levels, from the personal to the social to the political.

The question of external authority in religious life—god is central to life, the source of law, and requires obedience, while remaining distant from the world—may be said to reflect idealized patriarchal social structures. Indeed, some have suggested that the source of "underdevelopment" in some Muslim countries, notably the Arab world, is rooted in patriarchal or "neopatriarchal" structures (Sharabi 1988), of which religion is just one reflection. But it is difficult to test these presumptions, and it is far easier to see how the question of authority in general (and not simply "patriarchy") is multi-sided. That is, "obeying" an authority that resides outside of the sensed world is also a way of *exercising* authority vis-à-vis others in the world. In this sense, disempowering oneself vis-à-vis an external (divine) authority may be empowering vis-à-vis others. (It may also be, as Mahmood (2005) shows, empowering vis-à-vis perceived harmful aspects of one's own psyche.)

If we understand this dialectic of submission as source of empowerment, we are then able to isolate two particular points of emphasis that have come to characterize instrumental Islam, both of which are contested in hermeneutic Islam. The first involves how religiosity, understood as submission to an external authority, gives rise to a sense of superiority. The other involves how religiosity becomes then associated with a particular conception of collective identity. Both of these elements are evident in the literature of social movements that are informed by an instrumentalist approach to Islam. A sense of superiority, needless to say, is not specific to Islamic movements nor to a religious worldview by necessity. Secular variations on the sense of superiority based on nationalism, imperial grandeur, or technological accomplishments are abundant enough. The point here concerns only that outlet to the feeling of superiority that is provided by one's ability to submit to an external, otherwordly authority. In this respect, god compares quite favorably to modern tyrants, as Khomeini emphasized, and in obeying god *absolutely* one loses fear of modern tyrants and is able to topple them, in spite of their impressive modern power.

This sense of confidence is all the more important especially in contexts where modern states are contested. As I have argued elsewhere (Bamyeh 2005, 2009), Muslims were able historically to construct an elaborate civic life outside the state, which meant that "tyranny" (*Taghut*, endlessly denounced by Khomeini) needed little denunciation or no revolution before the advent of the modern state. That was because the modern state attempted to control society in more pervasive ways than old "tyrants" thought possible or even necessary. Totalitarian conceptions of power were thus accentuated in modernity because of the nature and capacity of the modern state, not because of the nature of religion. Modern states, as argued before, appeared as great power structures that invited struggles by all social groups affected to control them.[11] And since such states claimed to stand in on behalf of "the people" as a whole, they invited political aspirants to use whatever ideological tools available in order to gain control over other contestants. It is therefore important, when one observes a tendency for certain beliefs to give rise to feelings of superiority, to distinguish those aspects of superiority that are actually associated with conditions of vulnerability or defeat. In such a case, a posture of superiority probably acts more as compensatory feeling, and is to be distinguished from a posture of superiority that is associated with other social or political conditions: for example a large power structure (e.g., a modern state) that by its very presence invites all kinds of claims of being entitled to take it over.

Now this claim to entitlement to power may obviously be played out in democratic theaters. However, inducements to authoritarian uses of religion probably become particularly strong under one of two conditions: first, when the state's own authoritarianism, when it lasts for more than a generation, provides over time the only *familiar* template of politics; and second, when we encounter a process of social fragmentation, as in modern metropolitan centers in the global south, where connective bonds are threaded out of whatever discourses of social affinity may be widely shared. Modern Islamic social movements have emerged precisely out of such environments, and in fact remain most strongly represented

---

11. For an extended, global argument, see Bamyeh 2009, *Anarchy as Order*, esp. chapter 2.

in such theaters. To the above should be added that connective discourses may also gain more credence in diaspora situations, where a claim may be effectively made about the unity of a community in spite of its actual diversity and dispersion. A typical theater for such discourses of connectivity would be an Islamic mosque or center in any Western city that has migrants from broad expanses of the Muslim world. They may not have much of a reason to see themselves as anything more than a situational congregation, rather than a solid community. Yet, the fact that they are treated as a *single* community in host countries invariably invites the rise of forces within that diasporic constellation that do indeed seek to define the congregation as a community, and to speak on its behalf as such. In this case one *becomes* what one is treated like.

In the final analysis, instrumental Islam constitutes a social project, even though the clearest tasks are those connected to individual potentials, proclivities, responsibilities, and rights. The Muslim Brotherhood, as a prototype of instrumental Islam, represents in effect an organizational condensation of the intellectual heritage of nineteenth-century Islamic modernity. Much intellectual Islam in the public sphere remained content with its general formula until recently. Yet, instrumental Islam has not escaped basic criticism from other Islamic circles, as being based on a fundamentally flawed approach to religion: too instrumental, not spiritual enough, too close to daily battles, too beholden to the idea of divine "law" and thus not immune to authoritarianism—even when it may have great public following. These critiques have over time provided the foundation of the nascent hermeneutic movement in public Islam.

Hermeneutic Islam

From a hermeneutic perspective, the greatest conceptual weakness of the instrumentalist understanding of Islam is that it did not specify Islam itself as an *object of knowledge*, even though learning the faith was highlighted by groups espousing an instrumentalist approach. That is to say, from a hermeneutic perspective, the problem of instrumentalism lay in the assumption that the meaning of Islam was self-evident (or at least should be). In one sense, a hermeneutic approach involves an *awareness* that what one wants out of religion also influences how that person approaches religion. In another sense, the meaning of any divine message is extracted only through interpretive activity. Interpretive activity, in turn, is itself related to some kind of human interest. As such, the interpretive

activity reveals two things simultaneously: 1) some dimension of god's intention; and 2) the scope and capacity of human reason.

The instrumental method of knowledge was furthermore often seen
by its critics as ad hoc, reactive, and partial: Specific problems of modernity determined too directly how one came to know their faith. In this
mode knowledge accrued defensively: The Qur'an must be said to be "scientific," because the modern age is scientific; Islam must be said to recognize gender equality, because modernity implies such equality; Muslims
have a duty to fight their enemies, because colonial powers dominated
Muslim lands; and so on. This immediacy and defensive character of instrumental Islam led the prominent commentator Mohammed Arkoun
(1994) to argue that many modern Islamic movements were really secular movements thinly veiled in the garb of religion. Indeed, instrumental
Islam was and remains quite analogous to secularism in its closeness to
earth. Whether advocated as a social or political guide, instrumental Islam
addresses immediate goals and tasks, offering up Islam largely as the solution to all kinds of concrete problems.

The lack of specific elaboration of what such a "solution" might look
like under an Islamic government or in an Islamic social system, for example, may have to do with the instrumentalists' basic *agreement* with the
project of a developmental modernity. For the instrumentalists, an Islamic
consciousness would only add a sense of local cultural cohesion and independence *within* the larger project of global modernity, as Rashid Rida
argued early in the twentieth century, pointing to Japan as his preferred example.[12] But otherwise the instrumentalists wanted to fully enact all other
economic and political instruments of modernity. To modern social and political institutions, therefore, the instrumentalists only wished to add a certain moral character, rooted in tradition and thus more capable of carrying
out modernization without corruption.[13] Over time, the demand for an au-
thentic moral addendum to modernity acquired greater significance with

---

12. It is underestimated how much nineteenth- and early-twentieth-century proponents of
Islamic modernity were informed by efforts at modernization and contestations of European
colonialism by non-Islamic societies, such as China or Japan. The former seemed reminis-
cent of the ineffectual Ottoman empire, while the latter suggested a model of a culturally
and politically independent modernity that was worth pursuing. For preliminary notes see
Hamed (1990).

13. Indeed, most recently Yildiz Atasoy and Tugrul Keskin have argued, focusing on Turkey,
that successful modern Islamic movements are highly useful for legitimizing neoliberal
principles.

the increasing association of especially modern secular states with corruption and unaccountable elite rule. A clear example of how salient this simple message could be was the electoral victory of Hamas in Palestine in 2006, and also later in the revolts of the Arab Spring that, while not Islamic, were united in regarding pre-revolutionary states as corrupt and unaccountable. In the case of Hamas's electoral victory, the main issue for its electorate, as evident in post-election analysis conducted by the Palestinian Center for Policy and Survey Research, was the pervasive corruption of the ruling secular elite. In that context, Hamas's self-portrayal in the campaign as the more ethical force became quite credible, enough indeed to warrant entrusting the nation to a relatively new political force.

Yet, the political and organizational successes occasionally enjoyed by instrumental Islam did not mean that it was immune from criticism from religious points of view. In particular, its immediate worldliness was more likely to be criticized by religious intellectuals (for example the late Fazlur Rahman) than by secular nationalists, who generally had little training or interest in religious thought, and therefore could not reach the constituency to which politicized religious thought had become attractive. That meant that the real alternative to instrumental Islam was more likely to be a different form of Islam in the public sphere, rather than secularism. That was especially so because by the 1970s secular nationalism was already being widely perceived not to have carried out to fruition a developmental project around which there was a national consensus. Depending on location (Sullivan 1994; Clark 2003; Wickham 2002; Alterman and Hippel 2007; Benthall and Bellion-Jourdan 2009), that project faltered, produced uneven results, became laden with corruption, or was carried out outside the state by voluntary associations, many of which had a clear religious character.

In this light, it is possible to suggest that the hermeneutic approach itself gained more tract from the successes of the instrumental approach in establishing Islam as a reference point for social debates on modern solidarity, aid, and mutual help. Islam became broadly referenced as some sort of vague "solution" by the late 1970s and even more so since the end of the Cold War and the exhaustion of ideological alternatives. As one would expect of any idea that enters broad social circulation in vague forms, alternative interpretations of it immediately suggest themselves. This is especially so because it is far easier to package one's program in terms of a broadly familiar reference point, than to invent or use a reference point that few people in society share. The instrumental presentation of Islam

as a "solution" itself gave room for competing, non-instrumental understandings of Islam. In one sense, the rise of any idea may depend to a great
extent on the apparent success of an opposing one.

The alternative to instrumentalist religion was therefore a more complex and less immediate religion, one in which religion itself was posited
as an object of a theory of knowledge, and not simply as a ready guide for
action. Such an approach was of course always part of the long intellectual history of religion, but the modern challenge was to offer an Islamic
theory of knowledge with wide social appeal, that is to say a new *public* hermeneutics that would challenge the old public instrumentalism as well as
competing secular frames. This quest for new public hermeneutics began
in earnest in the 1960s. By the 1980s it had a substantial public audience,
though its political and social organizations remained uneven worldwide.
Employing Sufi traditions, Islamic hermeneutics, and an avowed scientific
outlook, this current evolved in different Muslim societies and took form
through the work of initially unconnected public intellectuals who nevertheless converged on a few pivotal points.

These points broadened the scope of religious activism beyond
questions of national development or even national culture. Whereas
the Brotherhood responded to modern models of collective identity—
preeminently the nation—by articulating them in religious language,
the hermeneutic movement in public Islam proposed a framework of
collective identity and practice that spoke to postnational as well as post-
modern tendencies. In contrast to the conscious mobilization and instrumentalism of the Brotherhood, the work of scattered public hermeneuts in
Sudan, Turkey, Egypt, and Iran converged on a central philosophical core,
suggesting an underlying similarity of fundamental tasks confronting
Islamic social philosophy across the Muslim world.

Whereas the primary tasks identified by modern instrumental Islam
were oriented to *organizing society*, those identified by hermeneutics aimed
primarily at *organizing knowledge*. Islam went from being a ready-to-use
"how to" instructional manual to being an invitation to contemplation.
Hermeneutic public intellectuals, operating in different countries and divergent in political fortunes and ambitions, converge nonetheless on key
common points. For Mahmoud Taha in Sudan, Fethullah Gülen in Turkey,
Muhammad Shahrur in Syria, and Abdolkarim Soroush in Iran, the idea
of "progress" is inferred not from a global developmental model, to which
one then merely adds a cultural appendage expressing "our" authenticity.
Rather, progress is seen as a natural eternal movement of humanity,

motivated by the perpetual desire of a space and time bound, and thus limited humanity, to approach that which is infinite and eternal, that is to say, that which by its nature must always exceed the cognitive and experiential capacity of humanity.

Some of the central ideas of the hermeneutic approach were also to be found in instrumental Islam, although they were subordinate to an activist program, within whose parameters their philosophical significance could not be fully appreciated. Most important among those was the notion of religion as an irreducible totality. In instrumental Islam this principle meant regarding Islam as a *total way of life*, informing daily practice; in hermeneutics it implied approaching Islam as a *total idea*, itself informed by life's pragmatics. That is to say, whereas in hermeneutics one begins from life so as to bring religion into alignment with it, in instrumental reason one begins from religion so as to bring life into alignment with it. There are of course occasions in which these two perspectives converge. But neither starting point presupposes such convergence. The starting point concerns whether the primary question should be posited as "how to know" (hermeneutics) or "how to apply" (instrumental reason).

Thus here one quickly reaches the end of the common ground between the two paradigms. From a hermeneutic perspective, the primary texts of the faith could not be approached selectively and defensively. An ancient holy text does not stand above a modern reader; the latter cannot be expected to only assimilate it passively, like an empty vessel being filled by knowledge from without. Rather, the process of understanding begins with the believer, not the text. The relationship to the text is dialectical rather than unidirectional. The reader understands in a particular, not absolute, way because the reader is a creature of a specific moment and circumstance. Only in that sense could an ancient text, according to the hermeneutic understanding, live on across vastly different epochs and speak to very diverse minds.

While some of the new Islamic hermeneuts, such as Shahrur in Syria or Soroush in Iran, focused only on propounding new interpretations in the public sphere, others became leaders of social movements, such as Taha in Sudan and Gülen in Turkey. The latter two emerged out of Sufi traditions, and their work, composed in the 1950s and 1960s, essentially represented a modern intellectualization of Sufism. By contrast, the works of Shahrur and Soroush in the 1980s and 1990s represent a different trajectory that was nonetheless inspired by the same basic way of seeing that characterizes the hermeneutic paradigm as a whole. The latter two emerged out of the sciences: Shahrur had been a professor of engineering at Damascus University before becoming a widely read author on Islam in the Arab world, while Soroush was educated in Germany and England as a philosopher of science before becoming one of the leading reform intellectuals of the Iranian Revolution.

One of the common conclusions of the hermeneutic paradigm entails rejecting or at least downplaying religion as a source of identity. Here Islam is often conceived as an evolutionary natural religion of humanity. In itself this is an old idea that could be found in Sanusi's nineteenth-century work and in Shah Waliullah's in India even before him (Dallal 1993). This same idea enjoys some appeal as well among secular public intellectuals sympathetic to the old classical hermeneutic traditions in Islamic history. For example, the late leftist activist-scholar Hadi Alawi recalled how he rediscovered Sufism after migrating to China in 1977, where the old sources of Sufism were not only available but also lent themselves to being mixed with the distinctly non-Islamic philosophy of Taoism (Alawi 1999:134–135). In modern hermeneutics, analogous arguments for the universality of Islam beyond the community of actual Muslims are further justified by arguments presenting Islam as a body of meanings that are naturally mutable as humanity comes to know more of its own truth. In the words of Taha:

> [Intuitive] Islam as such is the religion of humanity. Its intention is to entertain the human illusion inspired by the will to freedom, until it steadily surpasses it into a firmer wisdom whose fruit would be the conscious Islam. Islam as the religion of humanity appeared alongside Reason, and kept evolving alongside Reason in its long history, from a weak and naïve genesis into an acquired and wise conclusion. (2002:141)

Taha begins, as typical of Sufi thought, with the question of human existence in general. Only after lengthy deliberations does he move back to specific issues confronting Muslims. This method appears justifiable by the belief that god could not possibly be more concerned with the petty minutiae of earthly squabbles than with large issues of being and creation. However, humans in any epoch could only have a partial understanding of the larger issues, bounded as they are by the limited horizons of their specific time and place. God's universal nature is illustrated therefore in the structure of his revelation, and specifically in the otherwise baffling character difference in the Qur'an between the Mecca and Medina revelations. This difference is well known, but for Taha it held great hermeneutic significance: The Meccan Qur'an, with its peaceful, reflective, and universal verses, was *the* essential Qur'an. By contrast, the Medinian Qur'an, which contained the rules regulating society, conflict, commerce, law, and many aspects of everyday life, was derivative, situational, specific to its time, and therefore less binding on humanity.

Blasphemous as the idea might have been, it contained enough coherence and mobilized enough social backing for Taha to survive his first court trial for heresy in Sudan in 1968. Taha justified his novel interpretation with the aid of the very Qur'anic principle of *naskh*, or "abrogation." His originality consisted in using this principle in a way that was exactly opposed to its traditional use—an approach popularized in other ways by the legal scholar Abdullahi an-Na'im, one of Taha's most notable followers in the West.

The doctrine of *naskh* occurs in a couple of verses in the Qur'an. It suggests a way of reading the Qur'an that has traditionally been understood to mean that if a verse contradicted one that had been revealed earlier, the later was understood to have abrogated the earlier. Taha, however, claimed that *naskh* could not possibly mean abrogation. A plausible theological ground for such a rejection is that an all-knowing god could not possibly abrogate what he had just said. For Taha, then, *naskh* could only mean the postponement of the earlier, *more essential*, statement until the right time. A later statement could only be secondary or derivative, since it is the essence of religion that is revealed first. The Qur'an itself exemplifies this principle, as it moves away in Medina from the cosmic, contemplative philosophy of its Meccan period, and begins regulating everyday issues confronting the growing community of believers.

Thus in Medina the Qur'an spoke to a specific historical community in a language it could understand and in a way suitable to those transient conditions, whereas in Mecca the Qur'an spoke transhistorically to all humanity. The point did not lead by necessity to the conclusion that the Medinian Qur'an was less holy than the Meccan Qur'an. Rather, the point could be simply that god, in revealing both a primary and a secondary Qur'an, had meant by the latter to illustrate to humanity how the timeless message revealed in the Meccan text must be perpetually revivified by humanity in every epoch, and in ways that correspond to that epoch's limits and possibilities.

The idea that the Qur'an itself proposes a basic distinction between timeless and time-bound instructions is likewise arrived at later by Shahrur and Soroush (though by using different terminologies), independently of each other as well as of Taha (whose work, however, was eventually translated into Persian). The same idea that the holy text contains both timeless and time-bound material had likewise emerged earlier and independently in another very different context, as one of the central themes of *Risale-i Nur* of Bediuzzaman Said Nursi (1877–1960). Nursi, also combining Sufi reflections with modern science, emphasized how the holy book possessed different faces with which it could confront different epochs of history. In modern times the divine text spoke to believers in modern language (that is, the language of science), whereas to earlier generations it spoke in the prevailing language of their times. In doing so, god did not change his mind when humanity changed, neither did god obey science because we wanted Him to do so. Rather, in every epoch god spoke the *same* eternal truth, but in a way that could only be understood by people inhabiting those times. The idea of eternal truth logically dictates, from a hermeneutic perspective, that we can understand only one facet of it at any given time—because we ourselves are not eternal, and thus must abide by a limit to understanding spelled by the ancient *Corpus Hermeticum* (Bamyeh 2007:56): "like is understood by like."

Such a standpoint, which in some way echoes Feuerbach's thesis on Christianity, can be readily found across the spectrum of modern Islamic public hermeneutics. Soroush, for example, argues that god's intention will ultimately reveal itself to be synonymous with the collective intention of humanity. In many ways, these modern hermeneutic positions indirectly contest Max Weber's (1978) conception of the role of ideas in historical transformation, since what is apparent here is how different trajectories of action may emerge from the *same* foundation. It likewise shows the limits of Karl Marx's conception of the materialist basis of historical change. Here a religious idea is transformed from being a decree to accept god's verdict into a guide for action, as Robert Bellah once suggested when he observed Reformation-like movements (Bellah 1991:67). In the process, social action is intended to discern how god's reason and human reason may be merged, and consciously so. In this way, hermeneutics offer a religious outline of multiplicity and indeterminism that are otherwise said to characterize high (or post) modernity. By contrast, instrumental reason remains more attentive to those features of modernity that require a sense of authority, finality, and truth.

The convergence on similar interpretive standpoints from unrelated sources and locations is even more striking when we consider the vastly different sociopolitical and economic systems within which the modern hermeneutic perspective emerged. Another striking feature is the common root of hermeneutics in social movements that opposed modern states but did not seek to take them over, even as such states regarded them with suspicion and hostility. Nursi and Taha, for example, got in trouble with their respective states, indicating that governments did not view their work as harmless philosophical speculation. Nursi was repeatedly imprisoned and his work banned as a threat to the secular order, whereas Taha was repeatedly prosecuted because his work was seen as a threat to the religious order. He was eventually executed by the regime of Ja'far Numeiry in 1983, precisely as that collapsing regime sought, with desperate cynicism, to shore itself up by enlisting the support of instrumentalist Islamist forces led then by Taha's antagonist, Hasan al-Turabi of the Sudanese variety of the Muslim Brotherhood.

In both cases, however, the direct target of the hermeneutic critique was not the political order but a larger cultural problem. In Turkey, Nursi's apparent aim was not so much secularism as materialism and the erosion of spiritual life in modernity, whereas Taha aimed his critique at the obscurantism of the religious establishment and the tendency for religion to be appropriated for instrumental political uses. It could therefore be said that Nursi offended by offering anti-materialism, whereas Taha by offering anti-obscurantism; the former was a thorn on the side of a staunchly secular regime, whereas the latter was a serious challenge to religious forces allied to an unprincipled regime.

However, the programs of both Nursi and Taha were non-political, in the sense that they neither aimed to usurp state power nor had realistic hopes for such a project, even though states saw them as threats. Yet, this view of them as threats may be a result of the fact that the root *social* intent of their programs was not dissimilar to the basic intent of instrumental Islam. Like the instrumentalists, the hermeneuts wanted to strengthen the spiritual quality of society. Both hermeneuts and instrumentalists aimed to mollify through new forms of religious consciousness modernizing social trends toward anonymity, individual dislocation, urban growth, consumerism, and materialism. Both were explicit that they meant to do all of these things in a way that conformed to the knowledge-based character of modernity. Both sought to cultivate new, post-traditional forms of social capital as old forms were challenged by such factors as modern states, increased social dislocation, rural to urban migration, and the spread of materialist philosophies of life and social order.

These commonalities in social intent of two paradigms suggest the possibility of transition by any actor from one to the other (that is, to the extent that that actor maintains a religious commitment). We would expect such transition to occur when one experiences the limit of one paradigm, either through practice or accumulated knowledge: for example, the hermeneut who becomes weary of the inapplicability of philosophy, and longs for the taste of action that promises to change the world; or the instrumentalist who, having been party to a political experiment that ended in failure, becomes introspective.

The instrumental tendency was seldom far from political struggles, did not shy away from combining spirituality and *Realpolitik*, and could occasionally find support within the religious establishment. By contrast, the hermeneutic tendency stood at some distance from state-centered politics and faced vocal rejection by the religious establishment. The hermeneutic accomplishment lay in creating room in the public sphere for styles of interpretation that expanded the meaning of religiosity beyond the limits of instrumental reason. At the same time, it offered a style of thinking that was independent of immediate politics, a style that sought to protect the social fabric against a myriad of large new alien forces, *including* the modern state.

Nursi's career illustrates this well. At a time when the Kemalist state banned religious publications, his *Risale-i Nur* circulated as handwritten copies throughout Turkey. By the time it was finally printed in 1956, it is estimated that 600,000 handwritten copies of the sprawling 6,000-page text had been made and distributed by his followers over the two preceding decades. This impressive perseverance in the face of active government persecution indicated the substantial social capital that backed Nursi's movement. While it kept distance from formal party politics, the movement would contribute to changing the political climate in Turkey in its favor. Nursi called upon his followers to vote against the more extreme anti-religious faction within Kemalism in favor of Adnan Menderes and his new Democratic Party. That party then ruled Turkey throughout the 1950s, when it began to accept the notion of Islam as an ingredient in Turkish nationalism, rather than as a retrograde parasite—to be repressed and expunged—upon the modern national soul.

This political accomplishment opened the way to a gradual and unceasing growth of the *Nur* movement. Its most important contemporary expression in Turkey was the Gülen's organization which emerged onto world stage from a local grass-roots base (Yavuz and Esposito 2003). Until the sustained official hostility that crushed its operations in Turkey following the failed coup on July 15, 2016, the movement enlisted millions of followers, had a daily newspaper, a television channel, a radio station. It oversaw an abundant circulation of videos and cassettes and, perhaps uniquely among Islamic movements, organized several academic conferences devoted to its philosophy and activism at various universities in the United States, Europe, and Australia. Before 2016, The Gülen movement managed to recruit important intellectuals and establish seven universities and hundreds of schools in Turkey, the Central Asian republics, China, and East Africa.

While the influence of that movement was facilitated by its considerable wealth, estimated at $25 billion, that wealth could also be understood as a symptom and not simply a cause of the movement's success. After all, the movement's capital was generated over several decades and was largely the outcome of constant donations by a large spectrum of businesses and individuals, specifically the Anatolian middle class that has become more visible over the past few decades. Supporters who built up the movement, including its social networks and economic infrastructure, saw themselves as promoting a new type of piety that would provide the best guarantee of a moral public order. In Turkey in particular, the demand for such a public moral order became more pressing with the internal upheavals of the 1970s, for whose control the secular Kemalist ethics alone appeared insufficient, thus requiring an army coup in 1980 (which Gülen welcomed).

Before its virtual destruction in Turkey, the Hizmet movement emerged into the global public sphere from a strong base in the national public sphere, and in a way that is analogous to the trajectories of virtually all other social experiments of the new public hermeneutics. In spite of its size the movement was secretive, and hence easy to demonize and find itself embroiled in conspiracy theories. So much so, in fact, that after the failed coup of 2016 it became impossible to remember the role of its ideas in attracting so many followers. It tended to be seen as representing a "Turkish" Islam, even though its philosophy, typical of the more general hermeneutic trend, highlighted the question of knowledge rather than that of identity. Generally, hermeneutic movements, like instrumental movements, emerge in local or national environments, but over time they tend to understand themselves as part of a global ethic, and in practice do establish themselves when possible outside of their original national borders.

Indeed, rejecting restrictive forms of identity appears central to the hermeneutic program almost everywhere. Shahrur, for example, argues that the term "Muslim" is necessarily non-identitarian, since it refers to a universal moral behavior that may be practiced by non-Muslims who could, moreover, be regarded as Muslims from a hermeneutic perspective. While this suggestion may appear novel when expressed in the public sphere, it is in fact not far removed from old standard theological conceptions, since Muslim theologians have long been aware that the Qur'an itself makes a distinction between "Muslims" and "believers." But especially central for Shahrur, the Qur'an makes a related and even more important, though historically less noted, distinction between a timeless Qur'an and its other, more time-bound version, which in the Qur'an is simply called "The Book." The thesis of Shahrur was that the two terms are not synonyms, as commonly understood, but a divine dialectic expressing how the Qur'an, timeless and divine, ought to be approached by a time-bound human society. This dialectic expresses an inescapable duality of the infinite and finite: "Islam," true and divine, could be practically expressed at any given historical moment only partially as "Islamization," which is the best that a human society can do. According to this interpretation, the first Muslim community in Medina was nothing other than the first variety of this time-bound Islamization. That is to say, it used Islam as a means to solve practical problems it faced in its own time and place. As such, that community could not be said to have given later Muslims a template on how to Islamicize their own conditions at other times and places.

The hermeneuts thus envisage religious life, including its truth claims and whatever politics may emerge from it, as being necessarily situational. The instrumentalists, too, may accept this position, but as a matter of temporary practical necessity rather than as a philosophical principle. Thus, while hermeneutics and instrumentalism may actually appear similar to outside observers sometimes, the difference between them lies substantially in how practices that deviate from some ideal are justified. For the instrumentalists, they are justified by practical necessity. For the hermeneuts, situational "practical necessity" is itself the clue that there must be a universal (that is, *non-situational*) philosophical basis for it.

There are further important apparent similarities between the two standpoints, which may make outside observers lose sight of the difference between them. Both instrumentalists and hermeneuts agree that their common, *permanent* enemy is materialist philosophies of life, not other religions or nations. Hasan al-Banna, for example, recommended once to his physician a book describing the story of a Japanese physician who adopted Christianity and propagated it in Japan (Hathut 2000:53). In recent times, Farid Esack (1997), who represents a self-consciously pro-gressive understanding of Islam that emerged in the context of the struggle against apartheid in South Africa, likewise saw the common struggle in the modern world to be one between spirituality and materialism on a world scale, rather than between religions, nations, or civilizations. The struggle against materialism forms a general common thread across all varieties of modern Islamic consciousness, even though in their gov-erning practices, Islamic movements are sometimes, and not inaccurately, associated with promoting heartless neoliberal economic policies (Tuğal 2009; Atasoy 2009; Atia 2013).[14] But even in such cases, it appears that a spiritual appendage to crude economics makes the latter more tolerable than if such economics appear simply as an expression of pure materialist forces devoid of any humanity.

This observation does not necessarily suggest that this religious con-sciousness consists simply of adding a cover to otherwise crude material processes. Quite the opposite, it shows how religion is sometimes essen-tial for undertaking projects that would not be publicly supported other-wise. The point is not that bare economics is camouflaged with a spiritual garb. The point is that spirituality itself continues to be important enough for enough people to invite its being used in that fashion (even though that is certainly not its only use).

Thus while the struggle between hermeneutics and instrumental reason ends at the gates of materialism, it goes on everywhere else they meet. The core idea of hermeneutics—that there are two facets of the faith, one permanent, universal and essential, and another that is situational, local, particular, and human—diminishes, at least in theory, the capacity of religious authorities as well as states to use religion as an instrument of limitless power. The fact that any human understanding will always be limited and partial means that there can be no authority that could offer a transcendental and transhistorical interpretation of religion. In the case of Soroush, this led to an immanent critique of the Islamic Republic of Iran,

---

14. Interestingly, few studies cite the older example of Saudi Arabia, where this formula has been dominant for decades: extreme religiosity married to unimaginable levels of corruption and unaccountable governance.

the founding intellectuals of which he was among. While Ali Shari'ati before him might have foreseen the value of a hermeneutic critique in his own prerevolutionary times, Soroush as well as the revolutionary generation of 1978–1979 could experience a hermeneutic awakening only after having had to live with an Islamic republic that was entirely based on instrumental religion. Soroush's critique—whatever one may think of his credentials as an activist—was based on the principle, more recently reiterated forcefully by Adbullahi an-Na'im, Radwan al-Sayyid, and many others, that the very health of religious life requires it to be pursued for its own sake rather than because it is tied to an official position. In Iran, the first scent of political triumph of the hermeneutic program became associated with the consolidation of the reform movement around former President Khatami (1997–2005), even though that movement lost subsequent political battles. But that experience did show that hermeneutics, just like instrumental reason, could form the philosophical basis for a strong social movement. The two are tied: In this case, hermeneutics emerged as instrumentalist governance revealed the practical limits and situational nature of instrumentalism.

The two perspectives, thus, inhabit the same social and political environments, which facilitates their struggle as well as their communication. They are able to communicate because they do share an ultimate intent to modernize religious life, and in that they both oppose traditional, ritualistic religiosity. But they differ in how to respond to the demands of the national and transnational environments they cohabit. This is evident, for example, in their respective relation to nationalism. Instrumentalists make nationalism into their own cause, but fill what they regard as its cultural vacuity with what they regard to be a solid, and presumably long-established, religious identitarian foundation. Hermeneuts also identify a problem in the vacuity of national culture in its secular form, which, like the instrumentalists, they wish to supplant with a spiritual foundation that is also claimed to be part of a suppressed or forgotten heritage. But while the unity of society in the instrumentalist program resides in its common *identity* (Islamic), its unity for the hermeneuts resides in its common *discourse* (Islam). Thus both perspectives tend to see secular nationalism to be vacuous in so far as it lacks a spiritual foundation. But they differ on how the vacuity of non-spiritual collective identity ought to be supplanted: For the instrumentalists, it is supplanted with a more historically rooted understanding of what we really are; for the hermeneuts, it is supplanted with a more sophisticated appreciation of the fact that our public discourse seems to rotate around recurrent, common reference points.

A view that regards social realities as discourses does not necessarily imply that discourse is a weaker substitute for supposedly more solid facts. The question, rather, concerns how to resolve a possible contradiction between social consensus on the one hand and pluralism on the other. And that is best done, from a hermeneutic perspective, by regarding the agreement on what the common reference points should be as something that has already been accomplished by religion long ago, but disputing the proposition that such an agreement could be *forced* by any single authority. This quasi-Habermasian argument is evident in many ways throughout the literature of modern Islamic hermeneutics. Soroush, for example, could in the same breath both defend "religious society" *and* attack "ideological government" (by which he implies *religious* government). The distinction is easy to understand, especially if what is meant by "religious society" is society that agrees not on how religion should be followed, but only that religion should be a central reference point and a source of acceptable arbitrations and value judgments. That this discursive "consensus" means practical pluralism has indeed been the historical reality of virtually all Muslim societies and is evident in the multiple evolution of the *shari'a* itself, which has never been a unified body, nor consisted of a single school, nor was it expected to be so by Muslims themselves. An agreement on standards of judgment is not the same as an agreement on judgments. The former is what makes deliberative civil society possible, and the latter is what justifies governments. And religion, from a hermeneutic perspective, can only flourish in the former.

In short, the *social* (rather than purely philosophical) question in hermeneutics concerns how to regulate social life in light of faith if the human understanding of that faith can only be partial and particular. Here hermeneutics confronts a problem: the rules that guide *situational* interpretations of religion need to be *constantly* justified; at the same time, any justification may plausibly lead in different directions. Virtually all hermeneuts advise as a starting point a philosophical reflection on the actual experience of social existence, rather than starting out from the holy text. Soroush's method, for example, consists of quasi-Nietzschean[15] prioritization of "life" (2002:39–53). That is, our thought begins not with

---

15. Soroush, of course, does not call himself Nietzschean, but the underlying similarities are striking. That being said, his major references include various Islamic philosophical traditions, Western philosophy of science, and Sufi poetry (notably Rumi's *Mathnavi*).

abstractions but with basic principles that we deem necessary for life. Such principles, for example "justice" or "truth," are accepted intuitively as embodying self-evident virtue. Intuitive acceptance implies that these principles are latent in our customary practices already, that is to say, in our life. Truth and virtue cannot be imposed on life from without.

According to such hermeneutics, if we start out from earth rather than from god's mandate, we are in a better position to evaluate the value and role of all principles in a pragmatic way, while maintaining a spiritual life. If the mandate to *live* is the starting philosophical point, then we pursue all high principles, including divine principles, in so far as they serve life and not because they are external to it. This includes "truth" or "morality," which we pursue because they are necessary for our lives and not because they precede life or exist outside of it. All high principles are immanent in life; they do not simply descend upon us from a transcendental realm. In the final analysis, if the capacity to assimilate them does not already lie within us, there would be no mechanism by which we can genuinely accept them. This is why, for Soroush, official pronouncements cannot teach us what is proper or virtuous. We are predisposed to know those in our own way, simply because we need them in order to live. Our very acceptance of religion itself is rooted in that religion fits our own already existing predispositions toward practical morality and justice.

Now this priority assigned to life pragmatics does not mean that religious consciousness or even religious rules are simply derivative or dismissible at will. Rather life, from a hermeneutic perspective, needs that which is not yet in it precisely because life is about becoming rather than being, as Shari'ati argued in his earlier, quite popular expression of an existentialist Islamic philosophy. But even the propensity of modern Muslims to accept or at least listen to such a proposition is rooted in a deep heritage that seems to have survived the cataclysms of modernity and its institutions. "I am ephemeral; I do not want another who is thus": This paradigmatic statement of Said Nursi expresses the concept of life from the point of view of hermeneutics, even though his expression is still laden with old Sufi mysticism. It is rooted in the Islamic principle of *tawhid*, which means the oneness of god and correspondingly the unity of existence. As such, this principle has traditionally meant for Sufis that the goal of life was to become incorporated into the substance of god, and in the process overcome the experience of oneself as an ego entity, separate from others as well as from god. In its basic form this old idea has survived in modern hermeneutic elaborations of such concepts as "life" or "becoming." Hermeneutic reason then emerges out of the clash between the recognition of limits (ego existence; separation from others; limits to human life), and a desire to transcend them (in rejecting being in favor of becoming; *tawhid*; contemplation; and so on).

Of course, these concerns are not exclusive to hermeneutics. In instrumental reason as well, we can find an underlying concern with basic human recognitions of the realities of limits, including death and finitude. These are inescapable questions for any religious perspective. But the conclusions differ. In the instrumentalist case, the limits of humanity indicate that it is required to abide by a law external to it, a law whose totality and authority reside in god's ultimate custodianship over life and death. And this obedience, in turn, elevates life by supplying it with propensities that it cannot cultivate otherwise, such as discipline and self-control. In the hermeneutic case, by contrast, the limits of humanity indicate that it should seek to become more than what it is, since its limits exist in the context of god's hints—His *words*—that invite it to ponder the infinite. For hermeneuts, this attitude is a more properly spiritual condition than simply living by god's law, which for the instrumentalists should be valid even where it may not appear to fit real conditions or if it makes life actually more difficult for a while. God's law, from an instrumentalist point of view, must be regarded as universally valid and objective, whereas human-made law (*wad'i*) is by definition secular—meaning situational, myopic, and subjective.

Put simply, the two paradigms may be encapsulated by the priority assigned to "law" in the instrumental case and "life" in the second. Indeed, the concept of "life" seems central to important public Muslim hermeneuts in modern times, most explicitly Ali Shai'ati and Abdolkarim Soroush, in which case the validity of religion is evaluated on the basis of how close it is to the requisites of life. This means than we as humans tend to accept most readily those aspects of religion that are closest to the precepts of our human reason. If this is the case, then in the final analysis finite human reason is so programmed as to be in communion with infinite divine reason, rather than simply living at its mercy or apart from it.

The point here is not that one paradigm is more true to religion than another. Rather, the existence of such conflicting and highly visible paradigms in the public spheres of several large Muslim societies suggest that there is a remarkable vitality and demand for a philosophically justifiable religious life. In itself religion is not hermeneutic or instrumental; it is not liberal or illiberal. Sociologically speaking, religion is what religious people make it to be. The question then becomes why there is still such a profusion of philosophical religious reason in the public sphere, especially given that such public religious philosophy is unlikely to produce uniform conclusions.

The first element of a possible answer, I think, has to do with the fact that even though most of the Muslim world survives until today under secular rulers, and even as cultural life was (though increasingly less so) dominated by secular cultural producers and products, no Muslim society experienced a systematic *rejection* of religion. Muslim societies rarely experienced any broad anti-clerical "revolution from below." All modern anti-clerical "revolutions" in Muslim societies came from *above*: Kemalist Turkey, Soviet Central Asia, Enver Hoxha's Albania, Reza Shah's Iran. The implications of this general absence of an anti-clerical revolution in modern Muslim societies became apparent even in Turkey as it moved into the twenty-first century, that is, in the country that was dominated for most of the twentieth century by a self-consciously secular elite. Nowhere in the Muslim world do we find throughout the twentieth century a demographically significant secular revolution in cultural life, in which religious consciousness is set up as the *opposite* of secular consciousness. The common pattern, rather, seems to be of parallel or overlapping existence of both in the same mind, rather than of setting them as opposites.

This symbiosis of the secular and the religious is of course not unique to Muslim lands. For example, Robert Bellah's outline of American "civil religion," already visible in the country's Declaration of Independence and in the pronouncements of US presidents down to the present, is neither anti-clerical nor militantly secular (Bellah [1970] 1991:180–181). For Bellah, one attribute of this mindset is that it allowed average Americans to see no contradiction between the religious and the secular, and thus facilitated commitment to national goals. Those, in turn, were never justified (for the nation as a whole) as aligned with any specific religion, although politicians always found it useful to anchor them to a generic, non-confessional "god."

The variety of the modernization thesis introduced by Bellah suggests therefore that modernity requires no anti-clerical revolution by any necessity, and that the French model should be regarded as an exception rather than the rule. In the Muslim world, such revolution appeared even less necessary, since self-consciously secularist and religious people did not disagree on the main national and developmental agendas: sovereignty, anti-colonialism, material progress, and modernization. Even the history of communist parties shows that such parties were most successful in countries where they tended to contest religion least, such as Iraq, Sudan, or the former South Yemen.

In the former South Yemen, for example, no eyebrows were raised when the Marxist president lead the faithful in prayer. And when the great intellectual movement of soul searching among the Arab secular intellectuals began in the aftermath of the 1967 defeat, a large number of them, beginning with Sadiq Jalal al-'Azm's, Adonis, Muhammad 'Abed al-Jabiri, Husayn Muruwwah, Tayyib Tizini, and many others, went back to the Islamic heritage in search for critical answers. This intellectual activity may seem curious, since Islam had nothing to do with the Arab defeat in 1967, and no one fought then in the name of Islam, only of anti-colonial nationalism. The fact that studying the Islamic cultural heritage seemed necessary then, precisely by those intellectuals who had no religious commitments, suggests widespread conviction among intellectuals in the continuing relevance of Islam as a venue for understanding cultural patterns (but not necessarily religious commitments).

While one reason for the survival of religion may reside in the simple fact that it was never rejected and never had to face a secular revolution against it, another reason becomes more apparent when we recognize how both instrumental and hermeneutic paradigms reside in ongoing experiments aimed at establishing a modern moral order supported by a common public philosophy. In fact, it seems that there can be no public philosophy without some sense of a common good (Salvatore and Eickelman 2006). In this sense religion may be said to survive today for the same reasons it had survived historically: not because it is an "illusion" (as Freud postulated) to be corrected in due time as we enhance our rational toolkit or arrive at psychological maturity. In either instrumental or hermeneutic forms, the modern public intellectual systems of religion supply to social and personal life meanings that are both simple to understand yet broader in their scope, more profound in their apparent implication, and more participatory in the way they engage common intellects that any other *familiar* idea.

A simple example of how the interpretive work performs these social roles is the sacrifice of Abraham, commonly cited by Muslims, who devote to its commemoration their longest common festival every year. The aborted sacrifice is usually interpreted as an apprenticeship for social responsibility. First Abraham surrenders to god, completely, and only *then* does he learn that the sacrifice is meant for society. After all, unlike society, the high monotheistic god needs no sacrifice. So here, what Durkheim suggested as the hidden essence of religious life is brought to the forefront and freely acknowledged by religious people themselves. Such avowed earthliness makes religion no more profane, since alternative sources of modern morality have not planted comparably deep roots: Where *else* do we get a similar guide for binding ethics in secular modernity? Wherever moral ideas today—for example social responsibility—are grounded on sources other than religion, they correlate with an institutional structure that is still unique enough in the world: Western Europe. That region continues to be the great exception to the worldwide religious revival today (Berger 1999). It also happens to be the place that has gone furthest than anywhere in assigning social responsibility to secular social systems that continue to be broadly seen by their citizens to be legitimate. Everywhere else, including the Muslim world, social responsibility, especially in expanding urban locations, resides in whatever networks and civic cultures that could continually produce what is necessary for common social life and is otherwise missing: a philosophy of binding and participatory morals.

It is difficult to see how any religion would disappear without the establishment of a credible alternative to it, not simply as a moral philosophy of life but also, and correspondingly, as a discourse that regulates the social ethics of mutuality, responsibility, and obligations. And even then, with the rise of such an alternative, religion may still be maintained as a reserve philosophical compass so long as such an alternative—as in the United States for example—does not require the rejection of religion. If society remains substantially religious, meaning not only that large enough segments believe in god but also find it important to reference religion as a source of social ethics, there are precious few practical ways to separate religion from either public philosophy or even the state—even if the state officially defines itself as non-religious. A religious society will tend to evaluate all significant issues with reference to religion, not because religion presumes any particular answers, but precisely because a *living* religion will be living in so far as it means different things to different interest groups or social strata.[16] A religious society is not a uniform society ruled

16. This feature appears to be the basis of the idea that Islam promotes cross-class alliances (e.g., Atasoy 2005:167). Yet the notion of "alliance" misconstrues larger roles played by Islamic social discourse. These seem connected less to creating common agendas across the social fabric than to establishing structures of moral accountability and means of adjudicating conflicts.

by the same dogmas, practices, and levels of commitment. Rather, religion can be an aid to living only because it speaks to each individual or group in a language and concerning issues they understand and appreciate. This variety is precisely what gives religion a continuing license on social life. That is, a religion living across any differentiated or stratified society must by definition have varied social meanings or commitments that are coterminous with the social spectrum it covers.

That a religious society so understood will also compel its state to be religious regardless of its law, is a point that Marx well understood, even though he had the United States and not Islam in mind. (Indeed, his remarks about the United States are perhaps even more valid today than they were in 1843.) However, hermeneutics would qualify this observation: If such a state and such a society accept a hermeneutic rather than an instrumental approach to religion, any religion, then they also accept lack of finality and limited authority as also elements of the same faith.

Religious hermeneutics operates as an alternative to both secular reason and religious instrumentalism. If religion is a voluntary and uncoerced part of social life, it cannot meaningfully be separated from the state, because it cannot be separated from any issue of public life. But if this same religion is understood hermeneutically rather than instrumentally, then it itself develops in the same way as society does, since hermeneutics presupposes the absence of a frozen, single, authoritative, and immutable understanding (even as it proposes the existence of a divine reason that is timeless, though inaccessible to us). From a hermeneutic perspective, the presumption that humans can access an immutable meaning of religion violates the infinite, eternal, and incomprehensible nature of god. Nor could such a religion be instrumental, in the sense of being simply a spiritual counter-image of secular ideologies, including nationalism or neoliberalism. Rather, because in hermeneutics religion is understood as living in the same way that we ourselves live, its developmental or cultural projects are broader in scope, and more universal, than what specific national projects, fixed collective identities, or any specific policies may suggest. In this form religion, as any living idea must, evolves alongside humanity's reason, because humanity rarely seemed to wish to live by reason alone.

IN THE FINAL analysis, this hermeneutics is a religious perspective, and is not to be confused with secular reason. The philosophical complexity of hermeneutics does not mean that it is free from the prison of the holy text, especially where the text aligns with a moral standpoint that a hermeneut endorses—for example, Shahrur's justification of what he understands to be a Qura'nic ban on homosexuality. Like any other thought system, therefore, the hermeneutic experiment may always hit a limit prescribed by some local morality, even though the philosophical system is couched in the deliberative language of universal morality.

For the time being, hermeneutics offers another way of making religion conform to common sense and the realities of complex society. A good example of this concerns the status of *hudud*, or the antiquated Qur'anic "penal" code, whose significance is exaggerated in spite of its lack of use in most Muslim societies and miniscule textual volume, especially if compared to the even more antiquated (yet more profuse) code of *Leviticus*. The question, of course, is what to do with texts that are so arcane and ridiculous that most religious people themselves prefer to ignore them. Hermeneutics here comes to the rescue by suggesting that the legal aspects of religion should not be taken at face value, for two reasons: first, the very idea of a high, unimaginable god must by definition place him above petty or situational legalism. Second, if it is true that we have an intuitive capacity to understand the idea of "justice," there should be no need for a divine authority to spell out its minute operational details.

This is not an issue that a secular reason needs to confront, since it simply rejects the whole concept of *hudud*. In reality, that is precisely the case in almost the entire Muslim world now, in spite of minor though highly publicized exceptions—and even those appear to be very complex and require scrutiny of the local sociological details of every single case, rather than general pronouncements about what "Islam says" (e.g., Eltantawi 2107). From any religious perspective, *including* hermeneutics, the rejection of the legal part of religion requires justification. Shahrur in particular regards the legal aspects of religion to be its least compelling part. In particular, he regards divinely specified penalties not as a guide to what punishments humans should mete out, but as their absolute upper limit. This interpretation relies to a certain extent on linguistics, since the word *hudud* means "boundaries" or "limits."

But while this method may reveal that within modern hermeneutics there are styles of analysis still beholden to traditional interpretive approaches that rely on linguistic analysis (to which Shahrur devotes a lengthy, complex final chapter in his magnum opus, *The Book and the Qur'an*), we know that that sort of analysis of the same text can produce several meanings. The copious historical genre of *tafsir* testifies to this fact, as does the consensus of religious authorities that the holy text includes a certain (undefined) portion characterized by being *mutashabih*, that is, text that houses multiple meanings. After all, the Qur'an itself says as much about its own nature, most clearly in 3:7 (also suggested in 39:23).

Hermeneutics shares with the general tendency we call "fundamentalism" the philosophical proposition that if the Qur'an is valid for all times, then it must speak directly to us, without mediation, and we should be able to understand it without the weight of centuries of commentaries and interpretation. However, the hermeneutic variety of this standpoint proposes that we are able to understand only if we know *why* we are reading an ancient text *today*. That is, if we are able to identify the *modern* agony or problem that has set us in a religious direction. Reflexivity here becomes important. Muhammad Shahrur is a case in point: Formerly a secular intellectual educated in the former Soviet Union, he dates his interest in examining religion precisely to the catastrophic Arab defeat in 1967. That event was of such magnitude that it compelled him, along with many other Arab secular intellectuals, to spend many years searching for anything that had the appearance of being a "root" cause. If our whole "'heritage," along with the ways of thinking it gave us, was responsible for such a defeat, then one felt special responsibility to go to that source, even if one had no prior connection to it. An entire range of encyclopedic heritage projects (alluded to previously) emerged precisely out of 1967, of which hermeneutics was only one part.

Whatever the limits of hermeneutics, it emerges, like instrumental reason, from earthly problems. In modernity, god exists for a reason, and that reason has to be spelled out or at least explored by the modern believer. Perhaps the greatest difference between the traditional and the modern, if we want to use these terms, is not that religious sentiment is stronger in one than in the other. Rather the difference concerns whether a religious sentiment is taken for granted and appears natural, or that its source must be found and actively defended against alternative worldviews, both religious and not. Modern religion is brought out of nervous energy that characterizes all modern life. But in religion this nervous energy is discharged either as an intellectual elaboration of the meaning of faith, or as a *new* feeling, rather than as a mechanical fulfillment of ritual. The very statement one hears from modern religious people that religion provides them with "calmness" (Holt 2006; O'Connell and Skevington 2005; Ellison 1991) reveals one defensive aspect of modern religion against uncontrolled chaos. That modern religious perspective splits into more than one approach suggests that the pathways by which modern nervous energy transforms into any other feeling, be it calm repose or confidence, has to do with a *decision* in which the religious person chooses a certain perspective. But if it is *decisions* (and not "determinations") that matter, we may expect modern nervousness to deliver neither uniform meanings nor standard feelings.

Until a single authority becomes capable of enforcing at least the appearance of orthodoxy, a religiosity that is elaborated by each person on her own and that takes form in the internal cauldron of nervous energy may resemble a social anarchy. There is no necessary contradiction here: We know that part of the anarchist tradition has affinity to religion, and that some religious traditions have been claimed to contain anarchist principles (Christoyannopoulos and Adam 2017).

In this case, an unconscious affinity to anarchism is especially evident in some of the main propositions of hermeneutics. These include:

1) accepting uncertainty of knowledge;
2) rejecting human capacity to arrive at totality;
3) dialectics of reader and text: the text speaks not by itself but through the reader;
4) even this authority of dialectics is moderated by the finite interpretive capacity of the reader;
5) simultaneity of eternal truth and partial knowledge of it;
6) the limited meaning of particular group identities, including religious identity;
7) the emphasis of immanence (of the divine) in life rather than its transcendence over it;
8) the synonymy of god's intention with the collective intention of humanity;
9) the reliance of truth on its voluntary acceptance.

The list of principles above could be expanded further, especially if we consider them in a historical light. Then we discover why religion has lived for so long: not because it has been "applied" by any authority, but precisely the opposite. Historically, Islam had meant different things to different people, and the literature proving that point now appears endless, even though the point still needs to be repeated. Even without hermeneutics, Islam was made to fit the specific and varying needs of a large number of social groups, individuals, and conflicting classes, across immense distances and over centuries. In the next chapter we will see how even the shari'a had historically anarchic features, which were themselves responsible for its longevity. The shari'a was never "applied," as Islamists want it to be today, by any ruler who resembled the miscreants we have today. Rather, it functioned as a broad and flexible repertoire that helped social groups arrive at a modus vivendi that was voluntary, multiple, intuitively persuasive, and had the character of compromise. At the same time, like any other anarchic system, the shari'a could be replaced by practical wisdom when needed.

In the modern case of hermeneutics versus instrumental reason, the choice determines how one relates to religion. The two general pathways, which are expressed in public philosophies as well as social movements, include within each the entire spectrum of religious ideas. In the instrumental case, god speaks to the world from without, while in the case of hermeneutics, he speaks to it from within; in the instrumental case one lives according to god's law, while in the hermeneutic case one follows the grand intentions of such a law. In the first case one wants to use religion to solve social problems; in the latter case one regards social problems as manifestations of poor knowledge; in the former case, thus, one wants to organize society, whereas in the latter one wants foremost to organize knowledge.

These different expectations of religion are also part of its long philosophical history. The one modern issue that concerns us here is the fact that these paradigms enter modern public philosophy, where they must develop further against counter-arguments and become part of the learning experiences of Islamic social movements. The fact that both public philosophy and social movements operate simultaneously within national theaters and in global networks complicates the picture very quickly. This variety suggests that one may identify further sub-paradigms, and perhaps eventual overlaps, although the broad convergence of Islamic public philosophy into two distinct paradigms suggests similarity in the types of basic problems that Islam is asked to address—whether problems of social order, progress, identity, or knowledge. What is clear is that the evolution of paradigms and the increasing public density of their philosophical elaboration ensures a social life of religion in which it is not simply a set of rituals or a taken-for-granted tradition with an obvious meaning. Its meaning has to be sought and elaborated, in public and against counter-arguments (except in special cases like Saudi Arabia, where no counter-arguments are allowed, and in which case primitive, unresponsive religiosity is maintained by sheer authoritarianism rather than because it has persuasive capacity).

In sum, modern religion is necessarily expressed in the form of public philosophy. The degree to which such modern religion could be said to be socially alive is indicated by the degree to which it produces contending paradigms rather than uniform answers.

3

Islam as Global Order

PRAGMATICS OF HISTORICAL STRUCTURES

ISLAMIC SOCIAL MOVEMENTS and the public philosophies associated with them constitute visible dimensions of the contemporary Islamic experience. These, in turn, are unthinkable if Muslim organizations and intellectuals did not see themselves as positioned in some way, whether critically or otherwise, in relation to a rich, world-scale historical experience. But what is so distinctive about this historical experience? Rather than exploring how it is *remembered* (which is the subject of much existing scholarship), or simply *invented* (e.g., Aydin 2017), I would like in this chapter to do something else, and that is to identify some of the main sociological structures of this historical experience. We should be aware that there is evidence that social scientists in important parts of what is supposed to be the "Muslim world" rarely use that concept as an analytical category. This suggests that they do not think that the "Muslim world" constitutes a meaningful sociological entity (Bamyeh 2015:59), even though they do discuss Islam, Islamic social movements, Islamic thought, etc. This does not affect the analysis that follows, which focuses on historical structures as a way of understanding the present. But the point is not to argue that the "Muslim world" is any more meaningful than, say, the "Christian world" or "the West," all of which, I am sure, are profoundly misleading ways of thinking about the world. Nevertheless, we need to explore the historical processes that, at the deeper levels, made those categories take hold in our imagination.

This chapter will show how, as a discourse for organizing society, Islam gained historical longevity, and thus a hold on part of the imagination of the present, due to certain sociological structures that possess global features. When we explore these structures, we realize that the historical experience of Islam is broader than Islam proper: It is inseparable from recurrent general formulas for organizing a global society. As a universalist religion Islam is already part of a very old formula for organizing society at a global level.

In an earlier book (Bamyeh 2000) I sought to show how global cultural processes have historically served to humanize otherwise pure economic processes—the cold, heartless part of the story about which we seem to fixate entirely today when we discuss what we call "globalization." Yet, the historical tendency has always been for global culture to be inseparable from other global processes. Global culture, in turn, consists not of uniform propositions but of intersecting experiments. These include pronouncements of faith (thereby supplying ready credentials of global citizenship); universalization of ethical and business standards (especially among the trading communities); and loose political arrangements (that made possible the simultaneity of autonomy and communication).

The argument presented here is that the Muslim world, or Dar al-Islam (the abode of Islam) as it was historically known to Muslims, appeared as a predictable world system, and acceptable as legitimate to most of its inhabitants, only to the extent that it adhered to three fundamental principles: one political, another social, and a third cultural. They were namely the principle of partial control, the principle of free movement, and the principle of cultural heteroglossia. As will become apparent, these principles are not strictly "historical"; that is to say, they represent not simply features of an antiquated system. Rather, they are basic norms with the aid of which any global system could function with maximal systematicity and minimal interruption. Thus one should not be too surprised to see that these principles are analogous, in their spirit, to some emerging conceptions today regarding how to construct a modern global system characterized by maximal systematicity and minimal interruption, while at the same time remaining non-imperialistic. In fact, in its general patterns globalization today can be regarded as an attempt, so far inconclusive, to return from the age of nation-states and colonial power politics to older political, social, and cultural concepts that once regulated and humanized a well-connected global life. In this sense globalization is a very old story, so old that it is yet to be fully remembered. We will return to this point at the end of this chapter.

The three principles listed above persisted remarkably well throughout Islamic history, with many occasional interruptions, the latest and most enduring of which occasion the modern colonial epoch and the formation of modern states. The vitality and remarkable career of these principles had little to do with the benevolence or conscious strategies of any particular government or sovereign in Islamic history. In fact frequently they persisted against the expressed wishes of governments, which until the modern period had simply no means by which to establish total control, prohibit population movements, or impose common cultural orthodoxies.

It was only during the epochs of both colonialism and then the modern state when systematic attempts were made in order to replace these principles, which had provided global Islam historically with its "convivial" nature (Roy 1988). Yet such modern epochs managed only to replace this well-organized conviviality, conducive to global commerce and predictability, with nervous systems that could only rely on violence and power as primary guaranteeing mechanisms of predictability. Those mechanisms, costly as they were, were still not as efficient in reaching their goal as much as older patterns that seem to us loaded with medieval features of social organization. What follows will elaborate on how each of the three principles had operated historically, and in conclusion will suggest how each may be in the process of being reinvoked today as a pillar of global life.

Partial control

Until the state modernizing reforms of Muhammad (Mehmet) Ali in early-nineteenth-century Egypt, the Egyptian state had exemplified a pattern of partial control that had typified Muslim polities throughout history and distinguished them from European city- and then nation-states. These reforms are often said to have their roots in political and economic developments that had been taking place gradually in the latter half of the eighteenth century, including attempts at a more central and unified government and early capitalist development (Gran 1979). But undoubtedly they were greatly accelerated, and took on a far more sustained character, in the aftermath of the brief French takeover of the country in 1798–1801, an event that exposed the weakness of the old political system (Jabarti 1993). Unlike European states, which especially during the nineteenth century came to be seen as ultimate organizing embodiments of society, the Islamic state was historically regarded, by constituents and rulers alike, as only one among several sources of legitimate authority in society. Its control was territorially limited to major cities. Beyond the cities but sometimes even within them control had to be shared with other authorities, including religious scholars, tribal networks, merchant and professional guilds, Sufi orders, and vast networks of extended families.

Thus a variety of social networks, rather than state agents, governed more or less all aspects of life at the local level—except for imperial taxation, which was usually assessed on a region or a town as a whole, but subdivided according to local rules; and the office of the *muhtasib* or market inspector, who usually provided a service broadly appreciated, except by hoarders and speculators. Otherwise, it was local elites that meant anything in terms of familiar power structures. The most common form of relation of such local elites to local populations was one of a patron-client. But sources of local authority were multiple in form, ranging from family notables to important merchants to tribal elders to religious scholars and judges. A delicate balance had to be maintained always between these sources of authority, which often reinforced each other but also kept each other in check. The same applied to how all of them collectively related to state power above the local level. In some sense local elites could benefit from their expressed allegiance to an expansive Islamic state, since such a state gave their authority more reason. The distant state saw them as mediating between it and the local level, and in any case the state could efficiently deal only with a relatively small number of partners in each region. However, local elites also never wanted more state control than was needed to augment their purposes, which were to either have more say over a specific aspect of local life, or protect their constituency as needed, rather than to rule local society as a whole.

The fact that for much of its history the Muslim world was nominally governed by territorially expansive, loose states rather than confined city-states, meant that local civil society, social networks and collective identities could exist and evolve at some distance from state doctrines. Islam itself was elaborated historically by networks of scholarly communities largely operating out of their own schools rather than through official position in government. The faith was disseminated in society on the basis of their work, and spread geographically through long-distance trade that connected local economies to world systems. States themselves, in spite of their religious claims usually found it necessary, convenient, or less contentious to leave the task of elaborating Islam to other authorities, namely the scholars of religion and various independent religious orders. Indeed, according to at least two recent major theses and also an older one (Hallaq 2012; an-Na'im 2008; Abd al-Raziq 1925), the concept of an "Islamic state" is incompatible with Islamic thought theologically and Muslim traditions historically. In either case, the argument is based on both an interpretation of the traditions of the early Muslim communities, especially in Medina under Muhammad, and (especially in the case of an-Na'im) actual histories of states that claimed to stand in for Islam. These states, an-Na'im argues, must be understood as political and not religious entities.

Whether this difference is meaningful depends on the extent to which Muslims themselves noted it. For most of their history, authorities that were able to define Islam in ways that were actually followed were always authorities that were close to an actual population. That fact had something to do with the nature of authority in Islam, and specifically how it differs from Christianity especially in Europe. In recent literature one encounters an overstated claim regarding how Christianity "essentially" involves a separation of church and state, since Jesus taught that Caesar and god had different requirements. But the historical reality has obviously nothing to do with this standpoint. While the first three centuries of Christianity are characterized by activism from below, with the conversion of Rome to Christianity, religious authority in Europe tended to have an avowed program of political alliances for which the hierarchical structure, particularly of Catholicism, lent instrumental credibility. This would not change in practice until the consolidation of the authority of modern states in the nineteenth century. In this connection it should be noted that the Peace of Westphalia in 1648 affirmed as an elementary proposition that each state would follow its own distinct religion, the only difference now being that it is determined by its sovereign ruler. The conflation of the religious and the political was most clearly institutionalized in England, where the monarch has officially been the head of the Church of England for the last five centuries.

In Islam, by contrast, while the ruler was expected to be a Muslim, it was never expected that this should be enough reason for the population to follow his particular creed. Religious authority operated largely in civil society and the *ulama* were staples of civic life. This was the case even among the shi'a, who had a more hierarchical structure but rarely their own state, apart from the Ismaili Fatimid state (909–1171) in North Africa and the Levant, the Safavid state in Persia as of the sixteenth century, and the Buyid state five centuries earlier. The two centuries of rule over Egypt by the Ismaili Shi'a Fatimid dynasty (969–1171) did not occasion a demographic dominance of their creed, and overall the country lived for six centuries with a Muslim ruler and a non-Muslim majority. None of these states seemed to consider the enforcement of a uniform religious culture

to be one of their roles, except in Savafid Persia, where the ultimate outcome from the enforcement of Twelver Shi'ism was the consolidation of
the power of the clergy as an independent force that outlasted the Safavid
dynasty. In the other two cases above, neither state showed much interest
in enforcing any orthodoxies, and they seemed resigned (or at least not
to have a problem with) ruling over a population the majority of whom
remained non-Shi'a. The point is even more clear when we explore the
history of Sunnism, commonly understood as the mainstream of Islam,
although "Sunni" is a large category, having in common a general allegiance to the "way" (*sunna*) of Muhammad, interpreted variably within the
loose networks of religious scholars.

This is clear from the evolution in Sunni Islam of the *shari'a*, today mis-
understood as Islamic "law," even though it had the exact *opposite* properties
of what we understand as "law" today. A proper definition of the *shari'a* is that
it is the sum total of practical ways of being a Muslim in the world. These
practical ways far exceed in their scope and purpose legal matters and what
we generally understand by "law" today—including such matters as questions of faith, daily manners, rules of hygiene, proper composure, mourning
rituals, and thousands of other details concerning how one should lead one's
own daily life as a good Muslim. Indeed, more appropriate than the concept
of "law" would be to regard the *shari'a* as an anarchic system of social organization. The anarchic features of the *shari'a* become evident when we consider
its three distinctive historical properties:

1. The *shari'a* has never been a uniform body of rules. It is elaborated
   according to the methods of different interpretive schools, both historically and in the present. The four surviving schools in Sunni Islam
   accept the *multiplicity* of *shari'a* as a basic historic and contemporary
   property of an Islamic way of life.
2. The *shari'a* may involve contradictory advice that does not require synthesis or resolution. A learned *shari'a*-based judgment (*fatwa*) may be
   contradicted by another. Sociologically speaking, the validity of the
   judgment depends on the extent to which it is followed, and not on its
   inner logic or consistency with tradition.[1]

---

1. Countless examples of this reality could be offered from all time periods. A prominent example from recent times concerns how *fatwas* issued during the Arab Spring were ignored
or followed depending on whether they adhered to prevailing sentiments. For example, prior
to the downfall of President Mubarak in Egypt, the country's highest religious authority

3. The *shari'a* was elaborated in civil society by scholarly authorities, and not by state legislators. It was not state-oriented in the sense that it did not describe the functions of the state, only how individuals should behave. State matters were addressed in different genre, *siyasa*, which emerged *explicitly* because the *shari'a* did not cover its scope. (This point will be addressed in some detail in subsequent pages.)

The *Shari'a* developed over several centuries in historical Muslim societies to become a comprehensive but flexible guide for life. The careers of the founders of the main Sunni schools of *shari'a*, of which only four have survived out of more than twenty schools that flourished at some point or another during the first three centuries of Islam, consistently show a dogged distance from state affairs. Abu Hanifa, one of the first founders of such schools, preferred to decline the offer by the Abbasid caliph to be the chief judge of Baghdad. This show of independence did not go unpunished. The caliph ordered Abu Hanifa's arrest, and he eventually died in prison. It is reported that nearly 50,000 people attended his funeral, which testified to the early development of a civic culture around independent learned authorities, including in this case someone who had defied the caliph.

In its general outline this same story is typical of the clash between the authority of learning, oriented toward elaborating Islam as a basis of an autonomous civic culture, and political authority, which with few exceptions saw Islam largely as a means to its own consolidation. The few exceptions were, as they still are, well-noted by Muslims themselves, precisely because they are exceptions: the first four caliphs, known collectively as *Al-Rashidun*; the Umayyad caliph 'Umar Ibn Abd al-Aziz; the Murabitun state founder Yusuf Ibn Tashfin; and a few others. But the general expectation was that the authority of learning and that of the state followed different rather than synergetic requirements.

A spectrum spanning the most orthodox and most libertine among the celebrated founders of the *shari'a* was unified by a perspective that regarded the authority of learning to be higher, or at least of a substantially different nature, than that of state leaders. Thus Ahmad Ibn Hanbal, whose followers are often seen to be inclined to play an authoritarian role

---

issued a widely ignored *fatwa*, prohibiting demonstrations against the government. Other religious authorities in the same country issued different rulings at the time, some similar to and others blatantly contradicting his judgment.

in policing civic manners and public spaces, also defied another Abbasid caliph on theological questions and ended up in prison, a fate that only increased his influence. The same is true of Malik Ibn Anas, whose school still dominates in North Africa and elsewhere in the Muslim world. Malik consistently defied political authorities, including pronouncing the invalidity of the people's oath of allegiance to a caliph when that oath is taken under duress, refusing to lecture in the camp of the caliph, and persisting in his lessons even when ordered to not do so by the city governor. He was tortured for his disobedience. His standard biographies all exalt his defiant qualities as signs of great learning, the ultimate outcome of which should be that one loses fear of temporal authorities and becomes confident of his own guiding role in civic life.

Indeed, in both Christianity and Islam, the narrative surrounding the earliest phase of formulation of religious doctrine is also a tale of such knowledge emerging in conditions of defiance and suffering—the period of the composition of the Gospels and the founding of the *shari'a*, respectively. However, an important difference here is that whereas the foundational period of Christianity produced the early martyrs at the hands of non-Christian powers, in Islam the foundational period of the *shari'a* produced suffering at the hands of *Muslim* authorities. And it is perhaps here that one can identify the genesis of separation of religion and state in Islam (although of course no one spoke that way in those times). The scholarly guardians of the faith had to struggle against the caliph for their right to define the faith, in a way that Christian bishops never needed to after the conversion of Constantine. Indeed, they would see no problem in attending a council convened by Constantine himself, in an attempt to arrive at consensus on the tenets of Christianity. Thus whereas with the conversion of emperor Constantine further elaboration of the principles of Christianity could develop out of a foundational gnostic period where they had already been in existence in one form or another, in early Islam the gnostic period occurred under the eyes of Muslim political authorities. The comparatively early formation of an Islamic state (or, more accurately, a state with an Islamic identity) was conducive for Muslim rulers trying to claim a role in defining the faith. This only meant that their claim would be contested by the other relevant authority, namely that of the religious scholars, in a way that was far less necessary in Christianity.

The authority of learning became so paramount and so fundamental to Muslim civic life that even when states fostered a specific religious direction that was favored by some established group of *'ulama*, it was the latter who gained the most power from the marriage of convenience between religious doctrine and state policy. Most illustrative of this dynamic was the Safavid state's case, in which the state's decision to convert then largely Sunni Persia into Shi'ism required inviting Shi'a clergy to disseminate their teachings among the population. But in the process those clergy came to acquire a lasting power base of their own in society, a base that survived the demise of the Safavids and all subsequent states in Persia. And when the Ottoman Sultan Ahmet, presiding over an empire at the peak of its power, built his famous mosque in Istanbul with six minarets to equal those of the Haram of Mecca, he faced an uproar that was settled only when he added a seventh minaret to the Mecca mosque, thereby reestablishing the prominence of the Mecca mosque over the sultan's mosque. (After that contentious episode, imperial Ottoman mosques went back to being built with their usual four minarets.)

That episode served as a lasting lesson on the limits of imperial power in the face of a religion whose institutions were regarded as grander than those of any temporal power. It is in the nature of empire to expand and transcend until it discovers a limit (Bamyeh 2007). In this case, the limit comes from opposition from below: The prophet's authority must always be visibly higher than that of the Sultan. The Sultan comes to accept that principle, but not before testing the limits to his power. This historical reality may be contrasted to what happened when limits to power are removed in modern time: Atatürk, for instance, was treated as a deity in a way that no previous sultan or caliph could have enjoyed.

Modern states in the Muslim world were all well aware of this dynamic, and therefore one of their first acts of "modernization" involved to some degree or another attempts to subdue or coopt established religious institutions. If there is a problem of authority in modern Islam, therefore, it can be traced to the nature of the modern state rather than to ancient dynamics. All modern states sought to either marginalize Islamic authority in civil society, whose space the modern state wanted to occupy, or co-opt such an authority for state purposes. Emblematic of this was the transformation of al-Azhar under Nasser into a state institution. Another event that looks very different is in fact similar in its underlying logic: the establishment of a Wahhabi state in Saudi Arabia, to be discussed later in this article, should also be seen as an example of modern state effort to transform religious life for its own purposes. The Wahhabi state was from the beginning based on a novel proposition that was unfamiliar to most Muslims, and that was the proposition that there should be no distance between the men of religious learning and the men of temporal power. And in this form Wahhabism itself was from its beginning in 18th century Arabia unenforceable without a program of political control that was integral to it from inception. The Wahhabi movement itself, operating in then largely isolated and resourceless central Arabia, could not possibly acquire any real prospects without the alliance of Ibn Abd al-Wahhab and Al Saud family. The fact that this movement is anomalous in Islamic civic history is clearly evident from the astonishing degree of violence it needed in order to reach its goals. As Hamid Algar reminds us (2002: 42), the second Saudi conquest of Hijaz, which included Mecca and Medina, beginning after 1913, was not a march into a friendly territory: 40,000 public executions and 350,000 injuries accompanied that horrible campaign, which laid down the foundations of a modern, authoritarian state whose ideology had no parallel in Islamic history and whose clergy, unlike the historical *'ulama*, have always required state support in order to enforce their dogmas.

Historically, the civic authority of the learned class was facilitated by the consolidation of charitable endowments (*waqf*), whose regulation was one of the earlier issues to confront the evolving *shari'a*. A *waqf* was typically a private endowment consisting of real estate, although it could also consist of any other property that is able to generate income into perpetuity. It could be used for any charitable purpose, and it was for example used to support hospitals, welfare for the poor, or the upkeep of cemeteries. However, the two most common recorded uses of *waqf* in Islamic history were to support the upkeep of mosques and for education, including support of schools, scholars, and libraries. The *waqf* institutions played an undeniable role in maintaining the independence of scholarly communities from governments, as well as in supporting their role in civic life. The very size of *waqf* endowments on the eve of the modern era testifies to their crucial role. For example, the land survey in Egypt in 1812–1813 showed that 24% of the cultivated land was held up in *waqf* endowments (Ramadan 1983:128), a percentage that after modernist reforms aiming to eliminate the *waqf* continued to be as high as 12% by 1949 (Qureshi 1974). In Turkey the share of *waqf* properties reached one-third of the land (Armagan 1989:335). About half of the land in Algeria in the mid nineteenth century was held as *waqf*, and one-third in Tunisia in 1883 (Qureshi 186–187). At the beginning of the twentieth century, all of Jerusalem's 64 schools were supported by *waqf* endowments (Asali 1983). Çizakça (2000) claims that the entirety of the health, education, and welfare functions under the Ottoman system were carried out through *waqf* endowments.

With the exception of Timur Kuran (2001, 2005), who sees *waqf* institutions as impediments to modernization and supports state confiscation of their resources, virtually all contemporary commentators are coming to see the value of the *waqf* both in economic development as well as in fostering social autonomy from the state. A common view is that the *waqf* has historically made it possible for the perpetuation of a non-state centered third sector, and thus was highly useful in furthering the autonomy of the public sphere (Assi 2008; Hennigan 2004; Çizakça 2000; Shatzmiller 2001; Hoexter 2002; Arjomand 1999; Deguilhem 1995; Sayyid 1989). Others further highlight the role of *waqf* in fostering family autonomy (Doumani 1998) or women's agency (Fay 1997, 1998), or how it allowed the circumvention of Islamic inheritance law, and in ways that compelled the *shari'a* schools to adapt to it (Layish 2008; Shaham 2000).

Given its traditional importance in providing bases of autonomous civic life in the public sphere, it is no surprise that all colonial powers as well all modern states in the Muslim world sought from an early point to control *waqf* institutions. One of the earliest forays by the modernizing state of Muhammad Ali in Egypt was to place al-Azhar's endowment under its control in 1812, so as to limit the autonomy of that ancient citadel of conservative, traditional Islamic higher learning. One of the first acts of French colonial authorities in Algeria upon occupying the country in 1831 was to take control of *waqf* properties as a way of subduing the religious leaders who were militating against the French (Abu al-Afjan 1985:325). Various commentators, exploring modern state-led transformations in as varied places as Zanzibar, Penang, the Soviet Union, Jordan, and Kenya (Oberauer 2008; Khoo Salma 2002; Pianciola and Sartori 2007; Fischbach 2001; Carmichael 1997), concur with similar conclusions, namely that colonial or modern state disruptions of the *waqf* institution had the overall result of weakening traditional, non-state centered elites, and a realignment of loyalties either toward modern states (which was the hoped for result), or mass movements (which was not).

What has not changed much, however, was the expectation that religious authority in social life must be based on accomplishments and reputation, rather than investiture in a state-office. The institutionalization of religion into state offices in Iran after the Revolution only tarnished the reputation of the clergy, and it appears that toward the end of his life Khomeini himself was becoming aware of that fact (Sadjadpour 2008:10). The clergy that served the Islamic Republic of

Iran discovered soon how the mandate of governing a state was different in substantial ways from those of providing moral leadership in society. For example, now invested in a state, the clerical establishment confronted a decision toward the end of Khomeini's life that would have been unthinkable without an Islamic state: the elevation to the position of a supreme leader of Khamenei, a decision that raised the ire of the clerical establishment in Qom since everyone knew that Khamenei's scholarly credentials were inferior to most other possible protagonists. Those included the previously designated successor Ayatollah Hossein Ali Montazeri, who served as a *marja'* or guiding authority to far more people than Khamenei, and who shortly before his death in 2009 openly rejected the Islamic credentials of the regime, as did another important *marja'*, Ayatollah Yosef Sanei. The diminishing reputation of the Iranian clergy was clearly on the mind of another grand Ayatollah, Ali Sistani in Iraq, who saw the authority of the clergy in society to rely on their distance from government, and who differed from Khomeini on the question of *Velayat-e Faqih*, or rule (of society) by a supreme jurist. That standpoint did not contradict an outcome that Sistani still favored, which was that religious parties he favored, but not clergy directly, should have some rule in governing a state if they were elected democratically. In fact, his own web site asserts that one of the primary conditions for the authority of any *faqih* is the popularity of his opinions among the believers.

This standpoint is hardly modern. Historically as well as today, the validity of any religious opinion, or *fatwa*, among Muslims rests entirely on how many people believe in it, rather than on its legal enforceability. And the extent to which a *fatwa* is believed in depends, among other things, on the reputation of the person issuing the *fatwa* (that is, on something that requires many years of active participation in civic life). Being dependent on a political power usually diminished such reputation, since reputation could be sustained only by verifiable moral independence. Al-Azhar, for example, while continuing to enjoy broad respect, lost much stature among ordinary Muslims after it was made into a state institution, and *fatwas* issued by its council are contested if they seem to reflect more governmental wishes than public sentiments. A good recent example is the public clash shortly before the Gaza war of December 2008–January 2009 between some of al-Azhar's scholars, who issued a *fatwa* supporting the Egyptian government's building of a wall to prevent smuggling into Gaza. By that action they were seeking to offer a counter *fatwa* to the one issued by the then vastly more popular satellite television preacher Yusuf Qaradawi, who had declared that the wall in question was forbidden in Islam because it would bring about more hardship to Muslims already under extreme duress.

The importance of reputation, rather than official position, has indeed been central to dynamics of intellectual life in much of the Muslim World historically, where intellectuals in general—including religious scholars—were expected to be public figures in some dimension, and thus evaluated not only by their peers but also to an important extent by a public sphere (Bamyeh 2012a). But an authority that relied on reputation had to contend with the reality of partial control, no matter how established or widespread one's reputation might have been. Indeed, the practice of soliciting *fatwas* always implied an element of partial control, since a *fatwa* might be unpalatable, impractical, or liable to be contradicted by another *fatwa* issued by a different authority. Sociologically speaking, therefore, while a *fatwa* is an exposition of learned authority, it may be said to be a democratic practice, since unless there is a state to enforce it, a *fatwa* requires only a believer's own judgment of its validity. And that judgment, in turn, may itself be a reflection of one's own preferences as much as an outcome of further conversation about it with other familiar or trusted believers.

Now the question of authorial reputation (and not executive power) was likewise central in the evolution of the *shari'a*. The well-known stories about the resistance of its founders to Muslim political authority is inseparable from their ability to consolidate a lasting historical reputation. Knowledge, therefore, was always seen as a mark of an authority that is morally superior to the kind of authority that relies largely on force. The Qur'an itself endorses this standpoint in addressing Muhammad, telling him that *after* the "knowledge" that has come to him, he should no longer be in a position to follow mere "desires" of other mortals (in this case, other monotheists, 2:120). The general proposition here, which Malik seemed supremely confident in, was that knowledge was authority, not power. Knowledge was authority in a cultural sense, not power in a political sense. That meant that knowledge implied authority in civic life, since knowledge liberated one from instrumental reason as well as from following arbitrary and unanchored "mere desires" that typify those who have no or less knowledge—including rulers. Knowledge is authority here in the sense that it validates the scholar's sense of entitlement to moral leadership in civic life.

This strong sense that knowledge provides an alternative source of social authority is symbolized by the well-known *hadith* "*al-'ulama' warathat
al-anbiyya'*: scholars are the inheritors of prophets." Scholarly communities tended to construct knowledge and power (in the political sense) in
some sense as opposites rather than complementary poles. This does not
mean that they never saw that knowledge and power could be possible
allies. Rather, the equation they seemed to entertain for the most part involved three basic rules:

1. The alliance of knowledge and power is pronounced by the *'ulama* to be
   unequal: Knowledge must rule over power, otherwise there is no basis
   for the alliance.
2. If this supremacy of knowledge is not acknowledged by political power,
   the alliance between the two can be postponed, indefinitely. Out of this
   position one obtains a de facto separation of religion and state in Islam;
   not in the sense of "give unto Caesar," but "ignore Caesar until enlightenment comes to him. In the meantime do your work away from him."
3. The distance between knowledge and power may further be justified
   by elaborating and cultivating a myth of virtuous, unmatchable past
   (for example the *Rashidun* period or the *Sahabah*, Muhammad's companions, elevated above a later generation, *al-Tabi'un*, which itself is elevated above subsequent generations). This traditional formula, readily
   accepted by most Muslims, could when needed possess the effect of
   elevating authoritative features, which the *'ulama* were better positioned than anyone else to elaborate, of some unexperienced past above
   the dictates of any existing authority at any given point.

These various ways of conceptualizing the relation of knowledge and
power allowed the learned communities to be always in a position to
place themselves, rather than distant or unaccountable office holders, at
the center of civic life. In that role they elaborated over centuries what
we today know as the *shari'a*, which was never "law" as we understand
it today but a means of regulation by self-organized society. This is evident from the fact that in spite of its scope and longevity, there never appeared a single authoritative book called "the shari'a." The historical *shari'a*
was a mix of multiple traditions rather than a uniform code, and until
the rise of the modern Wahhabi dogma, all traditions forming the *shari'a*
included an acceptance of other traditions. This meant that, as in fact is
not uncommon today, pious Muslims form new standpoints by mixing

different *shari'a* traditions—as when a woman preacher in Cairo opined that women could lead other women in prayer, since three of the four acknowledged Sunni traditions seem to accept the notion and only one rejects it (Mahmood 2005:87–88). This opinion, as Mahmood shows in her study, does not mean that the fourth position is rejected, only that it is not followed. Now it is impossible to understand the *shari'a* as "law" unless by "law" we mean a code that we are free to disregard and if, as is also evident from Mahmood's ethnographic work, we understand it more as a range of recommendations, rather than a uniform and non-contradictory code of rules, which is what "law" means in modernity.

The fact that the *shari'a* became not only a code of civic and personal life that had little to do with state politics or the art of administering a state is illustrated by the evolution in North Africa and the Middle East toward the tenth century and after of a different science, *siyasa* or the science of politics, that was explicitly distinguished from the *shari'a*. Tarif Khalidi (1996:193–200), who traced that evolution, showed that this science of politics covered three areas, one of which concerned acts of government that were not within the scope of the *shari'a*. The other two uses of the science of *siyasa*, compiled entirely by advisors to rulers rather than by religious scholars, illustrate what is meant by "acts of government that go beyond the scope of the *shari'a*." Those concerned effectiveness of state policies, and the management of the state itself (i.e., genres that are equivalent to what Michel Foucault described as "governmentality" in European sciences of state).

The very fact that those central preoccupations of state officers (efficiency, management) were acknowledged to have nothing to do with the *shari'a* is amply illustrated with any *siyasa* manual, in which even the ethics of rulers are usually evaluated in terms of the effectiveness of their public display rather than traced to any divine source—as the *shari'a* would. Some famous *siyasa* manuals openly disregard the *shari'a*. For example, Nizam al-Mulk (1018–1092 C.E.), an advisor to a Seljuk sultan and author of the *Siyasatnama*, a classic in the *siyasa* genre, devotes an entire chapter to the proper etiquette of drinking wine in the ruler's palace. In it he includes advice such as that guests should not be allowed to appear intoxicated in public (because such appearance diminishes the authority of the sultan); and that the sultan's wine cellar should only have the best quality (because it diminishes his authority in the eyes of his guests if they brought with them wines of superior quality).

The discovery in the Muslim world, several centuries before Machiavelli, that state politics was not divine and that therefore it required its own distinct science, meant a de facto arrangement in which *shari'a* and *siyasa* lived apart from each other and spoke to different audiences. No clash between the two was necessary, so long as the state did not claim for itself prerogatives of the learned communities that saw themselves as guardians of the *shari'a*, and so long as the state itself was not contested in the name of the *shari'a*. On the other hand, the *shari'a* co-existed as well with another source of regulation of autonomous civic life, namely local customary traditions, often distinguished from *shari'a* in being called such terms as *taqalid, 'urf, qanun, 'adat*, all of which referred to local traditions, customs or mores that were not originated by the *shari'a* but did not explicitly contradict it either. (See Table 3.1.) However, those terms connoted a local code that may be traced to tribal customs, highland tradition, or communal identity in a way that was distinct from the *shari'a*. The degree to which *shari'a* adapted to or replaced local codes is often difficult to assess, as both *shari'a* and local customs were marks of a self-organized civic life. But the main distinction between the two was that the *shari'a* claimed a divine source and thus universal validity, whereas something like a highland *qanun* tended to be "secular," in the sense that its authority derived from ancient familiarity and local rootedness, rather than universal divine mandates.

Muslim jurists knew from an early point that a viable *shari'a* code would be one that accommodates local tradition to some extent, even though it may transform them and also transform, over time, the manner in which they are thought about. Muhammad's own prophetic career included a few

Table 3.1 Historical genres of autonomy and control

Genre	Scope	Attempted earlier mixtures (first three centuries of Islam; continuing)	Attempted later mixtures (beginning circa fourth Hijra century)	Attempted modern mixtures (esp. twentieth century & since)
Shari'a	Universal civics	*Shari'a & 'Urf*	*Siyasa & 'Urf*	*Shari'a & Siyasa*
Siyasa	State rule			
'Urf (a.k.a. *Qanun, taqalid, 'adat*)	Local customs			

remarkable adjustments to local traditions. For example, as it was adopting Islam, the Asad tribe received Muhammad's permission to distribute the required Islamic alms within the tribe—in effect doing what it had always done, though now under a different name—*zakah* rather than *sadaqah*. After his conquest of Mecca he reinstalled many of his old enemies in their former positions, ostensibly adjusting to a tribal dynamic that, as the messenger of god, he was theoretically free to dissolve. But these adjustments also introduced new realities, since in each case the recognition of a local authority or tradition was a recognition of local autonomy in exchange for an expression of allegiance to Islam. This dialectic, quite unavoidable in any pragmatic social history of religion, neither meant that Islam was "sullied" by being contaminated with impure local matter, nor that local traditions simply lived on just as before, nor that the addition of an Islamic discourse changed nothing but the appearance of things.

Rather, the relation of *shari'a* and local traditions was often quite conscious, although the degree to which the learned men of religion actively encouraged or discouraged that relation largely depends on the specific context. Malik, for example, explicitly wanted his school of *shari'a* to reflect the local traditions of Medina, which he was confident approximated best the original intentions of Islam. Less explicit claims were the norm wherever Islam was elaborated in relationship to environments whose local traditions could not so readily be claimed to express the universality of the faith. In reality syncretism was the most practical norm for spreading Islam, whereby pre-Islamic practices and beliefs that play a significant role in local life became incorporated into a local variety of Islam, a process that usually made the faith more palatable and locally meaningful. This was evidently how Islam became acceptable to large populations in Southeast Asia, South Asia, and Africa. Indeed, syncretic pragmatism could even be observed as a very early Islamic practice even in Muhammad's own lifetime. Then, several important aspects of pre-Islamic religious and spiritual life were incorporated into Islam, including the pilgrimage to the sanctuary in Mecca, the veneration of one remaining "idol" (the black stone of the Ka'ba), or the notion of the "forbidden months" in which fighting was prohibited. All those were pre-Islamic practices that went on, now with an Islamic imprimatur.

Subsequently the *shari'a*, as a gradual and pragmatic way of elaborating Islam in a variety of social worlds, had to adjust to various localisms, thus the *variety* of its schools becoming an acknowledged fact from the earliest points of Islamic expansion beyond Arabia. The most inventive were those schools that flourished in new environments like Mesopotamia and Persia, where urban life and local customs required formulating answers to hitherto unforeseen questions. By contrast, the more orthodox and literalist schools, such as that of Ibn Hanbal, held sway largely in relatively isolated territories that saw little social change, such as central Arabia. This multiplicity of the *shari'a*, which reflected its adjustment to local conditions, required neither streamlining nor official rules to set the boundaries of orthodoxy. In contrast to Christianity, for example, the doctrines of Islam were never defined in any meeting like the Council of Nicea (or the following 20 councils).

Living religions always involve an element of local syncretism, even when their official dogmas or doctrines are defined centrally or hierarchically. On the other hand, the fact that Islam (and here Islam is hardly unique) could always be seen as something more universal and more true than any local tradition meant that at any point Islam could be invoked to discredit or disallow a local tradition. At that point the local tradition is regarded as a local error rather than a local representation of a universal message. The success of that argument, however, is never guaranteed, since unless one is willing to use force, the argument depends entirely on the willingness of the audience to whom it was addressed to listen to it.

However, that very standpoint, namely isolating at one point or another some local habit as a reflection of "tradition" (or "culture") rather than "religion" often proved to be an effective argument. It allowed fundamentalist movements, for example, throughout Islamic history to disregard local traditions as violations of Islam rather than as its manifestation. In the Islamic Enlightenment during the nineteenth and twentieth centuries, the reformers' most common argument was that what they were rebelling against was an error-laden "social tradition" rather than "true religion." Prototypical of this strategy was Qasim Amin's call in 1905 for the emancipation of women, an argument in which he admitted that he was committing "heresy," but only against tradition and not religion. In its general form this argument is far more common today: Your tradition, what you do by force of habit, is not necessarily true religion. Here religion is seen to be that which is beyond habit, and thus requires active implementation and thought. Seen this way, religion provides license to *reject* tradition. This style of arguing, which at least since Clifford Geertz's early work (1971) has often been associated with modernity, has in fact been a recurrent feature of Islamic learning throughout Islamic history. Al-Shatibi (d. 1388) was perhaps the first Muslim scholar to create a catalogue of local traditions as a means of evaluating them on the basis of their proximity to the original intentions of religion.

While in some form or another the *shari'a* had to constantly elaborate some form of relation to local traditions, its relation to the science of *siyasa* was generally less clear. Although *siyasa* developed later than the *shari'a* as a distinct genre, its first evident genesis could be detected with the rise of the Ummayads, the first dynasty in Islam, centered in Damascus and thus removed from the early austere abode of Islam in Arabia, and more informed by the arts of governing in neighboring imperial centers, notably Byzantium. But the *siyasa* guidebooks remained for a long time purely "Machiavellian" (even though they precede him), and popular literature in Islamic history that espouses any understanding of state politics (for example *Kalilah wa Dimnah*) saw states to be hotbeds of conspiracies and intrigues rather than governed according to stable rules. In those tales, hope sometimes resided in a wise sovereign who occasionally triumphs, but not necessarily because of any necessary rule of nature. Conspiracy was typically seen to guide the state's basic mode of operation. The *siyasa* genre sought to study systematically the arts of intrigue, symbolism, conspiracy, and alliance so as to better guide the prince.

Only centuries later was that science brought to some form of orderliness with the institutional consolidation of the Ottoman Empire. In that case an initial attempt to expand and systematize state law, Sultan Mehmet II's (1432–1481) *Kanunname*, was only in the most vague way concerned with being based on the *shari'a*. Even less so were the later, more extensive legal reforms associated Sultan Sulayman the Magnificent (1494–1566), otherwise known as Sulayman al-Qanuni, "the lawgiver." The fact that both Mehmet II and Sulayman thought of the word *qanun* (and not *shari'a*) as the namesake of state law suggests that there was no expectation that the *shari'a* should inform even more *permanent* legal features of a political system, even though that system was an Islamic empire. This could be understood from the fact that their problems, especially Sulayman's, had little to do with the *shari'a*, and that furthermore the *shari'a* could not solve them since problems of state were not the *shari'a*'s traditional problems. Sulayman, who was also the first Ottoman sultan to end the standard practice of strangling all other potential claimants from among his brothers once he assumed the sultan's office, clearly thought that a system like the one he was governing required more permanent rules that relied less on accident and intrigue. And that stability was associated with what came to be known as *qanun*, not *shari'a*.

It is at that point that the notion of *qanun* assumes a different meaning than it had in its Greek origin or Albanian usage—as a "canon" of local customs. According to Richard Repp (1988:124–125), the Ottoman institutionalization of the notion of "Qanun" relied precisely in its usefulness as a different source of state authority than the *shari'a*. He identifies three main areas that over time came to define what a state (as opposed to social) *qanun* was:

1. *Qanun* organized state matters that were seen to lie clearly outside the scope of the *shari'a*, including taxation, land laws, and citizenship.
2. *Qanun* covered criminal law. (It is interesting here that the *hudud*, the supposed penal code of the *shari'a*, had no relationship to the *qanun* penal code; the latter expressed state rather than religion's sovereignty over bodies, life, and death.)
3. *Qanun* served as an expression of the Sultan's judgment. (The fact that the empire was Islamic in terms of its identity did not readily lead to the *shari'a* becoming its organizational legal principle, since everyone knew, in ways that are no longer clear to Muslims and non-Muslims alike today, that the *shari'a* had nothing to do with the state or its laws. Indeed, until today it is the word "qanun" or analogous words, and *not* *shari'a*, that is used to connote state legal codes in *all* Muslim countries.)

In this respect, calls during the twentieth century for making *shari'a* into a *qanun* in Muslim countries appear to be without historical precedent, and in fact to be confusing two categories in ways that earlier generations of Muslims had kept in separate conceptual compartments. These calls do have something to do with the nature of the modern state, namely its increased claims over society and the weakening of traditional (including religious) elites.

The reduction of the social scope of the *shari'a* that results from expanding the social scope of the state increasingly makes the state itself appear as a logical depository of a *shari'a* that now has fewer other autonomous social spaces into which to be deposited. Clarity here is essential, since any misunderstanding leads necessarily to catastrophe: When one asks the state to "apply" the *shari'a* one is in effect changing the whole purpose of the *shari'a*. It then transforms from being an art of disciplining the self, to a demand for disciplining others by the state.

But often this call reflects not a desire to impose any specific law on society than a general will to add ethical substance to governance itself.

This is evident in the Pew Research Center poll conducted in 2013 in 39 Muslim countries. The poll found that 70% of Muslims favor making the *shari'a* into the law of the land, even though further questions showed they were only committed to religiosity as a general guide to ethics, but had no detailed knowledge of the *shari'a* itself (Bulliett 2013:18). In fact, the only portion of the state *qanun* that is evidently influenced by *shari'a* in some Muslim countries is personal status law, covering family affairs, which had always been regulated by the *shari'a* even before being incorporated into state law. (A country like Lebanon, with a weak state and a fragmented society, remains closer to the historical reality in this regard: The state does not have its own laws on personal status matters. Marriage, divorce, inheritance, and so on are administered by each of the country's 18 sects according to its own rules.) But even in such cases, personal status law does not remain static just because it has supposed sure-footedness in the *shari'a*. Egypt for example amended its divorce law several times in modern history, the most sweeping being the amendment of 2000, which reversed all precedents by allowing women to divorce without the consent of their husbands. That change was claimed to be based on the *shari'a*, just like the previous law, which stipulated an exactly opposite rule (also previously claimed to be based on the same *shari'a*).

The other invitation for this modern tendency to confuse *qanun* and *shari'a* comes from above, that is, from states themselves. Political opportunism and effort of state elites to enlist the support of religious forces is evident in all such cases. Anwar Sadat's famous declaration in 1971 that the *shari'a* formed the basis of Egyptian law led until today to state law being contested by religious forces, even though the evolution of Egyptian state law until then had very little to do with any *shari'a*. The claim itself was completely baseless, though politically understandable in the context of Sadat's effort to enlist the support of Islamic political forces against his more serious enemies, then the left Nasserites. The same is essentially true of the misadventures of Sudanese politics since the early 1980s, where two military dictators sought to impose a "shari'a" they could not possibly have believed in as they were fighting a myriad of internal enemies. Ditto for Pakistan since the regime of Zia ul-Haq, a military dictator with no known prior religious credentials, who nonetheless for the sake of political expediency heralded the modern drive to "shariatize" (Shaikh 2009) state law.

The fact that until the late nineteenth century, and in most places still later, states that ruled Muslim lands did not think that their rule had much to do with enforcing any *shari'a* may be demonstrated by many examples.

One little-known but highly suggestive example is worth noting. In northern Iraq in 1872 the elders of the Yazidi sect, sometimes known to their detractors as "satan worshippers," presented to Ottoman authorities that were introducing military conscription a document containing 14 principles of their faith, all of which were meant to show why the Yazidis should be exempt from conscription. The document explained, among other things, that the Yazidis could not serve alongside Muslim soldiers, since the prayer of the latter includes a denunciation of Satan, which is a taboo in the Yazidi's faith. Remarkably from today's perspective, that argument was effective, and the Yazidis were allowed to pay *bedel-i askeri*, or a special tax in lieu of military service (Fuccaro 1999:3). It is hard to imagine a modern state that would allow someone to be exempted from military service because Satan plays a great role in his religion, but even at that late stage the Ottoman state still did not see itself as responsible for enforcing religious doctrine, including in this case even the basic Islamic denunciation of Satan. "Liberal" does not adequately describe such a state, since its approach was governed not so much by an explicit liberal ideology than by the very old expectation that each religion or sect is defined by its own religious authorities. And a corollary to that was the notion than a large world system, which the empire was, was in effect a constellation of communities each with its own norms and institutions. All these could stay in place, from the state's perspective, so long as no rebellion was conceived and so long that taxes (which the empire assessed on local communities or regions as a whole, not on individual households) were paid.

The example above obviously characterizes a system in which everyone was expected to belong to a faith, and the faith itself provided the basis of the autonomy of a community from the state. This may have had the effect of strengthening communal religious association, since that was a realm protected from government overreach. Now this equation suggests that religious affiliation, to the extent that it was a basic norm of social organization, limited governmental power, even within empires.

At the same time, as we see in the Yazidi case, religious affiliation *as the basis* of community autonomy from government may require the faithful to elaborate their faith more than would be necessary for it to be logically consistent. Two significant facts about the Yazidi articles of faith document from 1872 are, first, that it was unique, and second, that the aspects of faith that were highlighted were those that interfered most with ability to do military service. The document's historical uniqueness suggests that the community rarely saw it necessary to explain its faith to outsiders before, though now it had to do so since its continued autonomy from the state required it. Moreover, what the document reveals about the community's faith is not necessarily how it was actually practiced by all its members, only what the leaders of the faith expected of them, and then only those expectations that interfered with their ability to serve a distant state and in the process be taken away from their local community.

In this respect, while the principle of partial control entails relatively large communal autonomy, it may also at times, especially when states seek more control, lead the community to elaborate the reasons for its autonomy in more detail than was needed before. This explanatory process may somewhat alter its own religion: Aspects of belief that may have been marginal may become amplified if they serve the cause of continued autonomy. Religious faith, after all, is rarely expounded in a vacuum, but usually in relationship to a specific audience with specific demands or needs. Communal faith was one important means of facilitating the principle of partial control. That was so not simply because the message of the faith could always be adjusted to speak to new political powers on behalf of old local communities, but moreover because it reproduced the spokesmen of religion as alternative, albeit multiple, centers of authority to the state.

Thus a change in the *interpretation* of religion does not in itself change the role of religion as material in the architecture of autonomy. That role remains until we encounter modern states with new techniques of governance and little interest in old autonomies. From a modern political perspective, autonomy from its total control that had been partially supported by old religious systems becomes associated with stagnation, backwardness, and underdevelopment. The weakening of Islam as a discourse of social autonomy throughout the first three quarters of the twentieth century is evident not only in secular experiments as in Turkey, but also in states such as Egypt where the clerical establishment became more tied to the state. In that case they were expected to play a state-related political role rather than defend communal autonomies.

Religious ideas therefore do not survive in pristine forms, nor do they simply serve, as Max Weber thought, to orient the faithful in the world with the help of ideas that were permanent and independent of context. If an idea may be said to be alive in a sociological sense, then it lives on just as any living organism lives on, namely by transforming, adjusting, copulating with other ideas, maturing, and declining as it gives way to other ideas.

We can appreciate this point further if we observe a distinction between two social uses of religion: on the one hand, religion as *discourse*, in
the sense that it is surrounded by social consensus that it should be a reference point in all important matters; and on the other hand, religion as a
constellation of specific *ideas* that could be openly rejected or altered. The
abandonment, transformation, or reinterpretation of any religious idea
does not on its own invalidate the status of religion as social discourse,
and in fact it is often possible to alter ideas precisely because religious discourse is strong enough to withstand such alteration. In this way, the decline of any particular religious idea does not mean the decline of religion
itself as a *common* discourse. A discourse lives at a level above the minutiae
of its ideas, and in most realistic daily scenarios religious people tend to
explore particular ideas. Robert Wuthnow argues that the pursuit of specific ideas or interests is a means of embedding religion in reality, rather
than belaboring abstract discussions on the overall relevance of religion to
life (Wuthnow 2006; also Orsi 2006). We shall revisit this point in some
detail in the coming discussion of heteroglossia.

This means that even long-lasting social expectations of religion, such
as serving as a source of communal autonomy, could, given certain conditions, come under assault even from a religious perspective, or could become a marginal aspect of religious life itself. Ironically, calls for merging
shari'a and *qanun*, or alternatively eliminating any distance between state
and religion, could be understood not as marks of a strong religion but
rather of a strong state—so strong, in fact, that no meaningful social discourse (religiosity, ideology) or category (nation, ethnicity, tribe, civil society) could meaningfully live away from it. To the contrary, all discourses
and categories come to be seen as empowered further by association with
it—even though the state may be nothing more than a massive black hole
that sucks in all surrounding social energy, allowing nothing to escape its
deathly grasp.

Thus the pull of religion, in recent decades, toward the state even in
previously more secular Muslim countries, must be seen in a larger context: Other social categories and practices have also experienced a similar pull toward that same center of gravity. Bedouin life, for example, has
always been seen as one of the clearest manifestations of independence
from all authorities that were external to the world of the Bedouins. That
included even their own larger tribe, to which they owed an allegiance and
which owed them support as needed, but from which the Bedouin family
lived largely away except for the seasonal gatherings. Now when a modern

state, especially one lacking in any historical foundation, takes whatever social material it could find in order to build its legitimacy, it finds it useful to incorporate tribes into its legal and hierarchical structures. But in doing so it changes the nature of the tribe. This is evident in the case of Jordan (Massad 2001:66–73), as well as in the case of the emirates founded by the British along the western and southern coasts of the Persian Gulf. In the latter case, loose confederations were made into national entities with clear borders, and sheiks whose previous role involved little more than providing arbitration and presiding over ceremonies became dynasts with real executive power.

A tribe as a pillar of state is no longer a tribe in the older sense of the world, since in the state the tribe signifies permanent authority tied to office, whereas outside the state the tribe is the opposite: It is another space of social autonomy. (Max Weber's distinction between traditional and legal rational authority may seem to describe this situation, but it does not help us understand the nature of the transition. Here, the "traditional" may seem to have provided the working materials for the "rational." But to describe what happened as a transition to a "rational" order is really an exaggeration here. A marriage of convenience between incompatible categories of legitimacy produces no rationality.)

Here, more telling that Weber's categories of legitimacy are memoirs of those who observed those changes as they were taking place. In the Middle East, many of those memoirs date from the early part of the twentieth century. They show keen awareness of how colonial polities were distorting older social categories and practice. The prominent Iraqi public intellectual Ma'ruf al-Rasafi, who experienced both Ottoman and British rule, saw that the various ways by which the British were seeking to establish more control over society converged on weakening Islam, the one discourse that offered a shared cultural reference point for all inhabitants, including non-Muslims. Some of the colonial mechanisms mentioned by al-Rasafi in that regard include elevating "tribal law" to a higher status by the new state.[2] That process rigidified local codes that were previously neither clearly defined nor required state recognition. Rasafi also notes, quite correctly, that colonial powers were creating new and less rooted elites who depended on foreign powers—and in the case of Iraq that was true even after the country's formal independence in 1932 and until the overthrow of

---

2. This was in fact a common practice in the colonial system, and not simply in Muslim lands. See for, example, Mahmood Mamdani (1996).

the monarchy in 1958. Further, Rasafi notes how colonial administrators were busy dividing the populations of Iraq into various categories, ethnic as well as religious, so as to facilitate their own rule.

While as mentioned earlier the notion of "communities" was basic to the Ottoman system itself and that people were more familiar with that reality than with the novel idea of Iraqi nationalism, the British recognition of communities had different consequences and intentions than the Ottoman recognition. Under the Ottomans, recognition of communities meant recognition of autonomous niches, whereas under British colonial rule recognition of communities meant no such autonomy. Rather, in the colonial system, recognition of communities was tied to the project of founding a modern state that was expected to rule society more thoroughly, even though that state was entrusted to a deliberately weak monarchy. New research (Duri 2013) suggests that Iraqi elites themselves regarded foreign support as vital, given the new state's weak roots in domestic society.

The example of the founding of Iraq after World War I illustrates a more general pattern of the colonial period, in which new political uses for Islam came to the fore. It was clear that there was no way back to the Ottoman system, but the underlying idea of "Islam" as a namesake of an autonomous society began to be expressed in larger terms: "Islam" as a namesake of an independent civilization—independent, that is, from colonialism. In that form Islam became quickly mixed with anti-colonial nationalism, and proponents of national independence then devoted little time to differentiate the two, since little in reality depended on making such a distinction. If it was still familiar to everyone then that Islam signified social autonomy, there was no compelling need to do away with it from an anti-colonial, nationalist perspective, even when that perspective was completely secular in every other ways. This was in fact the most typical story throughout the Muslim world as it came under the sway of Western colonialism.

Turkey was an exception for a while, in the sense that a clear distinction was made in the 1920s between secular nationalism and religion. But that difference was made only after the establishment of an independent Turkish republic, which was unique in the Muslim world not so much because it was secular as because it was *independent*. This is evident from the fact that Turkey's triumph over Western plans to dismember it between 1918 and 1922 signaled a praiseworthy accomplishment for many Muslim intellectuals around the world, even after Atatürk's anti-clerical credentials became clear. But in general and apart from the case of early modern Turkey, there was no compelling need in the rest of the Muslim world to make a clear distinction between religiosity and secularity, when one wanted to use one or the other as expressions of resistance to colonialism.

In this sense we can understand why someone like Rasafi, for example, can be both derisive of Iraqi nationalism and its defender at the same time. He is derisive of it because it has no historical basis and only serves the interests of foreign powers in erecting a separate "nation," in a region where that "nation" was neither distinct from its larger environment nor had itself called itself into being. The Islamicate character of that larger environment is what this new nationalism seem designed to do away with. On the other hand, that otherwise bogus nationalism itself possessed— at least in theory—a right to self-determination. That meant that the discourse of nationalism, even if it served colonial interests against larger Islamicate ideas, also provided a basis for eventual liberation from colonial rule, as well as for undermining the colonial project of dividing Iraqi society itself for the sake of effectively ruling it by forces that have no social roots in it.

In this sense, Islam complemented this understanding of nationalism, but from a broader perspective. It too offered a discourse of social integration that could in theory stand in the way of colonial population categories. At the same time, Islam seemed to offer a more historically rooted model of social autonomy than nationalism—which until then had existed only as an idea rather than a real historical practice with its own institutions. So Rasafi's standpoint, and that is perhaps what made him into a popular public intellectual, was typical: Islam meant independence, clearly, and so did nationalism, but the latter only up to a point. Colonial powers were interested in nationalism because they wanted to divide into meaningless "countries" a region that had always operated as a continuous Islamicate environment. At the same time colonial powers were also more interested in "minorities" and other categories within such created nations, because the only way they could rule such "nations" was by accentuating separation and competition among communities that, with the modern state, were being deprived of the only asset that had made them into communities before, which was their *autonomy*. Thus for Rasafi, the concept of an Iraqi nation may serve as a good discourse against colonialism *only* if it is qualified: Such nationalism should not contradict larger commitments to Arabism or Islam. The former incorporated local nationalism back into the regional realm of which "Iraq" was simply an integral rather than separate part; and the latter pointed this new nation, not yet independent in any meaningful way, to a model of communal autonomy in a global system whose experience had not faded away from memory. (Later public intellectuals saw it as their role to keep that memory alive in the public sphere, long after the passing of people like Rasafi and his generation of transitional intellectuals.)

The modern era therefore meant almost everywhere that Islam would be increasingly elaborated in the context of colonial struggles. However, one could still identify many local and even some regional struggles, where colonial effects were still relatively distant, in which case Islamic reform movements arose against older Islamic structures of power rather than against colonialism. An important example here, perhaps one of the last in which we see region-wide Islamic movements whose discourse is not yet shaped by the gravity of a colonial encounter, is in early 19th century West Africa. There we do witness a number of Islamic movements, at the center of which being Uthman Dan Fodio's jihad in what is now Northern Nigeria. That movement defined the role of Islam in society in ways that highlighted the role of the learned communities and education in general, sought to promote orthodoxy by "purifying" Islam (that is to say, distinguishing it more from local animistic religions), and gained popularity by protecting local populations from abuses, including heavy taxation, by older Muslim authorities. But apart from these exceptions, the learned Muslim elites in the course of the nineteenth century were becoming increasingly concerned with the more pressing specter of colonialism. And here the global record varies little, which is another way to say that when we speak of political dimensions, the only universal common in the modern career of Islam was a universal exposure to defeat and domination by Western powers. "Islam" therefore appeared vulnerable only because all Islamicate populations appeared vulnerable.

In this connection it seemed to make little difference whether a Muslim country was "modernizing" or not. The Egyptian state of the nineteenth century, at some point the most promising modernist project in the entire Muslim world—far more advanced than Japan on the eve of the Meiji restoration—lost its independence to British colonialism shortly before the advent of the twentieth century. Just a quarter century before the British direct takeover of Egypt, the Mughal state in Northern India, then little more than a shell of its former self, was formally dissolved (also by the British, whose rule saw the decimation of India's contribution to world economy from nearly 25% to less than 4% by the time of independence

(Maddison 2006)). The twentieth century began with the collapse and dismemberment of the Ottoman state, by then the largest and longest enduring Islamicate state. By the 1920s almost the entire Muslim World was
under some kind of European rule, usually British or French, but also
Russian, German, Spanish, and Dutch.

That reality gave Islam a new role as one discourse, among others, that
could lend itself to aspirations of national liberation. The situation was
of course different in parts of the Muslim world that were very marginal
or had historically known only ephemeral states at best, such as the Arab
side of the Persian Gulf region and central Arabia. While in modern times
those territories witnessed puritanical movements, no states existed into
which the puritanical interpretation of Islam could be deposited, and in
any case no stable pre-colonial state traditions that could have facilitated
that imagination existed in those desolate and sparsely populated territories. Nearby exceptions, such as Oman, Hijaz, or Yemen, were not the sorts
of entities that could easily facilitate the cause of puritanism. Oman had
long been integrated into the long-distance maritime trade of the Indian
Ocean; Hijaz, while not formally a state, possessed some enduring administrative structures and housed global scholarly networks that catered
to its spiritual prestige as the domain of the holy places and pilgrimage
destination; and Yemen had been a long-standing but relatively isolated
polity with its own traditions. All three remained internally resistant to
puritanical movements, including Hijaz, until its forcible takeover by the
Saudis in 1924–1925.

In this connection, Khaldoun al-Naqeeb (1990) identified the pre-
eighteenth-century political economy of the Gulf as a "natural economy,"
because all its components, including long-distance trade across the
Indian Ocean, lacked the services and supervision of a state apparatus.
Al-Naqeeb argued that such a natural economy was eventually destroyed
by British imperialism, which promoted new dynasties and authoritarian,
rentier states. Such states thus had to be run as official or unofficial pro-
tectorates. None of them were informed by any *familiar* Islamic tradition
of government, and none even claimed to pursue such a project, of course
with the exception of Saudi Arabia—a new state lacking any historical
precedent. Rather, the new styles of governing (and here Saudi Arabia is
less of an exception) consisted of an *étatisation* of tribal ethics, which in
the case of Saudi Arabia was mixed with an acknowledged guiding role
of the Wahhabi clergy. From the moment of their founding, such polities required Western protection, which served as an *alternative* to their

integration into the larger region in which they lived. Saudi Arabia's claim to be embodying an original or more pure form of Islam was not enough to ensure its survival without non-Islamic guarantors (originally British, later US).

We are hard pressed to witness a complete *étatisation* of society anywhere in the Muslim world, even in places like Iraq where the public sector, employing more than a third of the labor force, came to dominate economic life by the 1970s (Batatu 1978). Yet, the large size of any state does not inoculate it against being a stranger to society, and long-enduring authoritarian traditions seem to confirm that strangeness. In the Arab world prior to 2011, with few exceptions like Lebanon or to a certain extent Morocco, the only political theaters that could be contested were those not connected directly to running the nation state: boards of professional syndicates; student governments; and, occasionally, municipal elections. The fortunes of most people depended on familiar and trusted networks, which operated away from the sight and regulation of states that were only partially informed of the complexity of their own society (Singerman 1996; Ayubi 1996; Anderson 1987). The parasitic nature of the state could only be confirmed by its behavior, governed as it was more by conspiratorial than strategic thinking. That reality tended to be the case even in relatively wealthy states, like Saudi Arabia or Iraq before its wars, where the state expanded into society through a mixture of repression and patronage, both facilitated by oil revenue—which in those cases was little more than an accidental advantage landing in the hands of state elites.

In other places, where state elites did not have the unique advantage of sudden income, to various degrees the historical pattern of partial control held: The state continued to be regarded only as one actor among many in society, and the state knew that fact even as it claimed otherwise.[3] States that accepted this reality, such as Yemen until its latest civil war, survived in some form, and those that did not, such as Somalia under Ziad Berri or Afghanistan under Hafizullah Amin, did not.

Historically, the principle of partial control involved predictable structures, many of which are considered by some prominent sociologists to be antithetical to a common sociological vision of modernity that highlights

---

3. During a visit to Georgetown University (November 2002), former prime minister of Yemen Abdolkarim Al-Eryani freely acknowledged that Yemeni tribes tend to regard the Yemeni state as just another tribe, albeit one with more resources, but nonetheless one with which they negotiate in the same reciprocal way tribes negotiate with each other.

the centrality of states to social transformation (Giddens 1991). Yet, the survival of patterns of partial control (even without the memory of it or the institutions that were associated with it) may be evident in the persistence of highly repressive structures—precisely the kinds that Michel Foucault has associated with incomplete ("premodern") power. One of the most sustained explorations of the principle of partial control in Islamic history is Roy Mottahedeh's (1980) study of the Buyid, a dynasty that assumed control of Persia and Iraq during the tenth through eleventh centuries. The image of that society provided by Mottahedeh is one of natural fragmentation into status, occupational, clan, and other types of groups. Such a society strove not for the kind of governance that provided it with unity, but one that provided a semblance of general order and legitimate arbitration.

As a rule, the preeminent expectation from being governed was to insure what we today may erroneously call "law and order," although the historical name is more telling: "justice." The historical notion of "justice" had a meaning appropriate for a society accustomed to partial rather than total controls. As Mottahedeh explains it, "justice" meant not so much applying the "law" as *balancing* various interests, so that none of them would impose itself upon the others. (That idea of "justice," we should always remember these days, had nothing to do with any *shari'a*.) That conception of justice supposes a specific nature of governing. That is, far from embodying society or representing its collective mission, as it would be under nationalism at a later stage, the Buyid state could in effect only be rule over society by *outsiders*. That is because in a fragmented society that saw its fragmentation as natural and necessary rather than an obstacle to be overcome, the balancing of various interests and conflicts could only be performed by an arbitrator whose impartiality was most guaranteed by his status as an outsider vis-à-vis all concerned groups.

This process of arbitrating "society" with the help of one's outsider status, as is well known, was typical in Islamic political history. In fact in the very first real Islamic community, that of Medina, we already see the onset of this dynamic, namely in how a transtribal *umma* was formed by an outsider, namely Muhammad, then himself a stranger to Medina. Muhammad succeeded brilliantly in Medina, where the conflictual tribes, needing common adjudication, all expressed faith in Islam before even seeing the prophet, who at that point had lost all prospects in his own home town of Mecca. In other words, a transtribal society could be built only by someone with an ideology transcendent of the particularities of any specific tribe, and a personal genealogy that was distant enough from theirs and that of their adversaries alike.

Indeed, the success of early Islam consisted to a great extent in its ability to graft a common spiritual language upon all transtribal, voluntary public spaces of the pre-Islamic era in Arabia. All pre-Islamic institutions aimed at transtribal peace, trade, and civic life, such as the *haram* of Mecca, the pilgrimage, and the sacred months, were simply absorbed into Islam. Even more remarkably, Islam incorporated such common spaces without elaborating a clear doctrine of a common state. The contemporary Islamists' claim to the contrary lack any foundation: Muhammad left no instructions on an Islamic state, and the Qur'an says virtually nothing about such an institution, even as both sources provide profuse advice on the nature of the virtuous community and the psychological aptitude of the faithful individual.

This combination, namely unifying the institutions of public life under a common religious discourse but leaving the question of government open, corresponded to a society that was familiar with the principle of partial control, had already developed an institutional life corresponding to it, and was in need only of a mechanism of impartial arbitration to guarantee its functioning. Beyond that, there is no evidence anywhere in early Islamic history that a "state" as such or total control of society and panoramic supervision of social life was anyone's intention. And even at later stages, historical documents suggest that the role of the state in most people's lives remained limited. In his detailed study of the Geniza documents, which provided one of the most extensive references to daily life in the medieval Muslim World, Shelomo Dov Goitein finds that while their presence was certainly felt, " . . . in general, we do not find that people expect to receive directives or help from their governments, except for legal protection and defense against enemies and pirates, nor are there many complaints against excessive taxation or direct wrongs" (Goitein 1:267).

This reality needs to be seen in the context of medieval Islamic political philosophy, which with few exceptions such as Farabi's purely idealistic conception of the state, tended to regard the state as a body that operated according to a logic that was quite distinct from that of ordinary civic culture (Bamyeh 2009). Still, we are aware of the centrality that Shi'a thought originally gave to the idea of a guiding imamate (even though the notion is practically abandoned after the twelfth imam in twelver Shi'sm and is transformed into a concept of cultural guidance for the Ismailis after the eleventh century). We are also familiar with some Sunni theologians' defense of the idea of rulership over the *umma* as a necessary protection against dissension into chaos, meaning, as Ibn Taymiyya and also Ali before him famously stated, an unjust ruler is preferable to no ruler at all. But this stance confirms the point, namely that expectations from state rulers were minimal given the reality of a self-organized society. That reality implied that the ruler would be necessary only so as a guard against possible dissension into chaos. This, in turn, could be done by a just or unjust ruler. But the ruler himself was not expected to bring society into being.

The remarkable persistence of this point of view among much of the Muslim learned communities was attested to in the Arab uprisings in 2011, about which the learned men of religion were frequently asked to issue appropriate *fatwas*. The conservative elements, which typically opposed the uprisings and sided with the old regimes, gave a reasoning that upheld what they regarded to be a long-established view among the ʿulama on the unadvisability of rebellion, even to correct injustice. Typical of those is the late Muhammad Said Ramadan al-Bouti of Syria, a well-established scholar whose opposition to the rebellion against the regime of Bashar al-Asad cost him his life. What was interesting about al-Bouti's position was his reasoning, which he disseminated broadly through recorded video messages. Al-Bouti argued that a ruler must be accepted *not* because he was just; even an unjust ruler must be tolerated, so long as he stands in the way of the greater evil of *fitnah*—the kind of social strife whose consequences were unpredictable. In other words, the conservative view among the ʿulama did not so much support rulers as posit predictability as the higher value.

The traditional conservative Islamic learning has always favored a pragmatic acceptance of the devil you know, so long as that devil refrained from openly fighting the faith. Political authority (unlike the authority of "knowledge," namely that of the religious establishment), could indeed be unjust, even if based on Islam. From that point of view, what was expected of political authority consisted of little more than the prevention of civil war, and that was usually good enough. In the absence of civil war, other politics, including the politics of knowledge, those of Sufi orders, guilds, urban notables, tribes, and so on, could continue to elaborate themselves as the natural and more intimate sources of guidance for most ordinary Muslims. Some of these institutions, such as the guilds between the ninth and nineteenth centuries in the Levant and Egypt, had their own legal systems that regulated members' rights, duties, and penalties. Those were applied within the guild and according to its rulers, rather than according to state law. As autonomous societies, guilds, just like Sufi orders, could in times of crisis (for instance, during the Crusades), also produce their own militias that took part in the fight against invaders.

An even clearer picture of the rules governing this system of partial control is evident from Michael Gilsenan's (1996:95–115) study of the relation of lords and sheiks in north Lebanon. The former ruled the feudal system and exercised political power, whereas the latter were local religious authorities but held little wealth and no political office. Gilsenan shows that a basic expectation in that environment was that the lords' business consisted precisely of committing injustice, and that no one thought that that could be changed, since that was the nature of the position of the lord. A virtuous person becoming lord did not change that eternal reality, because his virtue will soon be corrupted by the evil which defines the oppressive nature of the position he occupies. This is quite close to the point made by Mottahedeh on another Muslim society almost a thousand years earlier, where the expectation was that an office of state would change the psyche of the person who occupies it more so than that office would itself be changed if occupied by a virtuous character. In the case examined by Gilsenan, the expected moral transformation brought about by becoming a lord is even more extreme. A lord became such only if he was a self-seeking monopolizer and usurper, violent and capable of showing ferocity[4].

That expectation from local lordship suggests that higher levels of power (except for god, who reverses things), could only do more of the same rather than be saviors of some sort. The old tradition of partial control was based not simply on the sheer difficulty of full control, but also on a moral formula that suspected distant political power to be defined by an irredeemable pollution. The moral formula could be translated into this philosophy of life: by putting someone pure into a place that is polluted, we would more pollute the person than purify the place. Thus in addition to practical difficulties of full control, preference for partial control was also associated with an old moral idea on the character of purity and pollution. That idea seemed verified by dearth of memory of its opposite, and cumulative records that only confirmed it.

On the other hand, as Gilsenan's study shows, this underlying logic also provides the sheiks with their social role. They are a category that

---

4. Individuals from the same region (Akkar) mentioned to me that the lords used to claim the right to possess the bride of any local groom on her wedding night.

represents social virtue, but they do not and cannot claim worldly power, which is reserved for the lords. Sheiks, however, play a crucial role in alleviating the eternal gloom of the picture by clarifying how there are different modes of power, of which worldly power is only one. Their role in society is to show that there are at least two kinds of power: spiritual and worldly. The sheiks claim the former, the lords the latter. Both lords and sheiks come to *agree* on this division of labor. The lords sustain the sheiks as spiritual authority, and show otherwise needless supplication in their presence—in effect giving them symbolic power—in exchange for the latter also accepting the same equation that the lords had already accepted, namely that spiritual and worldly powers exist in separate spheres to do different tasks, and that they cannot possibly be folded together.

Thus in this case we have, in essence, an effective separation of religion and state, without anyone needing to claim this to be the case, nor to have to go through the needless trouble of the usual acrimonies associated with such a proposition. But this separation means something very different from what it means from a modern secular point of view. It means that religion must stay away from the state because religion is pure and the state is corrupt; that mixing the two will corrupt religion more than purify the state. Some strands within the modern Islamic revival have been gravitating toward this point (Al-Sayyid 2013). But in general, that old position was rooted in seeing Islam as more universal than the state—the idea of *Dar al-Islam* itself being an expression of that universal conception of the world: For a thousand years already, *Dar al-Islam* was much larger, geographically speaking, than any Muslim state.

That there were occasional calls for strong authority in Islamic history, therefore, must be seen in the context of periods of turmoil and uncertainty, as those characterizing Ibn Taymiyya's times, where the argument was still made that injustice was preferable to civil war or social disintegration. But the argument was never about the virtuous nature of state authoritarianism. Rather, the traditionalist perspective saw as always that moral ideas were the purview of the learned communities. Intellectual arguments in Islamic political philosophy about the necessity of fusing temporal and spiritual authority, most systematically advocated by Farabi, were introduced more as theoretical propositions—in Farabi's case after the.model of Plato's *Republic*—rather than as guides for any realistic political program.

Indeed, Islamic states had historically little reason to violate the principle of partial control not only because of the enormous costs of doing

so, but because the very diffusion of Islamic culture itself led to the evolution of autonomous institutions and spaces that surrounded themselves
by ethos of immunity from government entry. One could get a measure of
their autonomy from the outcry following Shah Naser al-Din's violation of
the Abdul Azim sanctuary near Teheran in 1892 in order to arrest and de-
port the famous reformer Jamal al-Din al-Afghani, who for seven months
managed to use the sanctuary as a relatively free environment from which
to denounce the Shah to large audiences. That event is documented in the
sources as so exceptional that it could not go unpunished: Shortly there-
after Naser al-Din was assassinated by a follower of Afghani.

Sanctuaries, certain areas of public life carved out as autonomous
spaces, did not only consist of physical forms. Well-known is the economic
principle of *waqf* discussed earlier, which had supported autonomous institutions until it was undermined by modern states. Less discussed spaces
signaling even more autonomy include the institution of the *harem*, usually seen from today's perspective to exemplify the highest form of patriarchal prerogative, and not as an expression of an unwavering right
to privacy. Almost all literature on the *harem* focuses on either the most
outlandish expressions of that institution, usually associated with sultans'
households, its connection to wealth and status, and its role as a patriarchal instrument. The history of the *harem*, which dates to pre-Islamic
times and whose earlier history is associated with non-Islamic empires
as well, provides material for a discussion too vast to be covered here adequately. But in so far as techniques of partial control are concerned, it is
important to consider the overlooked role of the *harem* institution as perhaps the most successful instrument of privacy in history. The etymology
of the word connotes a space that is forbidden: this has usually been understood to apply to the space occupied by the women of the household,
although the *harem* could be any area that outsiders cannot enter, *regardless*
of their status or power.

This institution was therefore highly useful for all classes in society,
although as Leila Ahmed argues, only the upper classes were able to give
it an "architectural expression," whereby it was "designed to be the pleas-
antest part of the house, not just because the women spent most of their
lives there but also because the master spent most of his time there when
at home" (Ahmed 1993:117). The *harem* therefore did not simply signify a
form of sexual segregation that had its own end, nor could it only be explained as a way of employing masculinity and femininity as organizing
principles of public and private sphere—although those elements were

certainly basic to its definition. But why important organizing principles of public and private life were so organized requires us to take the question a step beyond the question of gender, since the focus on gender alone gives us in the final analysis nothing more than the tautological explanation that segregation was an expression of gender. And while of course it was, underlying the question of gender was the *harem*'s unusual effectiveness in safeguarding privacy and in the process, safeguarding the family itself as an autonomous space in society.

In general, the traditional Islamic state found itself sharing control over the public sphere with a diversity of groups and counter-principles, each with its own distinctive organizational character and logic. These groups and principles consisted of cross-cleavages of various interests and propositions, each with a definite social purview and form of relation to other groups in public life. Until the modern period, significant social categories that ensured the impossibility of total control by a central state included tribes, millets, families, urban notables (*a'yan*), sufi orders, merchants, professional guilds, and the educational networks of the learned communities. Islam itself was elaborated by those groups according to their needs, albeit in an intercommunicative environment characterized by a good deal of choice. The basic social expectation that Islam itself should be defined by its scholars, who lived closer to the people in any case, rather than by the more distant rulers, already confronted the 'Abbasids at the height of their power, namely during the famous episode known as the *mihna* (833–848 c.e.). During that episode, the caliph attempted to impose a single orthodoxy regarding the otherwise obscure theological question on the createdness of the Qur'an. That experiment was ultimately abandoned after stiff resistance, led by among others Ahmad Ibn Hanbal, who asserted the authority of the learned men in questions of faith.

In more recent literature on the history of civil society in the Muslim world, the *mihna* episode is sometimes cited as a foundational tale (Kelsay 2002; Eickelman and Anderson 1999). But this interpretation makes sense only if we understand "civil society" from the point of view of Islamic rather than European history: Civil society was the sum total of a constellation of ideas and practices, armed with institutions corresponding to them, that regarded collective social life to be controlled only in partial and thus always negotiated ways. Of course, no one elaborated an explicit theory of "partial control" as the governing principle of collective life, since it was always easier and more comprehensible to say that the governing principle was simply: "Islam."

Free movement

Corollary to the principle of partial control was a principle of free movement of pilgrims, adventurers, merchants, and various communities throughout the massive *Dar al-Islam*, in spite of the division of the Islamic world between various political centers of powers for most of its history. Travel eased the concentration of demographic pressures in resource-poor areas, built channels of communication between intellectual communities, provided for a distinct global civil society forged across the great urban centers (nominally under the jurisdiction of different sovereigns), and endowed especially the cities with a vibrant multiethnic fabric. *One Thousand and One Nights* may be regarded as one great literary expression of the principle of free movement: The protagonists there are more often on the road from one destination to another than at home. The reality of free movement is evident in the documented histories of scholarly communication within the Muslim world. Virtually all influential interpretive approaches to Islam established themselves in global circuits, and the dissemination of their teachings entailed the building of networks of learning, for which travel was essential. That was true of all Sufi orders and the more orthodox schools of *fiqh* alike, and the expectation of travel was typical of scholarly life in general.

The same is true of economic histories. Focusing on the Mediterranean, Goitein (1967–1993, 1:42) mentions that a "journey from Spain to Egypt or from Marseilles to the Levant was a humdrum experience, about which a seasoned traveler would not waste a word. Commuting regularly between Tunisia or Sicily or even Spain and the eastern shores of the Mediterranean was nothing exceptional." He further adds: "Mediterranean man in the Midde Ages was an impassioned and preserving traveler . . . the discomfort and insecurity involved in [travel] were insufficient to discourage travel necessary for administrative, business, or social needs" (1967–1993, 1:273–274).

The centrality of long-distance trade to wealth generation in the Muslim world was one of the defining characteristics of its economy from its earliest point. This is exemplified in one measure by the fact that in addition to illness, travel is the only other ground listed in the Qur'an for exemption from the religious requirement of fasting during the month of Ramadan. And at least one classic source of Islamic economic ethics, al-Hubayshi's fourteenth-century compendium *al-Baraka fi Fadl al-Sa'y wa al-Haraka*, highlights the metaphor of "movement" as the basic character of all economic activity. Geography, as a science of movement, was one of the first sciences established as a distinct genre among the Islamicate learned communities. More than two dozen classic geographic compendia, and countless lesser ones, describing roads, destinations, and manners of distant peoples survive in some form from the early and medieval periods. In more general terms, movement as a basic norm of religious and economic life meant that "borders," which may have meant much to sovereigns, would be given as little attention as possible by everyone else within *Dar al-Islam*. First, a strong idea of "borders," as would be attempted by nation-states, was not compatible with the notion of a global *umma* whose domain was defined more by ideational than political reach. There never developed a clear association in which the latter helped the former by necessity. Ibn Battuta's denunciation of attempts by Muslim rulers of his time to disrupt trade shows the priority he assigned to free movement, which was the basic form through which Islam itself spread into territories without the help of any Islamic state—for example southeast Asia or west Africa.

Just as with the principle of partial control, the principle of free movement originated out of dynamics having little to do with the foresight or planning of governments and sovereigns. It emerged rather out of other realities and dynamics: 1) the historical fact that the Muslim world in effect inherited the territorial space of older world systems; 2) a sociological dynamic that lends conversion to Islam the character of being a way to surround connections with global trade partners with a binding ethical cosmos, most notably in central Africa and Southeast Asia; and 3) a connective cosmopolitan urbanity, through which Islam itself appeared as primarily an urban religion appealing most immediately, although of course not exclusively, to the commercial urban classes (Muhammad himself being part of that class before revelation).

Religion therefore expressed rather than simply created global social realities. The clearest examples here may be drawn from early histories of conversion to Islam in Africa (e.g., Robinson 2004), where to become a "Muslim" was an expression of the fact that one belonged to a merchant class defined by its global connections. The further expansion of Islam into other social classes also relied on this awareness of global connectivity, as global schools within both Islamic orthodoxy and Sufism sought everywhere either to "correct" local Islamic practice or, conversely, adjust Islam to other local beliefs. Of course, the notion that Islam is one expression of global connectedness never meant that Islam meant the same thing to all Muslims, as we will see more clearly in the next section. In fact, there never existed good mechanisms to ensure that kind of unity of perspective, and in any case global religion, as one way of personally *feeling* global effects, highlighted more than anything else the expression of a Muslim *identity*.

Yet, it must be noted that if global religion is one way of expressing global connectedness, this same religion could under different conditions express precisely the opposite fact: that one is *excluded* from a larger system. This is most evident today in how Islam in Europe in particular is often discussed as a way by which a community of immigrants "ghettoizes" itself amidst a surrounding host society. This point of view is quite common, and one finds it expressed not only by xenophobes but also by well-meaning liberal observers and politicians (e.g., Schwan 2008). However, the "ghettoization" thesis puts the issue on its head. The historical perspective suggests that a religion that was integral to a global system should also serve as one cultural expression of that system. It could hardly be thought of to have encouraged ghettoization. The historical "ghettos," after all, tended to be impositions by external players and not free choices of the ghettoized populations. Today's "ghettos" operate likewise, although they are not imposed by legal orders. European Muslim "ghettos" today emerge out of exclusions enacted on behalf of a larger host society, rather than out of the dynamics of religious life. In Europe today it is easy to see how the questionable self-ghettoization of Muslim communities (Bade and Finke 2010; Jouili 2015), may be more easily traced to exclusions of especially the lower classes of such communities from various economic, educational, and social opportunities. In either case, religion may be expressing rather than creating an already existing reality. If a global religion could for centuries express the reality of connectivity, at other times it may express the reality of exclusion. In the contemporary European case, religion may appear to "cause" ghettoization only because immigrants, especially less educated ones, who are already excluded will tend to express their exclusion in terms that are either familiar to them, or at least that are used by others to justify excluding. As Ferruh Yilmaz (2012) demonstrates, in contemporary Europe terms of exclusion only in recent times began to highlight culture (including religion) rather than economics as compelling reasons to exclude someone. Thus in this case it may appear that religion encourages ghettoization, where in effect it only expresses it. The formula follows: The more one is excluded on the basis of religion, the more likely that religion will become a salient feature of one's identity. One *becomes* what one is regarded to be.

Apart from the factors mentioned above, the principle of free movement by its nature fostered the further evolution of networks that became over time engraved in the fabric of deep reality. One of these was common educational and mannerist expectations, which allowed for the easy circulation of at least the elites. The *rihla*, or travel narrative, emerged as a distinct genre in Islamic history, including countless great and small collections. The most famous and extensive of such travels, notably that of the fourteenth-century Ibn Battuta, shows not simply the massive geographic extent of *Dar al-Islam* but also the unusual ability of learned men in particular to be at home everywhere in that world. For example, trained as a judge in Morocco, Ibn Battuta could without any further training find employment as a judge as far away as India. Other travelers, whose recorded narratives became more numerous by the sixth century of Islam, reveal how travel itself was a process by which elements of social experience are mixed, so that the traveler could in the same voyage act sometimes as a merchant, at another time as a pilgrim, or an adventurer, or a paramour.

Free movement, stimulated as it was by the centrality of long-distance trade to the economy of *Dar al-Islam* and the religious requirement of pilgrimage (and the two often went hand in hand), had important sociological outcomes as one would expect. One of the most enduring of those was the creation of a global civil society maintained through various networks connecting the great urban centers of the Islamic world. Many of such networks forged together the learned communities, in essence creating a world civilization connected more by lateral social networks than hierarchical command centers (Lapidus 2002; Voll 1994b; Salvatore 2016). Those established global spaces for the dissemination of discourses and debates in philosophy, the sciences, mathematics, ethics, legal rules, and theology. Another type of network connected merchant cultures, in ways that were both extraordinarily complex yet characterized by predictability and governed by common ethos and expectations.

The efforts of historians have helped shed more light on patterns of connection among merchant and scholarly communities in the Islamic world (e.g., Goitein 1967–1993; Abu-Lughod 1989; Doumani 1995; Fawaz 1983). Some of these studies focus on macro-processes and structures, while others attempt to uncover larger dynamics of connectivity out of a detailed focus on a specific local setting. Some historians (e.g., Faroqhi 1994) emphasize the role of imperial governments in organizing such collective ventures as pilgrimage caravans. This does not however contradict the fact that free movement was organized by voluntary associations in other cases, nor does it suggest that they would have been impossible without governmental effort. Particularly in the case of pilgrimage caravans, governments obviously sought legitimacy out of supporting the venture. Richard Bulliet has argued that aspiring Muslim rulers who lacked the necessary credentials to be called "caliph" found that they could accumulate significant compensatory prestige by claiming that they were facilitators of pilgrimage and its sites. According to him, Saladin, the first non-caliph to adopt the term *Khadim al-Haramain* ("Servitor of the Two Holy Places"), was also associated with the evolution of the status of Mecca as a magnet for global scholarly communities, a process that ultimately resulted in that "pilgrimage to Mecca replaced the caliphate as the central unifying entity in Islam" (Bulliet 2013:8).

Historical literature shows the degree of institutionalization of merchant and scholarly networks. The merchant communities used caravans; caravanseries; the practice of using an agent to represent a merchant in distant lands; risk pooling societies (i.e., precursors to the modern "company"); and credit and insurance arrangements. The knowledge communities developed instruments of cultural capital, notably certificates (*ijaza*) that spelled out what a person has learned, from whom, and the branch of knowledge he may be entrusted to teach. The validity of an *ijaza* depended naturally on the reputation of the scholar issuing it, as well as on his location in a global scholarly network.

Throughout the Islamicate world, trade routes obviously benefited from conditions of political stability and security. But such routes were not dependent on rulers possessing any quality other than willingness to respect free movement. In fact, the practical inescapability of the principle of free movement in an urban-centered Islamic world whose wealth was derived substantially from trade ensured the demise of any political system that sought to suffocate it. The comments of Ibn Battuta on the Mongol invasion of Mesopotamia (Ibn Battuta 1969, 3:23–24) are significant here, because they depart from the usual pattern of supporting Muslim rulers fighting infidels. Rather, Ibn Battuta blames the invasion directly on efforts of Muslim rulers in Iraq and Persia to disrupt trade routes.

There was of course nothing specifically "Islamic" about trade and its routes, only the addition of a common ethical and ideational cosmos to an already old idea of free movement. In the same way that Islamicate empires inherited older global trade routes, Mongols did the same for a while as they came to dominate much of *Dar al-Islam*, and the eventual Portuguese, Dutch, and English powers grafted themselves upon older routes in that same system, while nourishing new ones. In this respect, it becomes possible to suggest that the later European idea of "free trade" signified a *retreat* from the older idea of free movement. For in the notion of "free trade," as opposed to "free movement," the focus turns away from the people to the *objects* that travel. This shift occasions the rise of governments that were more interested in policing populations, as Foucault shows us, and thus would be expected to be friendlier to the freedom of things than to that of people. The rise of European powers to the center of the global system was associated with the rise of more coercive drives within that system (Abu-Lughod 1989:362). That was probably because European powers had not developed by then the sorts of global civic networks that had provided connective civilizational service in Islamicate history, with little need for coercion. Until then, global civilization seemed to emerge atop foundations built through the free movements of all things and peoples, and not just of economic assets.

Heteroglossia

Islam has frequently been described as a house of harmony or at least well-integrated social order (e.g., Watt 1961). This view, held by many sympathetic observers, is likewise often held by detractors, who wish to highlight the conformity and authoritarianism that for them define the essence of Islam. In practice, however, Islam operated in the spiritual, legal, moral, and political realms as a highly hybrid and varied practice. The Sunni orthodoxy of mainstream Islam, which itself consisted of an assortment of schools and interpretive arts, had to live with a more customary Islam (Kurzman 1998) that characterized less orthodox practices through which Islam managed to maintain relevance to the pragmatics of everyday life.

That Islam was historically and is in the present a very diverse practice is well-known to any serious student of the faith. This point itself is hardly original, although in our age of ignorance, in the West and in the East, it requires being repeated until finally heard. In this repetition here, I would like to add a term that may help clarify the point, since the point here is not that "difference" should be "celebrated," only that it is an unavoidable sociological fact, produced by life itself, everywhere and at all times.

I propose to capturethis basic property of a sociology of Islam in the term "heteroglossia" (rather than "diversity," for reasons that should become clear shortly). The term "heteroglossia" was coined in the 1930s by the Russian literary scholar Mikhail Bakhtin, who used it to analyze the way by which a single literary work (usually a realist novel) habituated multiple voices originating in different social standpoints. There are two ways in which this formulation may be expanded to explain the sociology of any discourse that, like a novel, appears singular (such as "my religion"). The first concerns a distinction between "heteroglossia" and "diversity," the second the social unconscious of religion.

Heteroglossia is not simple "diversity" in the sense that the community of believers does not regard itself as diverse as the analyst may see it to be. As Bakhtin outlines it, voices in the novel inhabit the same narrative space, when in effect they originate from a diversity of social locations and interests. "Diversity," the term to which we are more accustomed, describes a condition in which a variety of narratives compete to tell their own story. "Heteroglossia," by contrast, describes a condition in which a single narrative imposes order, *but not unity*, on the variety of voices within it. Heteroglossia is imagined unity; diversity is proclaimed disunity. The former allows particular voices to express themselves as if they were the voices of all; the latter allows particular voices to express themselves largely to those that are alike.

Each is a different game of social communication, but the basic difference is that while diversity is recognizable at the borderlines of communities, heteroglossia is the unrecognized, and thus *unconscious*, property of the community. It is due to these properties that heteroglossia, unlike diversity, is better equipped to escape repression or censorship. Likewise, it is also due to these properties that heteroglossia is better equipped to advance toward universalism—*its only cause.*

Islam is of course not the only belief system with heteroglossic properties. What concerns us here however is how these properties evolved to become indispensable for the social life of the faith. No ideology that hopes to become universal could escape heteroglossia. Already at its founding phase, during Muhammad's own lifetime, Islam transformed from being an attempt to create a local, Mecca-centered tradition, into a universal belief system into which the interests and viewpoints of various social groups, classes, tribes, and styles of life could be incorporated (Bamyeh 1999). The point of departure could in fact be precisely identified with Muhammad's migration into Medina—in effect abandoning his hometown of Mecca, which had rejected his prophetic claims, for a larger world. That event commenced the consolidation of a self-conscious Muslim community and altered the character of the Qur'anic text, which in its Medinian phase became more worldly and less contemplative, expounding ethical rules in response to a variety of new social situations, issues, and problems. The early classic Muslim commentaries were well aware of this multiple situatedness of the holy text, and the fact that Islam really begins its global career in Medina rather than Mecca is indicated by Muslims everywhere in the commencement of the Islamic calendar with Muhammad's *migration*, rather than, say, his birth or even his first revelations. For it was in Medina that the seeds of the heteroglossic character of Muslim society were implanted, not in Mecca.

That different social forces and interests saw themselves as addressees of a single divine message meant that the further expansion of Islam worldwide could only do more of the same. Thus Islam could simultaneously in its long history be used to justify revolutions advocating communist equality; others defending inequalities of wealth. Movements opposed to any political authority not explicitly consented to by the *umma*; others praising the virtues of despotic rule. Practices oriented toward mystical Sufism; opposing doctrines requiring rational theological sobriety. Gender inequality *as well as* gender equality. Economic doctrines oriented toward the interests of the merchant class; others highlighting the needs of the poor. Sayings, all attributed to the prophet, praising austerity and modesty; others, likewise attributed to the prophet, defending the rights of the wealthy to live ostentatiously. It makes therefore little sense to take one hadith or Qur'anic citation as an embodiment of some essential sociological idea in Islam. (As does Max Weber (1993:263), for example, when he seeks to isolate such an idea by using a single saying attributed to Muhammad on the merits of wealth display: "when god blesses a man with prosperity he likes to see the signs thereof visible upon him.")

The basic character of heteroglossia is not simply that for every argument there is a counter-argument and for every position there are many possible opposites within the same tradition. The counter-arguments and the many positions are features of the *same* system, not of competing systems. Within heteroglossic systems, few talk of "diversity," but all talk about the meaning of the same sentence. And it is the toleration of such a divisive sentence, more so than the toleration of its multiple meanings, that holds together the heteroglossic system. For the only reason to hang on to such a sentence is because it is the only common reference point between "I" and "thou." And such social agreements exist, as Durkheim suggested long ago, not because they have any essential meaning, but in so far as they facilitate a sense that something we call "society" exists because I or thou are able to stipulate a common reference upon which it is presumed to stand.

But this common reference possesses by its nature a heteroglossic property, since it allows each person who uses it in her own manner to hypothesize that she is speaking of the *essence* of the system and not simply of a variation within it. On the other hand, heteroglossia, also by its nature, replaces the propensity toward civil war that is always latent in clashing essentialist standpoints, with a convivial social life characterized by organized anarchy, where authorities remain multiple and the final authority is reserved to god or postponed until his judgment. Until then, heteroglossia governs life on earth.

That formula is the longest standing mainstay of Muslim social systems, and as a global religion Islam almost immediately became heteroglossic in character, as early as the Medina period. The resolution at Saqifat Bani Sa'ida following the death of Muhammad may be taken as the first expression of the fact that the heteroglossic character of the Muslim community had already been in place but could be proclaimed only upon his death. For the entire point of that meeting was whether the Muslim community should remain united under a single leadership, even through everyone knew that it consisted of several communities that only a messenger of god could bring together, and it was far from clear that an ordinary notable could do the same. The meeting at Sqifat Bani Sa'ida, therefore, constituted the first institutional experiment with heteroglossia in Islamic history, whereby a unity was proclaimed even though the alternative—namely divided leadership—was explicitly present as an option. With the heteroglossic solution, the alternative option was not abolished, as much as *incorporated* into the social body of the faith, just as the Qur'an had earlier incorporated relevant parts of local pre-Islamic religious and biblical traditions.

The fact that heteroglossia as a social systems tends, whenever at all possible, to incorporate rather than simply eliminate preceding loyalties is also evident in the persistence of older patterns of tribal loyalties well into later phases of Islamic history. But under the banner of Islamic solidarity, tribal solidarity does not operate in the same old pre-Islamic way, when tribalism was its own reference point and had no clear universal alternative. Rather, heteroglossia means that new solidarities *join* rather than, as Durkheim had suggested, *replace* older solidarities. Islam at the beginning did not replace tribalism but established a new and more universal game alongside it. In doing so, Islam allowed tribalism to be challenged, but only when tribalism itself openly challenged the heteroglossic system, as it did in the *ridda* wars during the reign of Abu Bakr. As a heteroglossic formula, a transtribal system of solidarity (as Islam) is not designed to put tribal solidarity out of commission completely, so long as old tribalism lived at peace with the now professed transtribal allegiance to Islam.

Unlike diversity, heteroglossia is constructed in such a way that the variety of standpoints and special interests that it houses do not devolve into a sense of infinite chaos, regardless of how infinite the range of viewpoints may be. It is indeed a remarkable property of heteroglossic systems to insure precisely against this possibility, at the same time as they advance further and further along the path of universal recruitment of souls and establish themselves into the fabric of deep history with every passing century of their existence. Thus religion appears much older and much vaster than any soul that is implicated in it. So much so, that the soul has less of an incentive to see itself imprisoned by a vast time-space horizon, than to realize the practical advantage it could acquire by drawing on the heteroglossic resources already at its disposal. In doing so, whether its course takes it to where it wishes to be or allows it to resist impositions or persist in their face, that soul only *adds more* to an already inexhaustible cultural reservoir of heteroglossia.

Now the question is how that is accomplished: In other words, what are the working mechanisms of such heteroglossic systems? At least two operational levels of heteroglossia may be identified in the case of Islam, as is typical of global religions: namely the level of ordinary, syncretic Islam or what Charles Kurzman (1998:6) aptly identifies as "customary Islam"; and the scholarly networks that elaborate a high form of religion in the form of specific doctrines and orthodoxies, or "scholarly Islam." The latter was explored earlier, and is evidenced in the evolution of the *shari'a* as a multiple tradition, whose schools required no clear definition of jurisdiction— neither in a territorial sense nor in the sense of excluding each other from recognition. And since the *shari'a* was not, as discussed earlier, a simply "legal" tradition in the modern sense of the word, customary Islam was even less clearly so. As such both testify to the soundness of the proposition that cultural systems that are global in any sense cannot be based on a binding and enforceable legal character, and indeed it is difficult for them to be sustained if that is what they require. They only require heteroglossia.

At the scholarly level, heteroglossia tends to be stabilized by the establishment of centers of gravity around which arguments rotate in such a way that even at great distances, like planets around the sun, they are kept in the system. In the first five centuries of Islam, we see the gradual consolidation of such centers of gravity not only in the global networks of scholarly institutions, but also in the evolution of the notion of Islam as a *"wasati"* religion, that is, a compromise between extreme variations of it. (This conception may already be seen in the Qur'an's (2:143) description of the *umma* itself as possessing a middling character among the nations.) Three key figures could be identified with an effort whose results established the *tenor of inquiry* (to be distinguished from specific ideas) around which the entire Islamic heteroglossic system rotated for centuries: Muhammad Ibn Idris al-Shafi'i (d. 820), Abu al-Hasan al-Ash'ari (d. 936), and Abu Hamid al-Ghazali (d. 1111). Each constructed a lasting synthesis that highlighted *pragmatic conservatism* as the practical logic of the faith, and each tackled a particular area of knowledge.

The chronological order of those three figures shows something about how heteroglossic centers of gravity emerge. The first synthesis (al-Shafi'i) provided a foundation for adjudicating the validity of the sources of the faith itself; the second (al-Ash'ari) provided another foundation for unifying theological and philosophical approaches to inquiry; and the third (al-Ghazali) fused popular, mystical approaches and the more orthodox, rational approaches to practicing the faith. In other words, the first steps of the scholarly heteroglossia were oriented to establishing a shared traditionalist perspective. The second involved incorporating into the traditional consensus, or defending it from, modes of inquiry that had evidently originated outside of it but were addressing the faith's central themes. The third incorporated into the same consensus widespread, irrepressible popular practices that had aided in the transmission of the faith and endowed it with global social vitality. To put it simply, the three steps in building a heteroglossic system answered three successive questions of knowledge: First, how do I *know* my faith? Second, how does this faith live with its apparent *alternatives*, that is, relevant knowledge systems that are not based on faith? And third, how does knowledge *demonstrate* itself to be "true," that is, imprint itself upon the soul as an experience, after it had arrived to the mind in the form of mere concepts?

In al-Shafi'i's case, the basic problem consisting of resolving the emerging division of the scholars into two competing general camps, one highlighting the centrality of transmitted tradition and the other the role of independent judgment—or, as they were called, *ahl al-Hadith* and *ahl al-Ra'y*, respectively. The solution to this tension did have obvious consequences in matters of jurisprudence, and it is perhaps for having provided an acceptable synthesis that al-Shafi'i is often identified as the founder of *usul al-fiqh*, or the principles of jurisprudence in Islam. However, the ramifications of al-Shafi'i's synthesis, which asserted the centrality of tradition *and* established rational judgment as its basis, was not simply about legal issues. At its root the synthesis was about how to be a Muslim in the world. While the tension addressed by al-Shafi'i concerned what in our terms would be called "reason" versus "literalism," it is important to note that he rejected neither approach.[5] Indeed, his own work could be accepted only to the extent that it did not appear as another school (although eventually it would be treated that way), but as itself based on a sense of tradition, that is, referencing and acknowledging its earlier opposites, giving them their due space, but resolving apparent problems of extremism or unipolarity they had generated.

The second step in establishing a center of gravity for the Muslim heteroglossia, namely the synthesis of philosophy and theology provided by Abu al-Hasan al-Ash'ari, would in effect repeat what al-Shafi'i had done earlier, but at a different level and concerning new forms of struggle between reason and revelation. The logic of the synthesis was similar: Philosophical propositions, as articulated by the philosophers (specifically, the *mu'tazila*), should be tempered with theology, which ensured that reason, which one should not abandon, is also validated by something other than itself. With this solution, around which Islamic thought rallied for centuries afterward, reason ceased to appear as a threat to theology, and theology, in turn, could become more reasonable. However, unlike the case of al-Shafi'i, who was recognized by Muslims as a synthesizer of opposite ways of seeing (even though he may have been closer to one side of the equation than the other), al-Ash'ari (like al-Ghazali after him) was often regarded as having saved the tradition against the arguments of the rationalist who threatened to undermine the entire basis of faith.[6] But a closer look at his work (as well as that of al-Ghazali), show him to be deeply

5. Important contemporary efforts that try to show that al-Shafi'i provided really no synthesis but rather delivered a lasting victory of tradition over reason (e.g., Abu Zayd 1996), can be properly understood as aspects of debates about the root problems of *modern*, not historical, Islam. What is important for us here is less the substance of al-Shafi'i's synthesis, but the fact that for centuries, Muslims generally *did* regard him as having delivered a synthesis with which they could live.

6. As in the case in the previous note, complaints raised later about the error of this perspective (as for example by Fazlur Rahman 1984), who blamed al-Ash'ari for freezing Islamic thought for centuries), are modernist critiques that evaluate tradition less on the basis of

philosophical, employing rational arguments he had mastered during his own earlier immersion in philosophy, but using them in such a way as to ensure that they do not undermine the pragmatically conservative center of gravity of a faith-based heteroglossic system.

The same could be said of al-Ghazali, who saw himself as following his predecessors' footsteps, but confronting new problems that required new synthesis. The question was still how to synthesize reason and revelation, but now that old question had acquired a new dimension. Reason, as before, did not seem sufficient to ensure certainty of truth and absence of doubt. But simply following a tradition did not seem to generate any better results either, as al-Ghazali tells his audience in his own biographic confessions. Rather, faith, several centuries after the original prophetic experience, seemed to require a personal *experience*, which he found in Sufism. The synthesis of rationalism and mysticism that al-Ghazali proposed adjusted well to the sensibilities of both the orthodox scholars as well as the more esoteric theologians whose teachings were already capable of generating a large popular following. With al-Ghazali, the last step of the project of consolidating an identifiable center of an Islamic heteroglossia is reached, with the removal of the distinction between reason and its erstwhile mystical nemesis. It is also noteworthy in this regard that al-Ghazali was capable at that point of doing what would have been impossible to do at the time of al-Shafi'i, and that was to establish a synthesis with an *acknowledged* weak basis in the tradition itself (specifically, the *hadith* part of it), highlighting instead what practices, behaviors and dispositions produce a morally virtuous life. In al-Ghazali's case, thus, we see a clear nod of scholarly Islam in the direction of customary Islam.

While the three steps above concern how heteroglossia is established at the scholarly level, one should also take note of how heteroglossia takes root at the popular level, even though a chronological account cannot be established here. Customary Islam, that is, the historical lay religion of Muslims, may be said to feed on four compelling sources. First, it provides a venue into a spiritual realm when that is seen as a necessary complement to material life, and in a way that is immediately practicable, requires little erudition, and makes material life itself more bearable. Second, it validates local traditions by linking them up to a universal message, and in the process supplies every local person, rooted in a locality as she might

---

problems that historical Muslim themselves regarded to be worthy of resolving, and more on the basis of what appears (erroneously, I think) as their modern result.

be, with an added sense or prestige of global citizenship. Third, it supplies the basic philosophical materials for lay intellectual education; that is to say, it corresponds to a lay philosophical interest in meaning-making, but in a way that is ennobled and legitimated by being elevated above the instrumental demands of material life. Fourth, it provides a set of methods for justifying and validating everyday choices that either require no specialized, learned opinion (*fatwa*) or perhaps even require avoiding its solicitation, for various practical or emotional reasons.[7]

Those four orientations provide the basic working materials for the heteroglossic customary system, since each acquires salience only in the context of a particular individual life, even though the discourse through which each orientation expresses itself appears universal. So customary heteroglossia emerges out of this duality: The ordinary person has intellectual orientations that, while rooted in his individual experience and everyday existence, are easiest to develop further, and as needed, by drawing on the philosophical raw materials of a discourse that is both familiar and shared with others. Therefore nothing that one eventually finds, even if no one else finds it, necessarily requires him to leave religion. (In this sense we can understand how Sufis, for example, could downplay what other Muslims would deem to be binding rituals, including even prayer, without ceasing to regard themselves as Muslims.)

The heteroglossic properties of customary and scholarly Islam may be separated for analytical purposes. However, since the scholarly communities saw themselves, and were also seen by lay people as guardians of the faith, the two levels of the faith were always in dialogue. The scholars' esoterics did not shield them from having to comment on popular traditions, and their opinion mattered regarding anything with an ambiguous status—including faith practices, issues of morality, or interpersonal transactions. Al-Ghazali, again, is usually regarded as exemplifying the unceasing attempts to synthesize the popular and the scholarly, and his work remained of central importance in Islamic learning for centuries after him.

---

7. Indeed, much of popular culture, including novels and films, rely precisely on this formula. In marriage situations, for example, a woman's choice of a partner in opposition to family preferences may be most effective—as for example allegorized in *Rana's Wedding*—when such violation is couched in the language of Islam rather than simple individual will to freedom. And in Naguib Mahfouz's novels, which are keenly attentive to the intricacies of neighborhood and everyday life in Cairo, the lay religious language of "fatalism" serves, as Halim Barakat (1990) has observed, as a mask for actors making their own choices.

Like al-Ash'ari before him, one of al-Ghazali's most sustained projects was concerned with distinguishing a specifically Islamic scholasticism from "philosophy," which for him meant Greek philosophy as well as the work of earlier Muslim philosophers that was based on Greek sources. That the Greeks fell outside of the Muslim tradition was more clear (or more important) for Ghazali than it was for earlier Muslim philosophers like Ibn Sina (Avicenna) or Farabi. But, as Ebrahim Moosa (2005) argues, in "refuting" the Greeks, al-Ghazali was actually Islamizing rather than dismissing Greek philosophical questions. Those questions included among others the nature of the universe, the character and place of human will, the explanatory status of cause and effect. In that way, Greek thought came to be recognized as part of the Islamic thought tradition itself, rather than as an import from alien sources.

Thus, the heteroglossic reservoir of Islamic gnosis was expanded by incorporating as "Islamic" logical traditions that other Muslim thinkers had earlier accepted with the full knowledge of their non-Islamic identity. That was done precisely by a "refutation," which proved to be precisely the way by which Greek philosophy could be fully Islamicized. This approach to knowledge, namely incorporating into one's logical system precisely those questions that one is criticizing, is not unique to al-Ghazali, but a basic heteroglossic procedure of knowledge. It may be compared to the early Islamic critique of the biblical tradition, in a way that made that tradition itself into an integral part of Islam. The same applies as well to the Islamic critique of pagan traditions, which only dismisses those portions of them that clearly contradict monotheism, but incorporates everything else. We see that procedure of "critique" most clearly when the Qur'an (2:189, 196–200) told the early faithful that the old pagan pilgrimage was now god's own ritual, and that they should follow it, but under the new banner of Islam.

If one of al-Ghazali's contributions consisted in setting a more clear boundary between Islamic and non-Islamic thought (namely by translating the core concerns of the latter into recognizable Islamic idioms), his second contribution consisted of unifying Islamic thought itself. That, too, is a classic heteroglossic procedure. That consisted, as mentioned above, of synthesizing Sufi and orthodox thought, which according to him was motivated by his own earlier crisis of doubt from which he was saved not by orthodoxy but by Sufi practices. The latter allowed him to recognize the light of god implanted in his breast, which he could not have experienced through rational reasoning alone. Watt's argument (1953:14–15) that al-Ghazali's contribution here consisted largely in allowing orthodoxy and Sufism to coexist with relative peace also suggests another facet of the equation that became apparent to al-Ghazali: The basic orientations of customary Islam inform and are in turn informed by its scholarly orientations.

The outcome of this grand synthesis of the practice and philosophy of the faith, and the accompanying "refutation" of unbelief, was al-Ghazali's *Revival of the Religious Sciences*, in which ordinary faithful are instructed on a wide range of issues concerning religious rituals, social customs, moral attitudes, and habits of thought. In other words, the full range of sociability became systematized according to a spirituality more intellectualized than had been necessary earlier. Yet, Ghazali thought of his grand manual as a "revival" rather than a *new* invention. That is because it is a basic property of heteroglossic thought to regard what it discovers to have always already been there. In other words, heteroglossia is reinforced by the claim that what had just been discovered was actually something that already existed, and only needed restoration so that it may be presented again to a generation that had forgotten it.

In its basic tenor, this method is virtually indistinguishable from later Muslim revivalist movements, as evidenced in the Islamic enlightenment since the eighteenth century. In that case, the familiar argument of the reformers was not that they were "liberalizing" or "modernizing" Islam. Rather they saw themselves as "reviving" Islam, in the sense of rediscovering its true and forgotten origins or intent. Typically, the argument was based on making a distinction between "religion" and "tradition" (or between "religion" and "culture"). The argument was that tradition (or culture) were what had become *familiar* to lay people and scholarly communities alike. But "true" religion was no longer familiar. True religion, according to that argument, was not that which simply reinforced existing habits. Indeed, true religion required *rejecting* existing tradition. The Qur'an, after all, repeatedly (2:170, 5:104, 7:28, 10:78, 21:53, 26:74, 31:21, 43:22–23) denounced as logically insupportable what it presented as the main argument of pre-Islamic polytheism, namely the notion that what justified polytheism most was its being based on the *habitual* obligation to follow the traditions of the forefathers. On the other hand, the Qur'an's own best argument against such traditionalism was that it was *reviving* an earlier and forgotten tradition (namely that of Abraham).

This familiar style of arguing, in which true religion is presented as something that is liable to be repeatedly forgotten and replaced by habit (or tradition), forms the mainstay of all revivalist claims. All revivalist claims,

including the liberal variety, involve an attempt to stamp out the historically heteroglossic character of religion so as to replace it with a uniform
meaning. Yet, the ultimate outcome of all revivalism is for the revivalist
claims themselves to become part of the heteroglossic reservoir. That is
because no religion that is global and old enough could possibly be uniform, especially on those matters that speak to the non-uniform everyday
pragmatics of the endlessly differentiated faithful.

A good example of the liberal variety of revivalism concerns the question of women's equality. The basic structure of the argument today remains similar to that of Qasim Amin's famous pamphlet on the topic in
1905, in which he sought to provoke his opponents by acknowledging that
his demand for women's emancipation was a heresy, though one against
tradition rather than religion. That way of making the argument continues
to be a basic starting point for contemporary advocates of women's emancipation from an Islamic point of view. That the argument is questioned or
moderated by more conservative Muslims means that it has come to form
an inescapable dimension of contemporary Islamic thought and public
philosophy: The argument for women's emancipation, from an Islamic
rather than secular point of view, cannot be simply ignored by any Muslim,
including the most staunchly patriarchal ones.

The proposition that such a conversational reality further expands the
heteroglossic reservoir of religion is most evidenced in the fact that both
advocates and opponents of women's emancipation find themselves compelled to delve deeper into the Islamic heritage itself for supporting arguments. Heteroglossia lives on by virtue of such intense contestations
that drive all parties to dig deeper into the same well. In the final analysis,
this activity contributes more to deepening the well than to resolving the
argument.

The revivalist critique, which appears to target everything that is practiced or thought habitually, is part of the historical character of heteroglossia. In other words, revivalism is part of the Islam that it critiques, in
the sense that revivalism is a mechanism through which religion is constantly modernized, that is, made to answer to contemporary concerns.
This does not mean that the answer given will be "correct," only that it
cannot avoid being given.

The more recent Islamic hermeneutics explored earlier likewise only
add to the reservoir of heteroglossia, even though hermeneutics appear to
place so much of ordinary religious reason in question. The hermeneuts
make their contribution to heteroglossia by taking the revivalist critique

a step further. While the revivalists' critique rests on making a distinction between true religion and tradition, the modern hermeneutic critique highlights another type of distinction: between true religion and *religiosity*.

This distinction is based on the following proposition: True religion does have a *definite* essence and meaning, but that definite essence or meaning escapes our capacity as humans to grasp it, since it corresponds to the boundless and timeless nature of god. As humans who are finite in time and space, we are at best able to approach religion with the cognitive capacities and social demands that emerge out of our specific age in history; but we cannot make final statements about its essential meaning. The terms vary by which this distinction is now made between an eternal, true religion and what we could possibly do as humans, that is, practice time-bound religiosity, which is all we could hope to do. "Religiosity"—the inclination to religion—is not to be confused with practicing "true religion," which exceeds human limits. Therefore, from a hermeneutic perspective, any religious *knowledge* is situated in a particular circumstance, even if *religiosity* is universal. Interpretation is all that a human mind could do (so long as no divine revelation is forthcoming).

The fact that the hermeneutic ways of refashioning an old distinction have gained both great following and hostility means that they too have become part of the heteroglossic house of Islam. That is because the hermeneutic argument is itself based on Islamic sources and a claimed commitment to religion, and thus a right to not be excluded from the Islamic public sphere. The case of hermeneutics shows that critique of any aspect of a religion from a religious perspective only adds to the heteroglossic reservoir of that religion .

Heteroglossia versus inquisition

Just like the two previous principles of historical Islam, namely partial control and free movement, heteroglossia thrives best when existing authorities do not have sufficient power to impose orthodoxies, whether against avowed or hidden heterodoxies, as attempted in the Spanish Inquisition (which has no real parallel in Islamic history, apart from the *Mihna* of 833–848). Global systems tend to give rise to some calls for strong ruling authority or empire, although global systems do not require empire by any necessity, nor even strong authority. The universalist culture of the system, which emerges in stable and voluntary forms only through heteroglossia rather than force, survives best when the system itself includes strong egalitarian claims. This was one of the great features of historical *Dar al-Islam*, negated in those modern environments where the opposite claim is made: that Islam requires force from above (Saudi Arabia being the prime and earliest modern model here; Da'esh being little more than a copy of that wretched system).

If heteroglossia has been such a central global property of this historical faith, how do we account for what appears to be its recurrent opposite, namely, attempts to impose a single and binding orthodoxy? Here I would like to explore this question in two ways: first by clarifying the distinction between heteroglossia and inquisition (see Table 3.2) as two facets of the social life of any religion; and second by discussing some conditions surrounding especially modern puritanical movements in Islam.

First, heteroglossia and inquisition must be seen as two complementary facets of the life of each religion. Both are two features of the same phenomenon, namely that religious life is characterized at one and the same time by fragmented reality and organizational impulse. The clash of the two features—reality of fragmentation and impulse to put it into order—should be more frequent the more global and older a religion becomes. That is because longevity and expanse expose religious ideas to the variety of the human experience. It is in fact only in entertaining and resolving a constant clash between heteroglossia and inquisition that a religion may be said to be living, since in so doing it reflects and then absorbs the complexity of humanity itself.

Both heteroglossia and inquisition are strategies of universalism. But while heteroglossia consists of the strategy by which encountered varieties in the human landscape are absorbed into an ever growing reservoir of religious conceptions, inquisition describes the strategy by which attention is increasingly directed at the real unity of the universal community. At

Table 3.2 Inquisition versus heteroglossia as strategies of faith management

	Heteroglossia	Inquisition
Method of organizing fragmented social reality	Organized by voluntary agreements on reference point	Organized by force
Method of observing faith	Observing exteriors	Observing interiors
Cost	Low cost	High cost
Duration	Constant	Recurrent, episodic

one level, inquisition may be said to be motivated by the fear of the fragmentation that heteroglossia fosters in its natural movement. Inquisition, therefore, is the recurrent rejection of the liberal excess of heteroglossia in religious life. Inquisition comes into being when it is suspected that heteroglossia is doing what it is indeed doing—namely using faith primarily as *discourse*, that is, as a way to facilitate common social life.

By contrast, inquisition consists of the belief that a common social life requires a source of commonality deeper than "mere" discourse. Commonality that is deeper than "mere" discourse can only be one that reaches into the interior of the soul. Therefore inquisition requires interrogation or active questioning, and a demand that adherence to an orthodoxy be verified not simply in externally visible rituals, but in such a way that the rituals may allow the observer to see into the interior of the observed. Thus settings that involve intimate and constant contact, as in the ideal of monastic life, reflect the highest hopes of a strategy of inquisition. The same is essentially true of all forms of religious education that involves lengthy contact between teacher and student, as well of social movements where members tend to spend much time together, either in fighting camps or when they live together as a matter of principle.

The demands on individual life of the heteroglossic strategy, by contrast, tend to be less intense. It is for this reason that heteroglossia always escapes the claws of inquisition at the last moment. Inquisition requires constant mobilization of precious resources (time, dedicated personnel, organizational resources, coercive capacity, supervision techniques, testing methods, means to overpower resistance, and so on). By contrast, heteroglossia requires little more than hiding away in times of inquisition. At all other times, heteroglossia thrives in the general tenor of pragmatic conservatism, and on the basic intellectual orientations of ordinary life.

One may say that inquisition is a way of taking religion more seriously. It is not clear, however, that those who are religious in other ways are necessarily any less serious about their religion. The *mihna* period in early Islamic history shows a clear attempt at an inquisition, but as discussed earlier it failed in part due to the resistance of some entrenched religious scholars, including Ahmad Ibn Hanbal, who was unquestionably committed to his own dogmas. Thus here inquisition failed not simply because of "liberal" resistance. It also failed because of a social reality that, even at the height of caliphal power and prestige, was still characterized by traditions of partial control that made it possible for most people to ignore

as irrelevant the high intellectualism and sophistry championed by the en-
forcers of the official dogma.

After all, Islam itself was originally motivated, as we see in the Qur'an,
by an explicit discomfort with the inquisition-like campaigns and purges in
Byzantium. Without those, Islam would likely not have emerged but given
way to a Christianity that was already spreading among the Arabs and was
well-entrenched throughout the Middle East by Muhammad's time. From
the early Islamic perspective as it was emerging with Muhammad, many
of whose mentors had close affinities to Christianity, the older religion was
no longer a viable option precisely because of its evolving sectarianism,
which itself was the product of inquisition strategies. Those strategies only
fragmented a church that should otherwise have been universal. Indeed,
the most *sustained* Qur'anic complaint about Christianity concerned a *social*, not theological observation, namely that the Christian community
had become deeply divided and strife-ridden (2:176, 213, 253; 3:19, 105;
5:14; 19:37; 43:65). In the Qur'an, references to that social fact clearly out-
number the few theological arguments about the nature of Christ.

Although Christian sectarian politics of the period concerned (at least
on the surface) Christological arguments, the resulting social sectarianism
seemed from an Islamic perspective to poorly correspond to an ideal of
communal unity presaged in the very concept of a monotheistic god. If
Islam emerged out of the reworking of contested elements of Christianity,
it can also be said that Islam had originally represented a heteroglossic revolt against the excesses of inquisition within known Christian traditions.

But that revolt was conducted in such a way as to signal the end of the
discursive unity of that tradition—after all, early versions of what would later
appear as distinct Islamic tenets of faith had earlier appeared as "heresies"
within early Christianity (for example Marcion (d. 160) or Arius (d. 338),
among others). It is noteworthy that inquisitions, which had become such
a dominant feature of Christian sectarian life in the Levant and Egypt by
Muhammad's time, could take place only in territories ruled by Byzantium,
just outside of Arabia. By contrast, the heteroglossic revolt borne in Arabia
benefited from the fact that it was borne in a place that had only known partial control and was far enough from the coercive arm of imperial systems.

But the new discourse of Islam, too, also became over time candidate
for inquisitions, since inquisition is an expected reaction to heteroglossia.
And heteroglossia, in turn, is an unavoidable consequence of the exposure of any expanding religion to a variety of social demands, interpretive standpoints, and perspectivist preferences associated with territorial

expansion and longevity, all of which compel religion to establish itself in a way that is answerable to social complexity.

While inquisition may involve an attempt to enforce a highly intellectualized dogma, like the createdness of the Qur'an during the *mihna*, it may also appear in an opposite, anti-intellectual form, which explicitly aims to strip away excessive intellectualism and, correspondingly, all adornments, whether physical or linguistic. In other words, in this latter case inquisition seeks to "return" religion to an austere and more pure essence. Thus puritanism in various guises is often (but not always) a preferred inquisition perspective. Puritanism tends to be the language of inquisition especially where there is a weak tradition of government, since the more esoteric languages of inquisition may not be easy to enforce without a commanding authority.

Modern inquisitions

In recent history, the trials and tribulations of more austere (puritan) forms of inquisition may be illustrated by exploring one of the deciding conflicts in the modern Middle East, namely the early-twentieth-century struggle over control of Hijaz between the Saudis and the Hashesmites. The Hashemites had for centuries been the traditional chiefs of Hijaz and guardians of its holy sites, a role long legitimated by their claim of descent from the lineage of Muhammad. This meant that it was difficult to challenge their religious pedigree. But there was usually no need for such a challenge, since heteroglossic Islam flourished unchallenged under them, as evidenced in part in the scholarly traditions of the learning circles in Mecca and Medina that were integral to several global revivalist networks in early modern times (Voll 1980; Ochsenwald 1984:76–83). The only religious view that could challenge this old and venerated reality had to have the character of a radical reformation, that is, the type of puritanism defined by an expressed intolerance for its alternatives. That was so since the religious heteroglossia that had existed under Hashemite aegis in Hijaz did not presuppose any demand for overthrowing them. The Saudi discovery of Wahhabi puritanism, therefore, was crucial to their struggle against the Hashemites, whose long-established, albeit partial, religious authority could be challenged only by unbending fanatics.

Wahhabism itself, as a modern puritanical movement and consequently a modern inquisition of the most intrusive, coercive, and violent kind, is therefore even today scarcely imaginable without being tied to a program of political domination. The alliance, beginning in 1740, of a local chief from the Al Saud clan to the equally marginal preacher Muhammad Ibn Abd al-Wahhab, whose constant denunciations of most Muslims of his day had earned him expulsion from everywhere else he had tried to preach, signaled a contract that until today survives as the foundation of the Saudi state. The contract divided up political and religious leadership between a royal family and the Wahhabi clergy. The latter could not impose their inquisition without the coercive muscle of the former, and the former relied on the latter to provide them with the only source of legitimacy they could possibly have.

The fact that in this case inquisition became "constant"—which is highly unusual for inquisitions—was only possible due to the vast expansion of the resources of the state itself after the discovery of oil. The relation between capacity for constant inquisition and vast resources becomes more evident when we compare the moderation of Wahhabism in other neighboring territories, notably the Gulf states (the UAE, Qatar, Kuwait). There, while Wahhabism was also part of the original contract of founding dynasties, it did not designate a permanent role for the Wahhabi clergy. Rather, elsewhere in the Gulf, small state size meant that legitimacy required being (at least initially) little more than an expansion and bureaucratization of already familiar traditional tribal and inter-clan alliances. By contrast, the tribal-religious alliance that formed the core of the unique case of the Saudi state was hardly traditional. The only remotely comparable case in modern history, namely the emergence of a monarchy in post-independence Libya that was tied to the Sanusi movement, was typified neither by puritanism nor a determined inquisition against internal enemies, but rather emerged, in complex ways, out of the dynamics of struggle against an *external* enemy—in that case Italian colonialism. The Saudis, by contrast, only fought other Muslims.

Thus while the emergence of the Wahhabi inquisition could be understood as a natural part of the history of religion, its unusual persistence could only be understood as a product of purely political, not religious, dynamics. The austerity of the doctrine corresponds to austere conditions: This means that so long as austerity persists, no further inquisition activity is necessary, since nothing that the austere dogma says contradicts experienced reality. Only when conditions of austerity give way to prosperity, as was the case in Saudi Arabia after oil, the austere religious dogmas *no longer* correspond to reality, and in every way make the enjoyment of wealth a suspect pursuit. Here, inquisition becomes difficult to sustain without constant coercive vigilance requiring enormous resources.

The psychic split that occasions this rift between austere doctrine and wealthy reality is an area that still requires much research. But the notion that puritanical inquisition is associated, at least initially, with austere conditions may be more evident if we explore the comparable case of modern Afghanistan. The emergence and success of the Taliban in that country toward the end of the twentieth century is comparable to the career of the Wahhabi *ikwan* in Arabia nearly a century earlier. Of course, Saudi Arabia and Afghanistan now could not possibly be further apart in terms of all indicators of wealth, social welfare, and quality of life. Yet in both cases, extremist ideologies seem to thrive on extreme conditions: one the wealthiest and one of the poorest countries in the world. There is less evidence that extremist religious politics enjoy broad support in middling conditions. This may be the case because middling conditions correspond to multiple centers of power and thus a negotiated system, which is the case even in Iran.

But the conditions facilitating success of extremist ideologies differ: Whereas in Saudi Arabia there was enough concentrated wealth in centralized hands to allow extensive patronage, in Afghanistan it required a severe crisis and complete destruction of the country in civil war *prior* to the Taliban takeover. But the *original* conditions were similar: the Wahhabi takeover of desolate central Arabia—the basis for what eventually became Saudi Arabia—itself was originally associated with very austere conditions.[8]

Thus prior to the puritan takeover, the two cases examined above (pre-oil Arabia and late-twentieth-century Afghanistan) seem to share three factors in common:

1) decentralized older governance with much local autonomy
2) little exposure to direct colonialism, and dearth of connections to a global system[9]
3) the correspondence of puritanical ideology to puritanical conditions of life

---

8. In both cases, there were also some geopolitical factors at play, namely eventual support of some important regional power for the insurgency: Britain in the case of Abdul Aziz in Arabia, and Pakistan in the case of the Taliban. Also in both cases, those powers withdrew support from earlier allies. But those geopolitical factors did not create those movements, only facilitated their success.

9. Of the territories that eventually made up Saudi Arabia, only Hijaz had regular and significant contact with the outside world, as it housed pilgrimage destinations and globally

The first factor is associated with heteroglossic religiosity, which so in-censed Ibn Abd al-Wahhab and became an affront to the Taliban, even though such sentiments *alone* were not sufficient to generate a social movement calling for an inquisition. The other factors seem important, each in its own way. The relative isolation of these two territories from global systems, including learning circles, meant that for much of their history they held scarce interest to outside powers, which saw little reason to divert sufficient resources to keep such movements under some kind of control. That was the case in Arabia under the Ottomans, for example, who contested the Wahhabis only when they sought to control Hijaz and southern Iraq, but did not pursue them into central Arabia. And the same is true of Afghanistan, which the Soviet Union (and later the United States) eventually calculated to not be worth the price being paid for controlling it, and which other powers subsequently left alone to disintegrate in civil war (only to rediscover it again, and only as a source of a global problem, after September 11, 2001).

The third factor above offers some complexities over time. It is easy enough to maintain austere conceptions of religiosity under austere con-ditions, which in the case of Afghanistan, after years of war beginning in the late 1970s, were coupled with broad demands for stability and ethical purity that only the Taliban seemed to promise. The situation is of course different in Saudi Arabia, where a cultural crisis now exists in the lack of fit between wealth conditions that invite an ostentatious life on the one hand, and officially sanctioned austere puritanical doctrines on the other. The future of such a crisis deserves its own study and cannot be adequately addressed here. But what can be said here is that the current inquisition in the social life of Islam tends to occasion extreme conditions. Without those conditions inquisition gives way, as has always been the case, to the heteroglossic norm.

Global order beyond Islam

There are two points to be made in conclusion. One concerns what happened or is happening in the Islamic world since the three principles outlined in this chapter—partial control, free movement, and cultural heteroglossia—came under severe challenge in modern history and increasingly came to

---

connected learned communities. It was also the region that offered most resistance to the Saudis.

be seen as unfit for modern states. The second concerns larger questions of globalization today in light of the historical structures that had given *Dar al-Islam* its sense as a concept of global citizenship, soverign historical continuity, culture dessiminated via networks of knowledge, and embeddedness in ordinary life. In other words, could something analogous to the three structures outlined here emerge in order to foster a humane global order today—something that possesses those same three global structures, but is not called "Islam," since in the final analysis it is the *structures* that matter, not their name? This point concerns not whether Islam could be "rescued" from one malady or another—a common concern in contemporary debates. It is rather whether the modern global world could learn something from the historical features of Islam as the organizing language of an older global system.

First, in much of the Muslim world, the three principles outlined here mutually reinforced each other through a delicate yet remarkably stable balance for several centuries. When they were violated in modernity,[10] no subsequent system managed to replace the sense of systematicity, certitude, predictability, and conviviality they had once provided. Rather, the colonial epoch was generally followed, especially in the Middle East, with an unusual period of almost uniform authoritarianism of a new and highly intrusive kind. The dynamics involved in nourishing authoritarianism were all implicated in the direct challenge posed to the three fundamental principles of *Dar al-Islam* since and after colonialism.

Indeed, some commentators, like Richard Bulliett, argue that authoritarian states in the Middle East became possible only after Islam had been weakened by colonialism. The argument here being that "Islam" had historically functioned as an equivalent to the concept of "the people" in the West, namely as the discourse most appropriate for placing a limit on the tyrannical tendencies of the state (Bulliett 1999). Likewise, Reinhard Schulze's (2016) analysis of the transformation of Islamic culture during

---

10. It will be useful to include some remarks on periodization, which means identifying historical points of departure from each of these patterns, but it is also useful to address likewise two methodological pitfalls in this regard. First, the point at which one or the other of the ruptures set in varies greatly across the Islamic world. In Afghanistan, for example, the principle of partial control is not substantially violated until the late 1970s, more than a century after the (inconclusive) Ottoman *Tanzimat*, itself about half a century following Muhammad Ali's reforms in Egypt. Second, the ruptures were not felt at the same intensity throughout the social and political fabric whenever they happened, and the prudent approach would be to sketch out a gradual process whereby the magnitude of the ruptures is felt more and more by wider social strata, and noted within various intellectuals circles over time.

the twentieth century focuses on the colonial effects. Factors highlighted by Schulze include the increasing relevance of state-centered politics in defining the scope of Islamic politics; the emerging capacity to translate central modern social concepts, such as justice or community, into Islamic idioms; and the increasing appeal of Islamic discourse to those urban nationalists who looked for reliable ways of liberating themselves from tradition, while remaining relevant.

It is unlikely that contemporary Islamic social movements would entirely share any of the understandings outlined above. Invariably, however, these movements address themselves to the problems of the postcolonial order. The persistence of both religious movements, as well as religious public philosophy, points to the persistence of a sense among broad enough sectors that society could resolve its manifold modern problems only if it reverts to some sense of "authenticity." This of course is not the same as anti-modernity, but in effect the opposite (Bamyeh 2002): It is an argument for a modernity that would not seem coercive or imposed by illegitimate, unaccountable, or outside forces whose expressions of concern for the well-being of the *umma* are unlikely to be believed. Unlikely, that is, not out of some "traditional" intractability. It is just that from a local perspective, there is no logical reason to take seriously expression of concern by outsiders, whether imperial or not, when such outsiders have no organic connection to those they try to help—only relation to them as aggregates and statistics. Successful modern Islamic movements, as we saw earlier, were all based on an experience of social rootedness in the everyday of constituents, and on a credible claim to representing at least some genuine element of a familiar heritage.

Second, any humane facets of globalization today could only be expected to mimic in some way the same historical principles of *Dar al-Islam* outlined here. That is because there is probably little that is unique about the Islamicate experience in fostering global systems fashioned by basic principles for the social organization of global life. The principle of partial control points to a present possibility, namely a global system run by a multiplicity of centers, including states, supra-state institutions, transnational bureaucracies, civil societies, social movements, and networked populations. The principle of partial control here indicates two facts that are already creeping into the scene: First, no one actor controls the global system as a whole. Second, within existing domains of "sovereignty," that is, states, other forces are being accepted as alternatives or partners to the state in some areas of life or with respect to some jurisdiction.

The principle of free movement is also part of this emerging picture, although in a still less developed form than the principle of partial control. So far, the principle is most evident in the most developed transnational society today, namely the European Union, and in that it testifies to how free movement has come to epitomize at the individual experiential level an already accomplished transnational institutional reality. Elsewhere, however, the principle continues to refer only to the "free movement" of capital and goods, and in some cases services, but rarely to the free movement of people. In the EU, by contrast, after years of vacillation we finally see the logic of free movement reaching a fuller maturity (except of course where it concerns migrants). The free movement of people is only a natural corollary to the free movement of things in general. Saskia Sassen (1988) has long argued that people simply follow in their own movement pathways already opened up by the movement of capital. If a global economy invites the free movement of things, and further ensconces that freedom as its primary act of faith, it will be impossible to separate people from their things. When this movement is made illegal, it will violate legality and go on. Global order, after all, does not consist only of that which is allowed.

Finally, it is already apparent that something we may call "global culture" is beginning to take shape, and much has already been written about it. Whether it will take a large heteroglossic form as we saw in the case of Islam is not something that can be definitely answered here. Its clearest expressions seem to be thus far in youth cultures, and parts of its form may be evident in emergent cultural genres like "world music," but it is also a clearly present dimension in visual culture (Halle 2014). But what is clear is that we are already beginning to see global social movements combining very different attitudes under the mantle of overarching, intercommunicative discourses—for example, global feminism, or global human rights approaches, or global peace and anti-war movements (Bamyeh 2010). This emergent culture was evident in the quick spread across very different countries of a global wave of protests in 2011 (Bamyeh 2012b), and in the earlier global movement against the Iraq war in 2003— perhaps the largest spontaneous social movement in world history.

In so far as religion continuing to serve as an aspect of global culture here, we begin to see how out of an old religious communal logic there emerge elements that communicate with a new heteroglossic formula, more adequate for a global culture, and unlikely to be defined by one religion or by religiosity alone, but by generic common ethics. Islam itself may come to be considered as simply another name for universal humanism

(Shahrur 2000), meaning that those who do not identify as Muslims could be regarded as such if they subscribe to a basic, undemanding, and uncomplicated moral code. Or it could be that Islam is less of a specific religion now, and more part of a global battle, being waged everywhere, between the forces of spirituality and the forces of materialism (Esack 1997).

In his recent book, *Sociology of Islam*, Armando Salvatore has proposed the concept of "civility" to describe many of the ethos associated with some aspects of what is here called heteroglossia, and other aspects of what in the parlance of modern social science is referred to as "civil society." While Salvatore draws on Islamicate history, the promise of the concept of "civility" is certainly broader, and is relevant to exploring the contours of voluntary global culture generally. One of the points stressed by Salvatore is that the priority of civility over legality in Muslim history meant that the Islamicate world faced less pressure to build a state based on the Westphalian model in Europe after 1648. The thesis reverses Norbert Elias's model of civilizational processes, suggesting that in the Islamic experience, unlike in the European one studied by Elias, civility emerges in lateral networks, rather than through a top-down process in which the aristocracy plays a decisive role (Salvatore 2016:63–64).

Civility here seems related to two simultaneous properties of global systems of knowledge: the imperfect knowledge of partners of each other, and their mutual expectation of some similarity to each other. In this sense, civility is the property of uncoerced (since coercion cancels out the need for civility) global systems. This civility, which comes from below and is learned outside of the state (or, as is usually the case in most of the world, in spite of it), is a fundamental building block of global culture. The fact that we learn about civility thus far only with the aid of specific civilizational histories—that of Islam in this case—does not mean that it is a property of any specific culture. Rather, it means that civility is the property of any cultural system that becomes global through voluntary dynamics.

The global order being attempted today is of course larger than the Muslim world, but it is striking to see features of the basic principles above being invoked into organizing it, in ways that are still inchoate and very far from being obvious or complete. Global orders are of course not new, and one can sketch a variety of models that have been proposed for it, including imperialism. But to the extent that a global order may remain humane, it would have to subscribe in some ways to the same basic principles showcased in the historical experience of *Dar al-Islam*, even though a modern global order will not be Islamic or religious. But it will have to have autonomies so that it appears intimate; it will have to operate as an open space because that is how a system is most systematic; and it will have to have ethics that are broadly and voluntarily shared. Those would be principles that humanize global order, enhance its intimacy, and make it useful and meaningful for the greatest number. And this means that such principles cannot be conceived simply as new ways to govern people, nor as another means of enforcing unsolicited dogmas, nor to retain the notion that people should continue to be forced to respect the prison walls called "border." Such a world would do well, I think, to reflect on the historical experience of *Dar al-Islam*, an experience whose profound nature, as an experiment in creating a global culture, has been lost to our imagination.

Conclusion

ISLAM AS RESERVE DISCOURSE

FROM A SOCIOLOGICAL point of view, Islam is what Muslims do. Just as the meaning of a word cannot be found outside of the use to which it is put, as Wittgenstein maintained, the meaning of a living religion cannot be found outside of the use to which it is put. A living religion cannot acquire meaning any other way. It dies out 1) when we can no longer find ways to make it useful for our lives; or 2) when other discourses provide meanings that are more effective for life than religious ideas; or 3) when its only remaining tool is coercion—indicating that it no longer possesses persuasive capacity on its own. Life always comes before religion, not the other way around: Only a living entity can cultivate religious ideas, as well as abandon them.

Living religion

By "living religion" I mean a constant struggle to interpret god's commands or intentions. Sometimes this interpretation is done because one needs to solve a problem; another time it is done to respond to alternative views or objections. In ordinary circumstances, an interpretation appears more compelling when god's commands or intentions align with the practical demands of life. Either way, it is the faithful who give meaning to a living religion.

There are, of course, alternative ways to understand religion as a social phenomenon, outlined most systematically by Max Weber. Weber wanted to answer the question of why had oriental cultures, including ones dominated by Islam, Buddhism, and Hinduism, not developed capitalism as Europe had done. Typical of his general approach, Weber's analysis of Islam focused on the role of religious ideas, whose real meaning he assumed to lie in Qur'anic passages and sayings attributed to Muhammad. The assumption was that religious doctrines, as outlined in the founding texts of the faith, formed the parameters of the faithfuls' social behavior.

However, a wealth of recent studies, especially in anthropology, has shown how reality is far more complex that what Weber's approach would permit. We are more aware now that a social action informed by the same religious belief can follow a number of very different directions. Most recently, Saba Mahmood (2005) has shown in an ethnographic study how religious reason, far from "determining" behavior, acts more as a flexible compass for various orientations. Those orientations may concern self-fashioning vis-à-vis others; providing the self with a sense of selfhood; opening up outlets for action on one's immediate environment; or meaning-making of the world in general. None of those possibilities are determined in advance or in standard ways.

This seems to apply as well to what at first sight appears to be traditional ideas of accepting the work of determining circumstances, such as "fate." In a relevant, earlier observation, Halim Barakat (1990) showed how in literary portrayals of demographics similar to those studied by Mahmood, the concept of "fate" is actually used to justify *chosen* and novel actions that defy traditional expectations, rather than to exemplify a traditional attitude of resignation and lack of individual effect. The underlying thesis was that innovation tends to be less challenged when embedded in "traditional" language (including fatalism), rather than if presented as a subjective (and thus apparently arbitrary or groundless) license to innovate.

From this perspective, a living religion exists only in society, only as a social practice, and not as a set of fixed, eternal ideas. It has to have a social meaning right now, just as it had a social meaning a thousand years before, when it was elaborated in a completely different society. A practice may be said to be *social* if, rather than being oriented only to individual needs, it also expresses relations to others. Hence a social practice always entails social communication, oriented to a shared understanding—in this case, of a religion. But a "shared" understanding is not the same as a "total" or "final" understanding. A shared understanding is a situational, pragmatic arrangement that for a while appears to provide a moral basis of togetherness; to be aligned with individuals' experience of religious life; and to not explicitly contradict those formal doctrines about which there is a consensus among the doctors of the faith. Such a shared understanding may or may not be proximate to the spirit or letter of state law. It can only be produced in society, not by formal legislation.

Outside observers of any religion, for example social scientists, may be able to prove easily that a shared understanding of any religion is a fiction. But even if this is explained to the believers it is unlikely to make much difference to them, nor to make it less compelling for them to pursue a shared understanding of their own faith—assuming, of course, that they take their faith seriously. Underlying religious belief is always the notion that there inheres in an idea in which one believes the capacity to generate a shared agreement on its meaning. The shared meaning therefore is assumed to be possible to arrive at through communication. But this is so because the "Truth" is assumed to be latent in the idea itself and not simply in our own capacity to communicate. Our failure to generate a shared meaning is therefore experienced as a failure in our communicative methods, even of our very will to communicate, but not as a failure of the idea itself—assuming, again, that we sincerely believe in the idea. The assumed capacity of a religious idea to generate a shared meaning also generates constant religious *social* energy—meaning that religion is regarded to be a social and not merely an individual or reflective practice.

A religion as a social practice exists as ordinary people experience it, usually at a distance from two important sources that have *other* concerns: the systematic orthodoxies of the learned religious establishment, and the worldly calculations of political forces, including the state. These two are not usually good sources of information about the social life of religion, although they certainly have other stories to tell. As social practice, religion cannot fulfill any particular expediency in an obvious way, since no meaning can be shared if it appears to be obviously wedded to anyone's *particular* interests, and since the truth and the dignity of the idea in which it resides require distance from that which is obviously mortal, local, particular, or individual. Religion as social practice rather persists to the extent that it appears to fulfill a basic role, and that is to structure social life as a grand compromise.

This compromise is most evident in situations in which one confronts the dilemma of choice between doing that which is necessary and that which is ethical. An extreme example of this sort of reasoning is given by the late Ayatollah Muhammad Hussein Fadlallah, one of the most renowned Shi'a Muslim theologians in the contemporary world. In a comment addressing legalistic "tricks" that allow believers to circumvent otherwise inescapable religious mandates, Fadlallah suggests a logic, presumably ancient, that saw a religious virtue in those same tricks (Rifa'i 2000:43). A man, according to the story, made a vow to god to sell his

camel for one thousand times less its worth. When time came to fulfill
the generous vow, the man balked at the heavy cost to him, and went out
to seek a religious opinion on the matter. It is said that the eighth-century
imam al-Baqir, one of the infallible imams of early Shi'ism, advised the
man in question to sell the camel indeed for the price made in the vow,
but to only sell it with its rope, demanding a thousand times more for that
otherwise worthless item. Fadlallah then pointed out that no one doubted
that that solution was simply a legalistic ruse around a vow made to god.
But al-Baqir's reasoning was that a ruse of this sort still had a virtue, in that
it allowed one to pass back from the specter of sin (*haram*) to the realm of
sanctioned behavior (*halal*).

The case above may be unusual only in the obvious nature of what
may appear as spurious ethical validation of materialist behavior. But it
is part of a continuum of validations of less obvious violations. The point
was not how action should be guided by religion, but how one may sustain a religious standpoint, precisely as one needed a pathway around un-
workable religious edicts or ideas. In other words, what was important
was not the deed itself, but how one strove to endow all transactions with
religious validation, that is to say, how one made religion *conform* to the
practical patterns and necessities of transactional social life. In such cases
the question is not simply what action may be sanctioned by faith; it rather
concerns how faith may provide life generally with a moral compass that,
precisely because it is also meant to be practical, must in some way cohere
with what one must do at each instance. Seen from a secular perspective,
this feature of faith may confirm that faith is superfluous. But seen from a
religious perspective, this feature is precisely what makes faith reasonable
and meaningful.

How social logic emerges out of metaphysics

The point is not that these are equally valid standpoints, nor that one is
more rational than the other. The point is that social ideas are meant to be
placed in some practice, even though they may merge out of a purely intellectual process, as in philosophical reasoning or metaphysical speculation.
In experiments of belief, metaphysical speculation may be translated into
social action—a process already prefigured in the evolution of the Qur'an
itself between Mecca and Medina, as it transformed in character from contemplative illuminations on the nature of the universe and existence, to
practical guidance of ethical life in relation to others. How is metaphysics

translated into a form of relations to others, and a source of regulating the self?

I would like to propose three steps for the evolution of such social logic out of metaphysics, all centrally pertinent to the discussion of the social career of religious ideas. First, a philosophical principle of metaphysics becomes an elementary ground for a social movement when it is compelling enough to be considered by more than one person. One could cite endless examples here: in Christianity, the doctrine of god becoming man, suffering and dying, and in so doing saving the world. Before this idea may become a ground for any ethics, it has to be considered first as a philosophical and metaphysical puzzle in its own right. It is untenable to propose that metaphysical thought comes to be shared by more than one individual because of some material necessity—for example, "to make collaboration easier." That is because the actual solution to the problem of collaboration in practical and necessary matters is to simply collaborate.

Religious ideas may be said to translate material relations into spiritual scripts. But such ideas themselves cannot possibly come into existence unless they find receptive minds hospitable to metaphysical contemplation in at least elementary forms. At the origins of Islam, the entire Meccan phase of Qur'anic revelation dealt largely with metaphysical questions, asking man to reflect on the order of nature, on the source of life, on death, on the root of desire, and so on. That was the earliest part of revelation, and it preceded any divine law. The metaphysical ideas of religion were its very first ideas, its stem cells so to speak, since in principle they could give rise to *any* system of social ethics: The metaphysical speculations had no *necessary* relationship to the social behaviors that religion would later prohibit or permit. The metaphysical ideas even preceded any elaboration of the *rituals* that would give religion a clear identity as a distinct faith.

A second stage of social logic is when metaphysics is proposed as grounds for ethics. This is also quite evident in religious history, when the "law" is given *after* the idea of god is established (or at least felt to be established enough in society). The "law" may of course be demanded directly, as we see in the evolution of Islam in Medina, where the Qur'an begins to take a more instructive form as it *responds* to various demands for clarification of rules pertaining to the practice of faith and arbitrating conflicts in a differentiated society of faithful. An erstwhile purely metaphysical idea, now widely shared, generates a basis for social peace and, concomitantly, necessitates clarifying the rules and rituals that would regulate this emerging togetherness.

The third stage of the evolution of a social logic out of metaphysics concerns identifying the *agency* of ethics. This could lead to a number of divergent directions. This is also the concern through which religious thought tends to be most profusely present in the public sphere, since the question of an agency that produces ethics is also a question of power and counter power. Ethical doctrines may be elaborated with reference to an earthly power, such as when the state comes to be seen as a custodian over ethics in the form of laws, policing, and enforcement of compliance. Here ethical questions are expressed primarily in terms of *effective guarantees* for their enforcement. This makes them appear to be the natural property of an apparatus external to the individual.

At the other end of the spectrum, ethical doctrines may be elaborated not in terms of effective guarantees of enforcement, but in terms that resemble in their character the metaphysical starting point: namely ethics themselves as contemplative activity, rather than as formal rules. Here, the guarantees of ethics are not formal institutions, nor is it the person, but an "intersubjective" entity: An outside force joins the subject through a dialogic process. One way by which this intersubjectivity forms is through feelings, as in love and fear, both of which are forms of relation to a god.

Love and fear (of a god) are two apparently contradictory impulses of religious life; they are certainly not unique to Islam. Generally, both fear and love are forms of relation to an external authority. When does one form of relation appear more appropriate as the proper relation, and what are the knowledge implications of each? Is it possible, for example, that a relation of love is more associated with a democratic mindset, and one of fear with tyranny? Can one love tyranny, more so than fear it? Are love and fear opposite tendencies, or could they be forms of relation of the same person to the same authority?

Within the history of any religion, countless examples may be given to illustrate the workings of either tendency. When Mohamed Morsi was elected as president of Egypt in 2012, I heard people say: "Finally we have a president who fears god." Put otherwise, this means: "We do not need to fear an authority that itself fears god." How do we know this? Because "we" ourselves fear god; our own fear of god is the one guarantee (or at least claim) of our ethics. Consequently, others' fear of god is likewise the one guarantee of their own ethics.

Yet, a loving god, an authority that loves humanity and one that we love, is a constant parallel to fear as a form of relation to god in religious life, and sometimes in the same mind, although typically love and fear are set as opposites and may indeed appear as opposing theological camps. When Mouhanad Khorchide argued that the essential Muslim relation to Allah should be based on love, he faced opposition from other Muslims who highlighted the fear of god as the primary character of that relationship. The same criticism faced the US evangelical minister Carlton Pearson, when he questioned how could a god who loves humanity so much be such a monster ("worse than Hitler," he said, since "Hitler burned six million people once, when our god promises to burn at least six billion people, forever"). In both cases, opponents of Pearson and those of Khorchide made the exact same argument, from the standpoint of two different religions: God must be feared, above all, because we could not be entrusted with ethics whose source is not feared. On the one hand, god's love for humanity is infinite, yet, as a lord of eternal damnation, god is also worse than the worst tyrants we ever had. How are the two attributes to be reconciled?

Until god himself answers this question, we are left with sociology: The two tendencies are expressions of social relations, which in turn are reflected in theological terms. Fear, or at least the specter of punishment, tends to be associated with relation to an external authority that is expected to remain external to the subject. The form of relation to such an authority tends to take a legalistic form: It gives you a law by which to live, and your obligation is to follow the law. In the process, you forget the most elementary proposition underlying legalisms: Legal relations are the form of relation among strangers, or at least among those whose obligations to each other are otherwise unreliable. Love relations, by contrast, are premised on the expectation of relocation of subject positions; put otherwise: I love what I want to know, intimately if possible. That was how mystics in all religious traditions have understood the idea, and that is why they approached divinity as something that they themselves could acquire—not as vanity, but precisely the opposite, as a way to eliminate selfhood, selfhood being understood as a separation from what they loved, meaning from what they could become. In mystic terms, therefore, love was a form of knowledge, and knowledge was not possible with fear, which only served to keep one away from truth.

But in so far as our concern with agency of ethics are concerned, both love and fear act in the same way, namely as dialogic processes through which one acquires capacity for ethics that are otherwise external to the subject. It is of course possible that a relation of fear is more likely to develop in the direction of calling for an external worldly authority (for example, government) as a guarantor of ethics. In that case, fear may become less needed for ethical purposes, since another earthly authority would be doing the work that personal fear of god had done.

The question of the agency responsible for implementing ethics also resides within the two polar opposites of Islamic public philosophy throughout the modern period that we explored in Chapter 2: instrumentalism and hermeneutics. It may appear that the instrumentalist perspective is more likely to define the agency of ethics as external to the self, whereas the hermeneutic perspective is more likely to define it as an outcome of a dialogic process. However, the map of possible propositions is complex. For example, the idea that ethics require an external apparatus may lead to conceiving that apparatus in any form, from a complete theological utopia governed by an enlightened despot, to a state whose law only partially accepts religious ethics as sources of its law. On the other hand, the alternative proposition, namely that ethics are unreliable if they are not internally generated and accepted, may imagine the intrinsic career of such ethics in a wide range of forms. They may range from simple moral reasoning that constantly brings god's law into harmony with daily pragmatics, to a position that aims to internalize and thereby overcome god as an *external* idea, rather than to submit to divine commands. And submitting to such commands is not the end of the road still, because submission itself requires answering further questions, beginning with: Do we submit because the commands come from a divine source, or because their logic is so incomprehensible that submission must precede understanding, and continue in its absence?

These three steps (metaphysical idea as basis of sociation,[1] sociation calling forth ethics, ethics calling forth an agency to carry them out) involve increasing choices and possibilities with each step. Thus the effort to control the diversity of possible approaches, and the counter-struggle against that effort, are natural corollaries to the history of any religion. What I would like to suggest, further, is that these are not simply "historical" processes, although one can most easily see them in historical dynamics. Rather, these steps seem also to be paralleled in individual biographies and individual lives of religious individuals. It is perhaps for this reason

---

1. "Sociation" is the English translation of Georg Simmel's *Vergesellschaftung*. The term shifts focus from "society" as an accomplished fact to "society" as an active process. The term "sociation" (as opposed to "association," for example) brings to the foreground the fact that it is actors who, as they develop networks and relations, bring into being something that appears to them as "society."

that the grand drama of historical processes assumes such a compelling hold on individual imagination, since history assumes a more compelling force and becomes more audible if it recalls in its narratives, however indirectly, what has been happening inside of an individual psyche.

Religious thought itself provides allegories of this kind of individual moral development, allegories that are usually meant explicitly as illustrations of some larger social lesson. A prototypical example of such moral development is the story of Abraham. Metaphysical thought in Abraham's story develops according to an *experimental* method (thus, akin to the votive religions, but at a more abstract level). The Qur'an (6:76–79) renders Abraham's discovery of god as a gradual process. Abraham first regards a star to be his god until it sets; then he shifts his faith to the rising moon, which also eventually wanes, causing Abraham to lose faith in it. Then it is followed by the bright sun that becomes Abraham's new god until it too sets. Finally, he is left with the conclusion that the real god must be the creator of all that he had seen, including the shiny appearances he had worshipped in error. The fact that the successive failure of cosmic elements to be permanently visible is registered by Abraham at all as a "problem" suggests what he is looking for: lasting, permanent, universal principles that are also external to the self.

That part of Abraham's story may be a commentary on an earlier, failed experiment in monotheistic thought, namely that of Akhenaten, who also looked for the sun as a permanent and only god, and banished from the ancient Egyptian pantheon all other deities that were less capable of being universally visible. Abraham's "improvement" of the metaphysical experiment of Akhenaton consisted of reverse procedure: contrary to what Akhenaton had thought, that which is unquestionably universal could only be universally *invisible*. This invisibility of god allows the human actor to become the story, that is to say unleash the full force of his psychic tensions as an earthly template of god's infinite reason. An invisible god could only speak through those who speak for him, and it is they whom we see, not god.

The evolution of ethics out of metaphysical search for lasting principles is clearest here in the divine command to Abraham to sacrifice his son. As we know, Abraham obeys, like all faithful are supposed to, without question. But also as we know the story does not end there, and it is hard to see how any religion of any consequence could have developed any further had the story been otherwise—i.e., as one of an appalling deed fulfilled as promised, with no amendment or further reason. Rather, Abraham's obedience to the external command, to the "law" so to speak, takes him *beyond* the law. Here, we learn that obedience is useful because it leads to learning a higher lesson than simple obedience. Sacrifice is meant, as the story is commemorated in the Islamic tradition, to a social good and not to god who, after all, needs no sacrifice.

It is easy to see how this portrayal may fit with Durkheim's outline of religious thought as a representation of society. But that is not exactly where the social logic that evolves out of metaphysical contemplation leads to. The story of Abraham, for example, provides an idealization of a specific path toward moral development out of metaphysics, but different lessons may be drawn from it. A religious mind does not simply idealize society, but explores options and contests other interpretations of the same story within the same religious tradition. And one may even take it further, still from a religious perspective: Abraham's story of spiritual evolution may express something we have not yet reached, to the extent that we are still at the stage of the law and of obedience. A religious person may say, for example, that Abraham's story seems to suggest that obedience is only an intermediate stage in moral development, since something more is learned after obedience. Yet, also from a religious perspective, one could make the exact opposite argument: obedience itself is the point, because obedience connects the finite reason of man, insufficient for its own good, to the infinite wisdom of god, sufficient for everything.

Whatever position one takes, it results in an argument about its validity. This is unavoidable to the extent that the alternative position is available or suspected to be such, even if only privately. As a basis of social communication, religions survive less by being followed than by being constantly interpreted, and thus modernized. (Sometimes, however, they survive by being ignored, which keeps them sheltered from error in periods in which most damage to society appears to be coming from a different source.) And interpretive activity typically resides in the decision to read a particular holy or founding text in a particular way, with a particular emphasis and in light of particular problems and issues that happen to bedevil a reader, at that particular moment. This view does not require contradicting any religious reason, since a religious person is always in a position to say that if god's intentions or laws are timeless, then they are meant for the here and now, for the particular and mundane reality of a mortal and passing moment. The sacred is meant for the profane.

Consensus and compromise

The major aim of this book has been to sketch out how Muslims have historically and in the present employed the faith as a practical means by which to foster global networks, public philosophies, and engaged civic lives. The overall conclusion is that Islam is a referent that in one part exists for the sake of being interpreted—that is, as *discourse*. But looked at as a historical and global experience, with attention to the needs of the here and now, Islam then lends itself as another way by which we may learn something more about our world. Such learning has something to offer Muslims and non-Muslims alike: On the one hand, it supplies a Muslim world perspective; on the other hand, it supplies a large and long-enduring story about techniques of managing life in a global society sustained less by power than by generalized conceptions of citizenship and heteroglossic cultures. In their general form, the questions explored in this volume— how to imagine a global society, how to guide life in the manner of a total philosophy, and how to relate to the world of daily struggles in organized or semi-organized civic forums and social movements—are not unique to religious life. But the career of a particular religion—Islam in this case— offers a focused empirical lens through which we may offer meaningful propositions about their more general forms.

Because it has operated as a namesake of a global culture, Islam has always been a pluralist tradition. It had to be so by sheer practical necessity, as would be expected of any referential system that is equally globally distributed, uncontrolled by any center, and old enough to have generated multiple schools and methods. This means that what we call "Islam" is typified above all else by constant internal struggles, again as would be expected of any referent that is equally old or vast. These struggles do not endanger religion: To the contrary, they are precisely what provide it with license for more life and relevance. One can even say that internal struggles themselves establish the very basis of global religion, and from the very beginning. When exploring the social origins of Islam in an earlier book (Bamyeh 1999), I traced its successful foundation (in an era that was teeming with other prophetic experiments) to its emerging status as a *plenum*. That meant that Islam was established as a general transtribal and cross-class referent precisely when it offered itself up as a way by which the worldviews and interests of divergent and contradictory social groups and classes could be expressed. The emergence of Islam did not end social struggles among competing groups. But it moved all social struggles inside the Islamic discourse itself, so that struggles could go on, but now in the name of Islam rather than in the naked name of a specific group, class or tribe. While it does not bring social struggles to an end, a common social discourse provides at least a regulatory framework for such struggles, and ways by which compromises may be made and justified.

Islam, therefore, was never strictly the religion of the poor, as leftist interpretations of Islam have argued in recent decades. It was of course the religion of the poor, but also of the wealthy, of the merchant class, of farmers, industrial workers, even of entertainers. A global religion becomes established neither because it resolves social conflict, nor because it stands in for the interests of just one group. Rather, it becomes established at the moment it moves all social conflict inside of it, so that social struggles could go on just as before, but now in an ordered way and with reference to a common discourse that regulates conflict and sets limits to it. "Harmony" is sometimes the word we use to describe this kind of conflict: A conflict governed not by the requisite of being resolved, only by the requisite that all partners to conflict should use the same reference points.

This persistent sociological character of Islam has been alluded to by Muslim jurists themselves, who from the very first century of Islam elevated the principle of "consensus" into one of the primary sources of jurisprudence. Consensus as a source of valid opinion or as an expression of the true intention of religion, was usually placed after the Qur'an and the transmitted traditions of Muhammad. That placement of consensus in the third place belied the fact that in communicative realities, nothing could supersede the priority of consensus, including god's word, since the most valid interpretation of god's word was the one on which there emerged the greatest consensus. In one sense, the ideal of consensus was the alternative to strong political authority, and in that sense it fit well the persistent sociological character of Islam as a body of thought and practices lacking a strong or effective central authority that could enforce dogmas across great distances.

However, the reality of a pluralist community of faithful meant that consensus was something to be sought. There are many exceptions that could be cited, but the general pattern was as follows: When consensus could not be established as an attained reality, its absence encouraged its pursuit as a communicative ideal. In that way, the ideal of consensus encouraged the scholars to elaborate doctrines in ways that incorporated older commentaries. In the final analysis, this process gave religion its basic conservative and conserving appearance. The emergence of the *sunna*, as a secondary body of religious practices over the first three decades of Islam can be understood as part of this communicative environment. That vast body of rules and teachings had the ultimate effect of enhancing the authority of scholarly communities in the lives of Muslims, and it served to highlight the decentralized authority of knowledge as the practical alternative to the usually distant or ephemeral authority of political rulers. The *sunna* was in the final analysis a collection of *sunan*, a multiple corpus produced by individual collectors, interpreters, and systematizers who pursued different perspectivist priorities and inhabited different social networks. Muslims themselves acknowledged the multiple reality of their reference points while condensing them in "Islam" as a unifying ideal concept, just as they recognized the resulting multiple structure of Islamic jurisprudence. The social pragmatics of the faith as they emerged out of those dynamics can generally be described as a usually conservative, though mobile, dialectic of consensus and compromise. However, given the right conditions this same dialectic equation could harbor a stunning revolutionary potential.

Elements of reserve discourse

This pragmatic perspective allows us to see better how Islam comes into use primarily as a discourse rather than as a social system. As it became obvious with the Arab uprisings in 2011 (and as used to be obvious before the Iranian Revolution), Islam is not mentioned compulsively by Muslims with reference to every problem they encounter. Rather, it is referenced in the manner of a *reserve discourse*. A reserve discourse is a resource that may come into use when needed, but lie dormant at other times when other discourses seem to be undertaking, effectively enough, a battle around which there appears to be social consensus (be it national liberation, development, modernization, or popular participation). This conception of "reserve discourse" allows us to understand how in most of the Muslim world, modern national liberation movements, for example, rarely found it necessary to reject the principle of Islamic solidarity, even though in theory Islamic solidarity contradicted the presumably alternative principle of national solidarity.

From this perspective, it is possible to understand how Islam owes its historical longevity to the fact that as a discourse it could live with other types of loyalties that were not at all religious in nature, including tribal, urban, regional, guild, class, or ethnic solidarities. For most of modernity until the late twentieth century, Islam was rarely a governmental or even serious opposition program, but was kept in reserve everywhere. While secular elites ignored it, even in Pakistan, Islam rarely had to face anti-clerical cultural revolution against it—especially one from below. This absence of a cultural revolution was one reason why Islam maintained its status as reserve discourse, and thus as a venue for expressing revolutionary and other types of social energies later.

A reserve discourse is not an alternative to the full complexity of social life, nor does it automatically invalidate the practice of multiple loyalties. Rather, its reserve nature means that it remains available when everything else fails, or when other types of loyalties lead to a type of crisis that require intervention in new ways. Indeed, given a century of secular political rule and the domination of national culture by secular elites in most of the Muslim world, it is not evident that the growth of Islamism in recent decades should serve as a real measure of the "natural" and everlasting strength of Islam in society. Rather, the rise of Islamism appears in this context to reflect more the scale of the crises (political, social, and economic) that other types of modernist experiments have generated. A reserve discourse avails itself not habitually, but when all else has failed.

In recent decades, awakening Islam from its deep slumber as a reserve discourse in several Muslim countries is evident in how it was made to address at least five clusters of collective issues that had earlier been entrusted entirely to secular authorities: 1) social solidarity; 2) participatory ethics; 3) political legitimation; 4) social justice; and 5) general civic ethics. As we saw especially in the first two chapters, these fields became gradually more occupied by Islamic discourses as well as Islamic social movements and organizations not out of any logic of historical inevitability, but in experimental ways. The salience of an Islamic discourse increased in proportion to the perceived failure of alternative discourses in giving a broadly accepted expression to the above mentioned five clusters of issues. After all, questions regarding the proper meaning and measure of solidarity, participation, legitimation, justice, and civics were inescapable in light of the modern character of virtually all Muslim societies; these questions required being asked in a modern and thus meaningful rather than ancient and forgotten ways. As it was called upon to answer these questions, religion itself was modernized, precisely at a time when its opponents thought that it ought to be abandoned.

The five clusters of issues above concern broad areas of modern transformations. They all concern how individuals understand the total mission of what they understand under "our society." But how does one arrive at them pragmatically? "Pragmatics," after all, are the daily issues of ordinary people. Those concern encountered, specific problems, and rarely are addressed in terms of such large concepts as "social solidarity." One path from daily pragmatics to large categories—perhaps the simplest to follow—is through accumulation of pragmatics, so that a large enough quantity of pragmatics leads into a qualitative judgment, that is, an arrival at a large concept that houses them all, thereby organizing one's observations and saving one from disorientation. One eventually says, "Finally, I can see that problems a, b, and c are not isolated. I had seen them one at a time, but now I have this large organizing concept that will bring them meaningfully together. This discovery will make my world meaningful and explainable, and in the process help me figure out what to do."

Pragmatics may be understood as a large reservoir of tactics—amendable, though their purpose always remains the same, and that is to give direction or meaning to life. A number of those tactics that came up in this volume include the use of religion: 1) as a vehicle for mobilizing dissent (as in Islamic social movements); 2) as a vehicle for emergency mobilization (as in some early anti-colonial struggles); 3) as a way of expressing moral superiority (which is the one dimension of religiosity that Nietzsche focuses on); 4) as a (passive) tradition (passive in the sense that it is performed ritualistically, largely out of habit and because everyone else who is familiar does it); 5) as an (active) tradition (in the sense of relating to it as an intellectual project, including constructing genealogies of ideas and references); and 6) as a mechanism of psychological defense in new conditions (this may apply to immigrants, but only when they are told that this is how they could defend themselves, or if they have few other cultural resources available for the task).

Two observations may be made about these items of pragmatics. First, they all are elements of *discourse*, and separating them for analytical purposes should help us better understand what "discourse" entails. Second, pragmatics are not everlasting conditions. Therefore, pragmatics could be ways of understanding social religion without essentializing it. However, some of the items above may by their nature be more temporary than others—for example, religion as a tool for mobilizing dissent; for emergency mobilization; or as mechanism of defense in new conditions. However, even those could become enduring, depending on how the "enemy" responds to these employments of religiosity. It would be best not to take all expressions of religiosity equally seriously or at face value. Much more important would be to understand the underlying conditions for the expression of religiosity—indeed, for the expression of any discourse regarding the organization of society.

If too much became asked of religion in the late twentieth century as a result, it is likely because other discourses increasingly fell silent, or became less credible, after having initially dominated the public sphere of most Muslim societies for about a century. The fact that too much is being asked of religion is evident in how it tends to be placed back on reserve, once alternative discourses present themselves as socially unifying and practically credible. Those alternative discourses do such work best when they appear as mindful of the old status of religion as a reserve discourse that should be left to play a reserve role in personal and social life. It is in this light that we can understand how, when non-religious discourses appear again promising in addressing the clusters of issues mentioned above (as in the case of the Arab Spring), religious discourse that only yesterday had appeared to be the only force capable of mobilizing millions suddenly reverts to its reserve status, allowing other experiments to begin. For a reserve discourse, with its sacrosanct prerogatives and assumptions, is too valuable for an ordinary believer's relation to the sacred, and too much of a nuisance for social communication as a whole, to be foregrounded constantly in social struggles, without emergency conditions and when alternatives appear equally sincere and dependable. A reserve discourse usually inhabits the background. It appears to occupy the foreground only when whatever had been standing there has collapsed.

Works Cited

Abd al-Raziq, Ali. (1925) 2000. *Al-Islam wa Usul al-Hukm*. Ed. Muhammad Imara. Beirut: Al-Mu'assassah al-'Arabiyyah li al-Dirasat wa al-Nashr.

Abdel-Latif, Omayma. 1999. "No Partners in Power." *Al-Ahram Weekly*, no. 461 (Dec. 23–29).

Abdel-Samad, Hamed. 2010. "Al Kaida ist eine Art Geisteshaltung." *Tagesschau* (Nov. 25).

Abu al-Afjan, Muhammad. 1985. "al-Waqf 'ala al-Masjid fi al-Maghrib wa al-Andalus." *Dirasat fi al-Iqtisad al-Islami*, pp. 315–342.

Abu-Lughod, Janet. 1989. *Before European Hegemony*. New York: Oxford University Press.

Abu Zayd, Nasr Hamid. 1996. *Al-Imam al-Shafi'i wa Ta'sis al-Idyolojiyyah al-Wasatiyyah*. Cairo: Madbouli.

Achterberg, Peter and Jeroen van der Waal. 2011. "One Nation Without God? Post-Christian Cultural Conflict in the Netherlands." In Dick Houtman, Stef Aupers, and Willem de Koster (eds.), *Paradoxes of Individualization: Social Control and Social Conflict in Contemporary Modernity*. Hampshire, UK: Ashgate, pp. 123–140.

Affendi, Abdelwahab El-. 2008. *Who Needs an Islamic State?* London: Malaysia Think Tank.

Ahmed, Leila. 1993. *Women and Gender in Islam: The Historical Roots of a Modern Debate*. New Haven: Yale University Press.

Ahmad, Mumtaz. 1998. "Islamization and Sectarian Violence in Pakistan." *Intellectual Discourse* 6:1.

Aikman, David. 2012. *One Nation Without God? The Battle for Christianity in an Age of Unbelief*. Ada, MI: Baker Books.

Akbar, Ahmed. 2008. *Journey into Islam: The Crisis of Globalization*. Washington, DC: Brookings.

Alavi, Hamza. 1997. "Ironies of History: Contradictions of the Khilafat Movement." *Comparative Studies of South Asia, Africa, and the Middle East* XVII:1.

Alawi, Hadi al-. 1999. *Hiwar al-Hader wa al-Mustaqbal*. Beirut: Dar al-Tali'ah al-Jadidah.

Algar, Hamid. 2002. *Wahhabism: A Critical Essay*. Oneonta, NY: Islamic Publications International.

Alterman, Jon B. and Karin von Hippel (eds.). 2007. *Understanding Islamic Charities*. Washington, DC: Center for Strategic and International Studies.

Amin, Husnul. 2010. *From Islamism to Post-Islamism: A Study of a New Intellectual Discourse on Islam and Modernity in Pakistan*. PhD diss., Erasmus University.

Anderson, Lisa. 1987. "The State in the Middle East and North Africa." *Comparative Politics* 20.

Arjomand, Said A. 1984. "Introduction: Social Movements in the Contemporary Near and Middle East." In Said A. Arjomand (ed.), *From Nationalism to Revolutionary Islam*. Albany: SUNY Press, pp. 1–27.

———. 1999. "The Law, Agency, and Policy in Medieval Islamic Society: Development of the Institutions of Learning from the Tenth to the Fifteenth Century." *Comparative Studies in Society & History* 41:2, pp. 263–293.

Arkoun, Mohammed. 1994. *Rethinking Islam: Common Questions, Uncommon Answers*. Trans. Robert D. Lee. Boulder, CO: Westview Press.

Armagan, Sevret. 1989. "lamha 'an halat al-awqaf fi Turkiyya." In Hasan al-Amin (ed.), *Idarat wa Tathmir Mumtalakat al-Awqaf*. Jeddah: Islamic Research and Training Institute, pp. 335–344.

Asad, Talal. 1986. *The Idea of an Anthropology of Islam*. Occasional Papers. Washington, DC: Center for Contemporary Arab Studies, Georgetown University.

———. 1993. *Genealogies of Religion*. Baltimore: Johns Hopkins University Press.

'Asali, Kamil al-. 1983. "Mu'assasat al-Awqaf wa Madaris Bait al-Maqdis." *Nadwat Mu'assasat al-Awqaf*. Baghdad: Institute of Arab Research and Studies, pp. 93–112.

Ashour, Omar. 2009. *The De-radicalization of Jihadists: Transforming Armed Islamists Movements*. New York: Routledge.

Assi, Eman. 2008. "Islamic Waqf and Management of Cultural Heritage in Palestine." *International Journal of Heritage Studies* 14:4, pp. 380–385.

Atasoy, Yıldız. 2005. *Turkey, Islamists and Democracy: Transition and Globalization in a Muslim State*. London: I. B. Tauris.

———. 2009. *Islam's Marriage with Neoliberlism: State Transformation in Turkey*. New York: Palgrave Macmillan.

Atia, Mona. 2013. *Building a House in Heaven: Pious Neoliberalism and Islamic Charity in Egypt*. Minneapolis: University of Minnesota Press.

Aydin, Cemil. 2017. *The Idea of the Muslim World: A Global Intellectual History*. Cambridge, MA: Harvard University Press.

Ayubi, Nazih N. 1980. "The Political Revival of Islam: The Case of Egypt." *International Journal of Middle East Studies* 12, pp. 481–499.

———. 1993. *Political Islam: Religion and Politics in the Arab World*. New York: Routledge.

———. 1996. *Over-Stating the Arab State: Politics and Society in the Middle East.* London: I. B. Tauris.

Bade, Klaus and Gunilla Finke (eds.). 2010. *Einwanderungsgesellschaft 2010: Jahresgutachten 2010 mit Integrationsbarometer.* Berlin: Sachverständigenrat deutscher Stiftungen für Integration und Migration.

Bamyeh, Mohammed A. 1999. *The Social Origins of Islam: Mind, Economy, Discourse.* Minneapolis: University of Minnesota Press.

———. 2000. *The Ends of Globalization.* Minneapolis: University of Minnesota Press.

———. 2001. "Postnationalism." *Bulletin of the Royal Institute of Inter-Faith Studies* (Autumn/Winter).

———. 2002. "Dialectics of Islam and Global Modernity." *Social Analysis* 43:3.

———. 2005. "Civil Society and the Islamic Experience." *ISIM Review* 15.

———. 2007. *Of Death and Dominion: The Existential Foundations of Governance.* Evanston, IL: Northwestern University Press.

———. 2009. *Anarchy as Order: The History and Future of Civic Humanity,* Lanham, MD: Rowan & Littlefield.

———. 2010. "On Humanizing Abstractions: The Path Beyond Fanon." *Theory, Culture & Society* 27:7.

———. 2011. "Arab Revolutions and the Making of a New Patriotism." *Orient* 52:3.

———. 2012a. "The Social Dynamism of the Organic Intellectual." In Mohammed A. Bamyeh (ed.), *Intellectuals and Civil Society in the Middle East.* London: I. B. Tauris, pp. 1–28

———. 2012b. "The Global Culture of Protest." *Contexts,* pp. 16–18.

———. 2015. *Social Sciences in the Arab World: Forms of Presence.* Beirut: ACSS.

Banna, Hasan al-. 1978. *Five Tracts of Hasan al-Banna (1906–1949).* Berkeley: University of California Press.

Banna, Jamal al-. 2010. Interview with Imad Sayyid Ahmad. *al-Masry al-Youm,* Dec. 20, p. 6.

Barakat, Halim. 1990. "Beyond the Always and the Near: A Critique of Social Psychological Interpretations of Arab Society and Culture." In Hisham Sharabi (ed.), *Theory, Politics and the Arab World: Critical Responses.* New York: Routledge.

Baroud, Ramzi. 2010. *My Father was a Freedom Fighter: Gaza's Untold Story.* New York: Pluto Press.

Batatu, Hanna. 1978. *The Old Social Classes and the Revolutionary Movements of Iraq.* Princeton, NJ: Princeton University Press.

———. 1999. *Syria's Peasantry, the Descendants of Its Lesser Rural Notables, and Their Politics.* Princeton, NJ: Princeton University Press.

Bayat, Asef. 2007. *Making Islam Democratic: Social Movements and the Post-Islamist Turn.* Stanford, CA: Stanford University Press.

Beinin, Joel and Joe Stork (eds.). 1996. *Political Islam: Essays from Middle East Report.* Berkeley: University of California Press.

Bellah, Robert N. (1970) 1991. *Beyond Belief: Essays on Religion in a Post-Traditionalist World*. Berkeley: University of California Press.

Benthall, Jonathan and Jerome Bellion-Jourdan. 2009. *The Charitable Crescent: Politics of Aid in the Muslim World*. London: I. B. Tauris.

Berger, Peter (ed.). 1999. *The Desecularization of the World: Resurgent Religion and World Politics*. Grand Rapids, MI: William B. Eerdmans.

Bohemen, Samira van and Roy Kemmers. 2011. "Secular Intolerance in a Post-Christian Society: The Case of Islam in the Netherlands." In Dick Houtman, Stef Aupers, and Willem de Koster, *Paradoxes of Individualization: Social Control and Social Conflict in Contemporary Modernity*. Hampshire, UK: Ashgate, pp. 141–155.

Boubekeur, Amel. 2007. "Post-Islamist Culture: A New Form of Mobilization?" *History of Religions* 47:1, pp. 75–94.

Boulby, Marion. 1999. *The Muslim Brotherhood and the Kings of Jordan, 1945–1993*. Atlanta: Scholars Press for the University of South Florida.

Bruce, Steve. 2011. *Secularization: In Defense of an Unfashionable Theory*. New York: Oxford University Press.

Brumberg, Daniel. 2001. *Reinventing Khomeini: The Struggle for Reform in Iran*. Chicago: University of Chicago Press.

Bulliett, Richard W. 1999. "Twenty Years of Islamic Politics." *Middle East Journal* 53:2, pp. 189–200.

———. 2013. "Religion and the State in Islam: From Medieval Caliphate to the Muslim Brotherhood." Occasional Paper no. 2. Denver: University of Denver Center for Middle East Studies.

Cammett, Melani. 2014. *Compassionate Communalism: Welfare and Sectarianism in Lebanon*. Ithaca: Cornell University Press.

Carapico, Sheila. 2007. *Civil Society in Yemen: The Political Economy of Activism in Modern Arabia*. Cambridge: Cambridge University Press.

Carmichael, Tim. 1997. "British 'Practice' Towards Islam in the East Africa Protectorate: Muslim Officials, Waqf Administration, and Secular Education in Mombasa and Environs, 1895–1920." *Journal of Muslim Minority Affairs* 17:2, pp. 293–309.

Casanova, Jose. 1994. *Public Religions in the Modern World*. Chicago: University of Chicago Press.

Christoyannopoulos, Alexandre and Matthew S. Adam (eds.). 2017. *Essays in Anarchism and Religion*, Vol. 1. Stockholm: Stockholm University Press.

Çizakça, Murat. 2000. *A History of Philanthropic Foundations: The Islamic World From the Seventh Century to the Present*. Istanbul: Boğazici University.

Clark, Janine A. 2003. *Islam, Charity, and Activism: Middle-Class Networks and Social Welfare in Egypt, Jordan, and Yemen*. Bloomington: Indiana University Press.

Cook, David. 2005. *Contemporary Muslim Apocalyptic Literature*. Syracuse, NY: Syracuse University Press.

Dagi, Ihsan. 2004. "Rethinking Human Rights, Democracy, and the West: Post-Islamist Intellectuals in Turkey." *Critique: Critical Middle East Studies* 13:2, pp. 135–151.

Dallal, Ahmad. 1993. "The Origins and Objectives of Islamic Revivalist Thought, 1750–1850." *Journal of the American Oriental Society* 113:3, pp. 341–359.

———. 2018. *Islam Without Europe: Traditions of Reform in Eighteenth-Century Islamic Thought.* Chapel Hill: University of North Carolina Press.

Deguilhem, Randi (ed.). 1995. *Le waqf dans l'espace islamique: outil de pouvoir socio-politique.* Damascus: Institut français de Damas.

Diamond, Sara. 2000. *Not by Politics Alone: The Enduring Influence of the Christian Right.* New York: Guilford.

Doumani, Beshara. 1995. *Rediscovering Palestine: Merchants and Peasants in Jabal Nablus, 1700–1900.* Berkeley: University of California Press.

———. 1998. "Endowing Family: Waqf, Property Devolution, and Gender in Greater Syria, 1800 to 1860." *Comparative Studies in Society & History* 40:1, pp. 3–41.

Duri, Saif al-Din al-. 2013. *Nuri Pasha al-Said 50 'Aman 'ala masra'eh wa suqut al-Nidham al-Malaki fir al-'Iraq 'am 1958.* Beirut: al-Dar al-Arabiyya lil-Mawsu'at.

Eickelman, Dale F. and Jon W. Anderson. 1999. "Redefining Muslim Publics." In Dale F. Eickelman and Jon W. Anderson (eds.), *New Media in the Muslim World: The Emerging Public Sphere.* Bloomington: Indiana University Press.

Eickelman, Dale F. and James Piscatori. 2004. *Muslim Politics.* Princeton, NJ: Princeton University Press.

Ellison, Christopher G. 1991. "Religious Involvement and Subjective Well-Being." *Journal of Health and social Behavior* 32, pp. 80–99.

Eltantawi, Sarah. 2017. *Shari'ah on Trial: Northern Nigeria's Islamic Revolution.* Oakland: University of California Press.

Enayet, Hamid. 1982. *Modern Islamic Political Thought.* London: Macmillan.

Ennab, Wael R. 1994. *Population and Demographic Developments in the WB and Gaza Strip Until 1990.* New York: UNCTAD.

Esack, Farid. 1997. *Qur'an, Liberation and Pluralism: An Islamic Perspective of Interreligious Solidarity Against Oppression.* London: Oneworld.

ESCWA (United Nations Economic and Social Commission for Western Asia). 2009. "Social Policy and Social Protection: Challenges in the ESCWA Region." Technical Paper 10. ESCWA 2:8, Dec. 9.

Faroqhi, Suraiya. 1984. *Towns and Townsmen of Ottoman Anatolia.* Cambridge: Cambridge University Press.

———. 1994. *Pilgrims and Sultans: The Hajj Under the Ottomans, 1517–1683.* London: I. B. Tauris.

Fattah, Moataz A. 2006. *Democratic Values in the Muslim World.* Boulder, CO: Lynne Rienner.

Fawaz, Leila Tarazi. 1983. *Merchants and Migrants in Nineteenth-Century Beirut.* Cambridge, MA: Harvard University Press.

Fay, Mary Ann. 1997. "Women and Waqf: Toward a Reconsideration of Women's Place in the Mamluk Household." *International Journal of Middle East Studies* 29, pp. 33–51.

————. 1998. "From Concubines to Capitalists: Women, Property, and Power in Eighteenth-Century Cairo." *Journal of Women's History* 10:3, pp. 118–140.

Fischbach, Michael R. 2001. "Britain and the Ghawr Abi 'Ubayda Waqf Controversy in Transjordan." *International Journal of Middle East Studies* 33:4, pp. 525–544.

Foran, John. 1993. *Fragile Resistance: Social Transformation in Iran from 1500 to the Revolution*. Boulder, CO: Westview Press.

Fuccaro, Nelida. 1999. "Communalism and the State in Iraq: The Yazidi Kurds, c. 1869–1940." *Middle Eastern Studies* 35:2, pp. 1–26.

Gallab, Abdullahi A. 2008. *The First Islamist Republic: Development and Disintegration of Islamism in the Sudan*. Hampshire, UK: Ashgate.

Geertz, Clifford. 1971. *Islam Observed: Religious Development in Morocco and Indonesia*. Chicago: University of Chicago Press.

————. 1985. *Local Knowledge: Further Essays in Interpretive Anthropology*. New York: Basic Books.

Ghamari-Tabrizi, Behrooz. 2016. *Foucault in Iran: Islamic Revolution After the Enlightenment*. Minneapolis: University of Minnesota Press.

Ghitani, Gamal El-. 2012. "Q&A with Gamal El-Ghitani: Politics Dominate Literature in Post-Revolution Egypt." *Al-Ahram Online*, Sept. 11.

Gibb, H. A. R. 1955. "The Evolution of Government in Early Islam." *Studia Islamica* 4, pp. 1–17.

Giddens, Anthony. 1991. *The Consequences of Modernity*. Stanford, CA: Stanford University Press.

Gilsenan, Michael. 1996. *Lords of the Lebanese Marches: Violence and Narrative in an Arab Society*. London: I. B. Tauris.

Goitein, Shelomo Dov. 1967–1993. *A Mediterranean Society: The Jewish Communities of the Arab World as Portrayed in the Documents of the Cairo Geniza*, 6 vols. Berkeley: University of California Press.

Göle, Nilüfer. 2000. "Snapshots of Islamic Modernities." *Daedalus* 129:1, pp. 91–117.

Gran, Peter. 1979. *Islamic Roots of Capitalism: Egypt, 1760–1840*. Austin: University of Texas Press.

Habermas, Jürgen. 1987. *The Theory of Communicative Action*, 2 vols. Trans. Thomas McCarthy. Boston: Beacon Press.

Hallaq, Wael B. 2012. *The Impossible State: Islam, Politics, and Modernity's Moral Predicament*. New York: Columbia University Press.

Halle, Randall. 2014. *The Europeanization of Cinema: Interzones and Imaginative Communities*. Urbana: University of Illinois Press.

Hamed, Raouf Abbas. 1990. *A Comparative Study of Fukuzawa Yukichi and Rifʿah al-Ṭahtawi*. Tokyo: Institute for the Study of Languages and Cultures of Asia and Africa (ILCAA).

Hamzeh, Ahmad Nizar. 2004. *In the Path of Hizbullah.* Syracuse, NY: Syracuse University Press.

Hassan, Riaz 2002. *Faithlines: Muslim Conceptions of Islam and Society.* Oxford: Oxford University Press.

Hathut, Hassan. 2000. *Al-'Aqd al-Farid 1942–1952: 'Ash Sanawat ma' al-Imam Hasan al-Banna.* Cairo: Dar al-Shuruq.

Haykel, Bernard and Robyn Creswell. 2015. "Want to Understand the *Jihadis?* Read Their Poetry." *The New Yorker,* June 8 & 15.

Hennigan, Peter C. 2004. *The Birth of a Legal Institution: The Formation of the Waqf in Third-Century A.H. Hanafi Legal Discourse.* Leiden: Brill.

Hilgers, Irene. 2009. *Why Do Uzbeks Have to Be Muslims? Exploring Religiosity in the Ferghana Valley.* Berlin: Lit Verlag.

Hoexter, Miriam. 2002. "The Waqf and the Public Sphere." In Miriam Hoexter, Shmuel N. Eisenstadt, and Nehemia Levtzion (eds.), *The Public Sphere in Muslim Societies.* Albany: SUNY Press.

Holt, Cheryl L. 2006. "Perceptions of the Religion-Health Connection Among African American Church Members." *Qualitative Health Research* 16:2, pp. 268–281.

HSI (al-Hay'a al-Sihhiyyah al-Islamiyyah). 2007. Beirut: Statistics and Archive Department Reports.

Hudson, Michael. 1977. *Arab Politics: The Search for Legitimacy.* New Haven, CT: Yale University Press.

Ibn Battuta. (1325–1353) 1969. *Voyages d'ibn Battuta,* 3 vols. Paris: Éditions Anthropos.

Ibrahim, Saad Eddin. 1982. "An Islamic Alternative in Egypt: The Muslim Brotherhood and Sadat." *Arab Studies Quarterly* 4, pp. 75–93.

Inglehart, Ronald. 1997. *Modernization and Postmodernization: Cultural, Economic, and Political Change in 43 Societies.* Princeton, NJ: Princeton University Press.

Iqbal, Muhammad. 1934. *Reconstruction of Religious Thought in Islam.* London: Oxford University Press.

Jabarti, Abd al-Rahman al-. 1993. *Napoleon in Egypt: Al-Jabarti's Chronicle of the French Occupation, 1798.* Translated by Shmuel Moreh. Princeton, NJ: Markus Wiener.

Jaber, Hala. 1997. *Hezbollah: Born With a Vengeance.* New York: Columbia University Press.

Jouili, Jeanette S. 2015. *Pious Practice and Secular Constraints: Women in the Islamic Revival in Europe.* Stanford: Stanford University Press.

Kandil, Amany. 1995. *Dawr al-Munazzamat al-Ghayr Hukumiyyah fi Misr.* Cairo: Matba'at Wehba.

Kandil, Hazem. 2014. *Inside the Brotherhood.* Cambridge: Polity.

Kassem, Maye. 2004. *Egyptian Politics: The Dynamics of Authoritarian Rule.* Boulder, CO: Lynne Rienner.

Kelsay, John. 2002. "Civil Society and Government in Islam." In Sohail Hashmi (ed.), *Islamic Political Ethics: Civil Society, Pluralism, and Conflict.* Princeton, NJ: Princeton University Press.

Khalid, Adeeb. 2007. *Islam After Communism: Religion and Politics in Central Asia.* Berkeley: University of California Press.

Khalidi, Tarif. 1996. *Arabic Historical Thought in the Classical Period.* Cambridge: Cambridge University Press.

Khoury, Philip S. 1983. *Urban Notables and Arab Nationalism: The Politics of Damascus 1860–1920.* Cambridge: Cambridge University Press.

Kuran, Timur. 2001. "The Provision of Public Goods under Islamic Law: Origins, Impact, and Limitations of the Waqf System." *Law & Society Review* 35:4, pp. 841–897.

———. 2005. "The Logic of Financial Westernization in the Middle East." *Journal of Economic Behavior and Organization* 56:4, pp. 593–615.

Kurzman, Charles. 1996. "Structural Opportunities and Perceived Opportunity in Social Movement Theory: The Iranian Revolution of 1979." *American Sociological Review* 61, pp. 153–170.

———. 1998. "Liberal Islam and its Islamic Context." In Charles Kurzman (ed.), *Liberal Islam: A Source Book.* New York: Oxford University Press, pp. 3–26.

———. 2005. *The Unthinkable Revolution in Iran.* Cambridge, MA: Harvard University Press.

———. 2011. *The Missing Martyrs: Why There Are So Few Muslim Terrorists.* Oxford: Oxford University Press.

Lapidus, Ira. 2002. *A History of Islamic Societies.* Cambridge: Cambridge University Press.

Lauzière, Henri. 2015. *The Making of Salafism: Islamic Reform in the Twentieth Century.* New York: Columbia University Press.

Layish, Aharon. 2008. "Waqfs of Awld al-Nas in Aleppo in the Late Mamluk Period as Reflected in a Family Archive." *Journal of the Economic & Social History of the Orient* 51:2, pp. 287–326.

Leggewie, Claus (ed.). 2004. *Die Türkei in Europa: Die Positionen.* Frankfurt: Suhrkamp.

Lerner, Daniel. 1958. *The Passing of Traditional Society.* Glencoe, IL: Free Press.

Levitt, Matthew. 2007. *Hamas: Politics, Charity, and Terrorism in the Service of Jihad.* New Haven, CT: Yale University Press.

Livezey, Lowell W., (ed.) 2000. *Public Religion and Urban Transformation: Faith in the City.* New York: New York University Press.

MacLeod, Arlene Elowe. 1993. *Accommodating Protest: Working Women, the New Veiling and Change in Cairo.* New York: Columbia University Press.

Madbouh, Ghada al-. 2011. *Unpacking Inclusion, Tracing Political Violence: A Case Study of the Palestinian Authority and Hama's Governance Under Occupation.* PhD diss., University of Maryland.

Maddison, Angus. 2006. *The World Economy,* 2 vols. Paris: OECD.

Madrasi, Muhammad Taqi al-. 1998. *Al-Nahj al-Islami: Qira'a fi Masirat al-Harakah al-Islamiyya.* Beirut: Dar al-Jeel.

Mahmood, Saba. 2005. *Politics of Piety: The Islamic Revival and the Feminist Subject.* Princeton, NJ: Princeton University Press.

Mamdani, Mahmood. 1996. *Citizen and Subject: Contemporary Africa and the Legacy of Late Colonialism.* Princeton, NJ: Princeton University Press.

Massad, Joseph A. 2001. *Colonial Effects: The Making of National Identity in Jordan.* New York: Columbia University Press.

Mernissi, Fatima. 1992. *The Veil and the Male Elite: A Feminist Interpretation of Women's Rights in Islam.* New York: Basic Books.

Moosa, Ebrahim. 2005. *Ghazali and the Poetic Imagination.* Chapel Hill: University of North Carolina Press.

Moscaritolo, Alice. 2009. "The Role of Education in Transitional Societies: A Case Study of Educators in Kazakhstan." Paper presented at Muslims Between Tradition and Modernity: The Gülen Movement as a Bridge Between Cultures. University of Potsdam, Germany, May.

Mottahedeh, Roy. 1980 *Loyalty and Leadership in an Early Islamic Society.* Princeton, NJ: Princeton University Press.

Munson, Ziad. 2001. "Islamic Mobilization: Social Movement Theory and the Egyptian Muslim Brotherhood." *The Sociological Quarterly* 42:4, pp. 487–510.

Murad, Khurram. 2010. *In the Early Hours: Reflections on Spiritual and Self Development.* New Delhi: Revival.

Na'im, Abdullahi Ahmad an-. 2008. *Islam and the Secular State: Negotiating the Future of Shari'a.* Cambridge: Harvard University Press.

Naqeeb, Khaldoun Hasan al-. 1990. *State and Society in the Gulf and Arab Peninsula.* London: Routledge.

Nasution, Khoo Salma. 2002. "Colonial Intervention and Transformation of Muslim Waqf Settlements in Urban Penang: The Role of the Endowments Board." *Journal of Muslim Minority Affairs* 22:2, pp. 299–315.

Norris, Pippa and Ronald Inglehart. 2004. *Sacred and Secular: Religion and Politics Worldwide.* Cambridge: Cambridge University Press.

Norton, Augustus R., ed. 2005. *Civil Society in the Middle East,* 2 vols. Leiden: Brill.

Oberauer, Norbert. 2008. "'Fantastic Charities': The Transformation of Waqf Practice in Colonial Zanzibar." *Islamic Law & Society* 15:3, pp. 315–370.

Ochsenwald, William. 1984. *Religion, Society, and State in Arabia: The Hijaz under Ottoman Control: 1840–1908.* Columbus: Ohio State University Press.

O'Connell, Kathryn Ann and Suzanne M. Skevington. 2005. "The Relevance of Spirituality, Religion and Personal Beliefs to Health-Related Quality of Life: Themes from Focus Groups in Britain." *British Journal of Health Psychology* 10, pp. 379–398.

Orsi, Robert A. 2006. *Between Heaven and Earth: The Religious Worlds People Make and the Scholars Who Study Them.* Princeton: Princeton University Press.

Pandey, Gyanendra. 1999. "Can a Muslim Be an Indian?" *Comparative studies in Society and History* 41:3, pp. 608–629.

Pankhurst, Reza. 2016. *Hizb ut-Tahrir: The Untold History of the Liberation Party*. London: C. Hurst & Co.

Parsa, Misagh. 1989. *Social Origins of the Iranian Revolution*. New Brunswick, NJ: Rutgers University Press.

PCSR (The Palestinian Center for Survey and Research). 2006. "Results of PSR Exit Polls for Palestinian PLC Elections." Jan. 25. Accessed May 29, 2009. http://www.pcpsr.org/survey/polls/2006/exitplcfulljano6e.html.

Pianciola, Niccol and Paolo Sartori. 2007. "Waqf in Turkestan: the Colonial Legacy and the Fate of an Islamic Institution in Early Soviet Central Asia, 1917–1924." *Central Asian Survey* 26:4, pp. 475–498.

POMEPS. 2014. *Islamic Social Services*. Washington: Institute for Middle East Studies, George Washington University.

Popper, Karl. (1945) 2013. *The Open Society and its Enemies*. Princeton, NJ: Princeton University Press.

Pottier, Johan, Alan Bicker, and Paul Sillitoe (eds.). 2003. *Negotiating Local Knowledge: Power and Identity in Development*. London: Pluto Press.

Qureshi, Anwar Iqbal. 1974. *Islam and the Theory of Interest*. Lahore: Sheikh M. Ashraf.

Rahman, Fazlur. 1984. *Islam and Modernity: Transformation of an Intellectual Tradition*. Chicago: University of Chicago Press.

Ramadan, Mustafa Muhammad. 1983. "Dawr al-Awqaf fi Da'm al-Azhar." Baghdad: *Ma'had al-Dirasat wa alBuhuth al-'Arabiyyah*, pp. 125–148.

Rasler, Karen. 1996. "Concessions, Repression, and Political Protest in the Iranian Revolution." *American Sociological Review* 61, pp. 132–152.

Repp, Richard C. 1988. "Qanun and Shari'a in the Ottoman Context." In Aziz al-Azmeh (ed.), *Islamic Law: Social and Historical Contexts*. London: Routledge, pp. 124–145.

Richardson, Joel. 2009. *The Islamic Antichrist*. Los Angeles: WND.

Rifa'i, Abd al-Jabbar al- (ed.). 2000. *Manahij al-Tajdid*. Damascus: Dar al-Fikr.

Robinson, David. 2004. *Muslim Societies in African History*. Cambridge: Cambridge University Press.

Rosenblatt, Nate. 2016. *All Jihad is Local: What ISIS' Files Tell Us About Its Fighters*. Washington, DC: New America.

Roy, Olivier. 1994. *The Failure of Political Islam*. Translated by Carol Volk. London: I. B. Tauris.

———. 2017. *Jihad and Death: The Global Appeal of the Islamic State*. Oxford: Oxford University Press.

Sadjadpour, Karim. 2008. *Reading Khamenei: The World View of Iran's Most Powerful Leader*. Washington, DC: Carnegie Endowment for International Peace.

Salvatore, Armando. 2007. *The Public Sphere: Liberal Modernity, Catholicism, Islam*. New York: Palgrave Macmillan.

———. 2016. *The Sociology of Islam: Knowledge, Power and Civility.* Oxford: Wiley Blackwell.

Salvatore, Armando and Dale F. Eickelman (eds.). 2006. *Public Islam and the Common Good.* Leiden: Brill.

Samatar, Abdi Ismail and Ahmad I. Samatar (eds.). 2002. *The African State: Reconsiderations.* Portsmouth, NH: Heinemann.

Sassen, Saskia. 1988. *The Mobility of Labor and Capital: A Study in International Investment and Labor Flow.* Cambridge: Cambridge University Press.

Sayyid, Abd al-Malik. 1989. "al-Waqf al-Islami wa al-Dawr alladhi la'ibahu fi numuw al-Ijtima' fi al-Islam." In Hasan al-Amin (ed.), *Idarat wa Tathmir Mumtalakat al-Awqaf.* Jeddah: Islamic Research and Training Institute, pp. 225–304.

Sayyid, Ridwan al-. 2013. "Al-Dhahira al-Islamiyya wa al-'Alam al-'Arabi al-Mutaghayyir." Lecture at the Abdul Hameed Shoman Foundation. Amman, Jordan, May 5.

Schulze, Reinhard. 2016. *Geschichte der Islamischen Welt: Von 1900 bis zur Gegenwart.* Munich: C. H. Beck.

Schwan, Gesine. 2008. "What Legitimate Role Can Religion Play for Democracy?" International Sociological Institute's 38th World Congress of Sociology. Budapest, June.

Scott, James. 1977. *The Moral Economy of the Peasant: Rebellion and Subsistence in Southeast Asia.* New Haven: Yale University Press.

Shaham, Ron. 2000. "Masters, Their Freed Slaves, and the Waqf in Egypt (Eighteenth–Twentieth centuries)." *Journal of the Economic & Social History of the Orient* 43:2, pp. 162–188.

Shahrur, Muhammad. 2000. *Proposal for an Islamic Covenant.* Translated by Dale F. Eickelman and Ismail S. Abu Shehadeh. http://www.islam21.net/pages/charter/may-1.htm.

Shaikh, Farzana. 2009. *Making Sense of Pakistan.* New York: Columbia University Press.

Sharabi, Hisham. 1988. *Neopatriarchy: A Theory of Distorted Change in Arab Society.* New York: Oxford University Press.

Shatzmiller, Maya. 2001. "Islamic Institutions and Property Rights: The Case of the 'Public Good' Waqf." *Journal of the Economic & Social History of the Orient* 44:1, pp. 44–74.

Singerman, Diane. 1996. *Avenues of Participation: Family, Politics, and Networks in Urban Quarters of Cairo.* Princeton, NJ: Princeton University Press.

Soroush, Abdolkarim. 2002. *Reason, Freedom, and Democracy in Islam: The Essential Writings of Abdolkarim Soroush.* Edited by Mahmoud Sadri and Ahmad Sadri. New York: Oxford University Press.

Stark, Rodney. 1999. "Secularization, R.I.P." *Sociology of Religion* 60:3, pp. 249–273.

Starrett, Gregory. 1998. *Putting Islam to Work: Education, Politics, and Religious Transformation in Egypt.* Berkeley: University of California Press.

Sullivan, Denis J. 1994. *Private Voluntary Organizations in Egypt: Islamic Development, Private Initiative, and State Control.* Gainesville: University Press of Florida.

Taha, Mahmoud Muhammad. 2002. *Al-Risalah al-Thaniya min al-Islam.* In *Nahwa Mashru' Mustaqbali Lil-Islam.* Beirut: Al-Markiz al-Thaqafai al-Arabi; Kuwait: Dar Qirtas.

Tahtawi, Rifa'ah Rafi'. 1993. *Takhlis al-Ibriz fi Talkhis Bariz.* Cairo: Al-Hay'ah al-Misriyah al-'Ammah Lil-Kitab.

Tausch, Arno. 2009. *What 1.3 Billion Muslims Really Think.* Hauppauge, NY: Nova Science Publishers.

Therborn, Göran. 2003. "Entangled Modernities." *European Journal of Social Theory* 6:3, pp. 293–305.

Tuğal, Cihan. 2009. *Passive Revolution: Absorbing the Islamic Challenge to Capitalism.* Stanford, CA: Stanford University Press.

Tütüncü, Fatma. 2012. "Islamist Intellectuals and Women in Turkey." In Mohammed A. Bamyeh (ed.), *Intellectuals and Civil Society in the Middle East.* London: I. B. Tauris.

Umm, Mustafa. 2008. "Why I Left Hizb ut-Tahrir." *New Statesman*, March 3.

Vergès, Meriem. 1996. "Genesis of Mobilization: The Young Activists of Algeria's Islamic Salvation Front." In Joel Beinin and Joe Stork (eds.), *Political Islam.* Berkeley: University of California Press.

Voll, John. 1980. "Hadith Scholars and Tariqahs: An 'Ulama Group in the 18th Century Haramyn and Their Impact in the Islamic World." *Journal of Asian and African Studies* 15:3-4, pp. 264–273.

———. 1994a. *Islam: Continuity and Change in the Modern World.* Syracuse: Syracuse University Press.

———. 1994b. "Islam as a Special World-System." *Journal of World History* 5:2, pp. 213–226.

Vollaard, Hans J. P. 2013. "Re-emerging Christianity in West European Politics: The Case of the Netherlands." *Politics and Religion* 6:1, pp. 74–100.

Watson, C. W. 2005. "Islamic Books and Their Publishers: Notes on the Contemporary Indonesian Scene." *Journal of Islamic Studies* 16:2, pp. 177–210.

Watt, William Montgomery. 1953. *The Faith and Practice of al-Ghazali.* London: Allen & Unwin.

———. 1961. *Islam and the Integration of Society.* Evanston: Northwestern University Press.

Weber, Max. (1956) 1978. *Economy and Society*, 2 vols. Edited by Guenther Roth and Claus Wittich. Translated by Ephraim Fischoff et al. Berkeley: University of California Press.

———. 1993. *The Sociology of Religion.* Boston: Beacon.

Wickham, Carrie Rosefsky. 2002. *Mobilizing Islam: Religion, Activism and Political Change in Egypt.* New York: Columbia University Press.

Wiktorowicz, Quintan. 2003. *Islamic Activism: A Social Movement Theory Approach.* Bloomington: Indiana University Press.

Wood, Gary and Tugrul Keskin (eds.). 2014. *Perspectives on the Gülen Movement.* Special issue of *Sociology of Islam* 1:3–4.

Wuthnow, Robert. 2006. *Saving America? Faith-Based Services and the Future of Civil Society.* Princeton: Princeton University Press.

Yavuz, Hakan M. 2013. *Toward an Islamic Enlightenment: The Gülen Movement.* New York: Oxford University Press.

Yavuz, Hakan and John Esposito (eds.). 2003. *Turkish Islam and the Secular State: The Global Impact of Fethullah Gülen's Nur Movement.* Syracuse, NY: Syracuse University Press.

Yilmaz, Ferruh. 2012. "Right-Wing Hegemony and Immigration: How the Populist Far-Right Achieved Hegemony Through the Immigration Debate in Europe." *Current Sociology* 60, pp. 368–381.

Zubaida, Sami. 1989. *Islam, the People and the State: Essays on Political Ideas and Movements in the Middle East.* London: Routledge.

Index